On the Take

FROM PETTY CROOKS

On the Take

TO PRESIDENTS

William J. Chambliss

INDIANA UNIVERSITY PRESS
BLOOMINGTON & LONDON

Library of Congress Cataloging in Publication Data

Chambliss, William J
On the take.

1. Organized crime—Washington (State)—Seattle. 2. Corruption (in
politics)—Washington (State)—Seattle. 3. Racketeering—Washington (State)—
Seattle. I. Title.
HV6795.S5C45   1978   364.1'06'079777   77-15213
ISBN 0-253-34244-9

FOR STEVE

We have met the enemy and they is us.

—Pogo

Contents

PREFACE

As this book is going to press we are being treated daily to a potpourri of national and local scandals of the highest quality. A group of journalists and investigators in Arizona have declared that "U.S. Senator Barry Goldwater, his brother and a close friend have dominated Phoenix and Arizona for nearly thirty years while condoning the presence of organized crime through friendships and business alliances with mob figures." The governor of Maryland, Marvin Mandel, has been found guilty of fraud and racketeering while he was governor of the state. His practices were part of a Maryland tradition which included former Vice-President Spiro Agnew, who, according to the court record in his trial, took kickbacks for government contracts from the time he became Baltimore County executive in 1962 through the time that he was governor of Maryland and on into his days as vice-president of the United States: at the same time, incidentally, that he was making speeches across the United States decrying "crime in the streets" and demanding that we reinstate law and order. In neighboring Pennsylvania, Governor Milton Shapp has admitted to a grand jury that he accepted two paper bags each containing $10,000 in cash during the 1970 gubernatorial campaign. Shapp told the grand jury he could not remember what happened to the cash.

We learn today that President Nixon's source of the infamous "million-dollar hush money" that he told John Dean he could get was the Teamster Union pension fund. And we learn that the long-debated question of whether or not Lyndon Johnson was involved in rigging the election which sent him to the U.S. Senate in 1948 may finally be answered by his former political ally who, in his declining years, wishes to make a clean breast of things by admitting he helped Johnson steal that election.

Sadly there is no end to this list. Union officials—like Tony Boyle and Frank Fitzsimmons—presidents, vice-presidents, congressmen, senators, governors, and racketeers are implicated in a ubiquitous system of payoffs and favors, backscratching, stealing, campaign contributions, and personal aggrandizement. When such things happen from time to time it may be sensible to seek an explanation in the psychology of the misfits who cheat, steal, and connive. But when they are so commonplace that they are scarcely newsworthy we must seek the explanation in characteristics of the society. In the book that follows I have sought that explanation by studying and analyzing from the bottom up a system of racketeering, payoffs, and political empire building. Like the relationships described, the names and places of this study can be transferred to any city, any state, and any country with only minor changes in casting. The parts and the script are always the same. Where politics, illegal business, and corruption are concerned, every city in the United States is "America in miniature."

ACKNOWLEDGMENTS

Outside Oslo, Norway, in the woods up from Skädalen were three things that helped make this book possible. First is a log cabin where I spent the year 1974-75. Between hauling water, chopping wood, building fires in a fireplace that was eternally drafty, and running through the snow to the outhouse this book was written, mostly by kerosene lantern.

The second thing that helped make the book possible is a magnificent Norwegian friend, Helge Ingstad. Helge gave me invaluable advice on how best to tell what I had found in my research. I shall never forget sitting in front of the large window that overlooked the city, watching him ski up to the cabin one cold morning. He had in his rucksack a copy of the manuscript I had left with him the night before. Over tea he told me, "You mustn't give away the end of the story in the beginning. You must make the reader discover things the way you discovered them as you drank beer and talked with these fellows." After several more comments he became angry with me: "Why don't you argue with me? You mustn't agree with everything I say or I won't give you any more opinions." He slammed the book shut at that point. His advice, faith, and endless good sense were truly inspirational.

Third were the people with whom I shared that year. My best friend and companion, Lisa Stearns, whose strength of conviction and confidence in the project kept me from using the mounting piles of paper for fire starter. And my children: Lauren, who lived with us for a good part of that year and whose laughter helped warm the logs as her jeans joined mine in the snow when we fell on skis that would not stand still. Kent and Jeff added their voices to the stay in the Norwegian woods and showed patience not only with my writing but with my unerring sense of direction, which almost got us lost in the frozen tundra on Christmas Day before we came home to a Christmas dinner cooked over a pot-bellied stove that must be the finest meal anyone ever had.

Perhaps the warmth and love we all shared that year while I was writing this book, this book about people who have so little of either in their lives, is the final paradox of the story.

Others helped as well. Nils Christie of the Institute of Criminology in Oslo read the manuscript, encouraged me to continue with it, and made many helpful suggestions. So too did John Mack of the University of Glasgow.

In gathering the data, I found that people whose lives were touched most by the events described were unspeakably generous with their time and their consideration. Most of them must remain nameless. A few, however, whom I wish to thank publicly are Don Duncan of the Seattle *Times*, Reg Bruce of the Citizens' Council Against Crime, Ron Henson of KIRO Radio, and especially David Keown, who worked hard and creatively on part of the research which made this book possible.

To all these people and to the Norwegian woods I am forever grateful. I can only hope the result of our efforts is worth it.

On the Take

Introduction

MODERN WESTERN civilization produces strange things: an infinite variety of products differentiated by color, size, and shape and signifying nothing (see Alvin Toffler's *Future Shock*), a common despair among overly institutionalized children isolated and hardened by a competitive, irrational, and insensitive educational system (see Jules Henry's *Culture Against Man*), a mass of unemployed youth masquerading as students (see Charles Reich's *The Greening of America*), and a variety of crime the likes of which the history of living things has never before experienced (see any big city daily newspaper).

Money is the oil of our present-day machinery, and elected public officials are the pistons that keep the machine operating. Those who come up with the oil, whatever its source, are in a position to make the machinery run the way they want it to. Crime is an excellent producer of capitalism's oil. Those who want to affect the direction of the machine's output find that the money produced by crime is as effective in helping them get where they want to

1

go as is the money produced in any other way. Those who produce the money from crime thus become the people most likely to control the machine. Crime is not a by-product of an otherwise effectively working political economy: it is a main product of that political economy. Crime is in fact a cornerstone on which the political and economic relations of democratic-capitalist societies are constructed.

In every city of the United States, and in many other countries as well, criminal organizations sell sex and drugs, provide an opportunity to gamble, to watch pornographic films, or to obtain a loan, an abortion, or a special favor. Their profits are a mainstay of the electoral process of America and their business is an important (if unrecorded) part of the gross national product. The business of organized crime in the United States may gross as much as one hundred billion dollars annually—or as little as forty billion—either way the profits are immense, and the proportion of the gross national product represented by money flowing from crime cannot be gainsaid. Few nations in the world have economies that compare with the economic output of criminal activities in the United States.

This is the story of illegal business and how it works in one of America's largest cities, Seattle, Washington. It is the story of the ins and outs of the subterranean, often invisible world that surrounds the multimillion-dollar industry built upon gambling, drugs, usury, business fraud, prostitution, professional theft, and robbery. This industry is an important feature of the political organization and economic structure of modern life, but one that we often fail to understand.

At the turn of the century one of America's finest journalists, Lincoln Steffens, made a career and helped elect Theodore Roosevelt president by exposing corruption in American cities. Lincoln Steffens concluded that "the spirit of graft and of lawlessness is the American spirit." In *Shame of the Cities* he described the results of his investigations in most of the nation's largest cities in the early 1900s:

> In the very first study—St. Louis—the startling truth lay bare that corruption was not merely political; it was financial, commercial, social; the ramifications of boodle were so complex, various and far-reaching, that our mind could hardly grasp them . . . St. Louis exemplified boodle; Minneapolis police graft; Pittsburg a political and industrial machine; Philadelphia general civil corruption . . ."[1]

These things did not die with Lincoln Steffens or cease with the election of Teddy Roosevelt. In 1931, after completing an inquiry into the police, the National Commission on Law Observance and Enforcement concluded:

> Nearly all of the large cities suffer from an alliance between politicians and criminals. For example, Los Angeles was controlled by a few gamblers for a number of years. San Francisco suffered similarly some years ago and at one period in its history was so completely dominated by the gamblers that three prominent gamblers who were in control of the politics of the city and who quarrelled about the appointment of the police chief settled their quarrel by shaking dice to determine who would name the chief for the first two years, who for the second two years, and who for the third.[2]

In more recent years the task of exposure has fallen into the generally less-probing hands of government committees and social scientists who, unlike their journalistic predecessors, have gathered their information from police departments, attorney generals' files, and grand jury records. Unfortunately this difference in the source of information has distorted our picture of organized crime and has led to the premature acceptance of the Justice Department's view that there is an Italian-dominated Mafia or Cosa Nostra that manages most of America's vice industry. Donald R. Cressey, one of the social sciences' most articulate spokesmen for this view who based his conclusions on data gathered primarily from the U.S. Department of Justice and from a few state crime commissions, depicted organized crime in the U.S. in 1969 as follows:

> In the United States, criminals have managed to put together an organization which is at once a nationwide illicit cartel and a nationwide confederation. This organization is dedicated to amassing millions of dollars by means of extortion, and from usury, the illicit sale of lottery tickets, chances on the outcome of horse races and athletic events, narcotics and untaxed liquor.[3]

He also says:

> . . . an Italian organization in fact controls all but an insignificant proportion of the organized-crime activities in the United States.[4]

The stereotype of the Mafia is an interesting and pervasive one in America. Hardly a month goes by that there is not an article in *Playboy, Harper's, Newsweek,* or *Time* about some facet of Mafia life: a person is killed, a "hoodlum" is arrested who claims to be part of the Cosa Nostra, a politician is suspected of being under the control of a Mafioso. Movies abound: *The Godfather* tells us about the "secret government" run according to the characteristics and customs of Italian families as they become more and more assimilated into American culture, but always involved in criminality as a way of life.

The curious thing about these various characterizations is that they all rely on a very small base of data. A few imaginative and talkative persons, usually facing felony charges and long prison sentences, gain immunity from prosecution on at least some of the charges by "telling it all." Curiously, what these people tell never seems to culminate in any very substantial number of arrests. Their stories are always contradictory and the people doing the telling are *never* those at the top. Occasionally a book is written from interviews with one of the alleged leaders of the Mafia: Lucky Luciano and Frank Costello have recently joined the parade of Mafiosi who have told their stories.

Careful reading of *all* the data contained in these biographies as well as the mountains of official reports by crime commissions, government investigations, and congressional inquiries does not lead comfortably to any simple conclusion about the organization and structure of those who run, finance, and manage illegal businesses in the United States. Indeed, one is tempted to say that these data are rather more elusive than they are enlightening. The only sound conclusion we seem able to draw from the contradictory and varied interpretations of the data is that no single "picture," whether it is of a highly centralized organization populated principally by Italian-Americans or a complete hodgepodge of small time entrepreneurs, conveys a correct image.

It is likely that relying on police and other law-enforcement agencies for our information may lead to an overemphasis on the role of those who fit the stereotype of the "criminal" and a corresponding deemphasis on the importance of businessmen, politicians, and law enforcers as institutionalized components of America's political and economic system, which creates and perpetuates syndicates that supply the vices in our major cities.

Going to the streets of the city rather than to the records and IBM cards of the bureaucracies may bring the role of corruption and complicity between political, economic, and criminal interests into sharp relief. Organized crime may not be something that exists outside law and government but may be instead a creation of them—a hidden but nonetheless integral part of the governmental and economic structures of the society. The people most likely to be exposed by public inquiries may be outside the government but the network of which they are a part may be organized around, run by, and created in the interest of the economic, political, and legal elites who on the surface represent the noncriminal interests of "everyone."

If that is the case, then the view of organized crime as a coalition of Italian-American families operating under the rules and regulations of a law unto themselves may be a smokescreen behind which the reality of illegal businesses is conducted. There need not be a conspiracy of public deception on the part of political and other leaders. The Mafia may simply be a convenient scapegoat for some and a reasonable explanation of an otherwise difficult-to-account-for phenomenon for others. One need not posit an evil conspiracy behind every instance of pluralistic ignorance. History is replete with examples of whole populations being divided *not* by wicked manipulators of lies (though there is always an abundant supply of such types in any society) but by blinders that color the interpretation of the world and create false consciousness.

In the fall of 1962 I began studying "organized crime" in Seattle, Washington. At the time I was told by almost everyone to whom I talked that I had chosen the wrong city for such a study. Seattle, I was informed, was blessed not only by a ring of natural beauty and unspoiled wilderness, it was blessed also by clean government, sturdy law enforcement, and a paucity of organized crime.

In the course of the study I came to change my mind about many of the beliefs I held before this inquiry.

Trained as a lawyer and a sociologist, I was prepared to find that crime was understandable in terms of people socialized, stigmatized, and differentially associated with criminal behavior patterns. I expected also to find that law enforcers were inordinately stubborn in their insistence on a "crime control" model of law enforcement, sometimes ruthless in wielding their authority, often insensitive to the human problems faced by those whom they found committing criminal or deviant acts: but for all of this, conscientious people expressing the values and sentiments of the community of all "right-minded" citizens.

In short, when I began the study I was located politically and theoretically slightly to the left of the liberal side of the academic community. I tended to see things at first which confirmed that picture.

The prime value of training as a social scientist, however, is perhaps in teaching a variety of theoretical lenses which can be called upon when the one we begin with fails to fit and in teaching as well that good research comes from scratching where it itches. In the early days of the research I had the uneasy feeling that I had not yet found the itchy spot.

The unfolding of the research is the description of the findings, so I do not want to spoil the story by preempting it. The methods, the theory, and the findings unfold dialectically. To convey the process is one of the things I wish to communicate in this book. My way of writing sociology, however, is rather unconventional. It is customary among social scientists to begin their work with their conclusions, perhaps as a way of giving overly burdened audiences an opportunity to cop out of reading the entire work but still enabling them to recognize quickly the material when they hear or see it referred to. I apologize to those who would prefer that format. I fear, however, following it might rob the reader of that sense of discovery which was and is characteristic of the research.

It will not be giving away too much to suggest a few of the conclusions. Theoretically, the most important finding of this project has been the realization of how shallow and unfruitful was the perspective with which I began. Indeed, the theories of the law and of crime that dominate the academic study of crime (as contrasted with the street knowledge of crime) are in my view almost entirely misleading. I have come to believe we shall cut through the maze of misunderstanding about crime only when we come to accept the fact that its causes and the reactions to it are best understood as social relations reflecting political and economic systems. To put it succinctly, but necessarily too simplistically, crime is a political phenomenon which takes its character from the economic institutions that exist at a particular point in time.

From the perspective of political economy the most important theoretical model for understanding crime in general and organized crime in particular is the dialectic: criminality reflects and stems from contradictions that inhere in the political and economic structure of society; these contradictions create conflicts and attempts to resolve them. The resolutions forged, in turn, reveal other contradictions, further conflicts, and more resolutions. In this way the process of history unfolds. In this way the development and maintenance of illegal business and of organized criminal activities fit into, reflect, complement, and mirror the political economy of our time.

This model is best grasped in its use. It is the intention of the remainder of the book to show how the reality of organized crime in Seattle led to and helped develop this model.

One other, more concrete conclusion that came from the research may also help put the materials in perspective.

The picture of organized crime I draw differs from the picture drawn by others in two important ways. First and foremost, I do not believe that organized crime is run and controlled by a national syndicate with a "commission" or "board of directors" who have a feudal-like control over underlings spread across the nation. Second, the idea of a Mafia, Cosa Nostra, or simply an "organization" that rules organized crime is deceptive for it implies that organized crime is run by a group of private citizens. My research has shown very clearly that organized crime really consists of a coalition of politicians, law-enforcement people, businessmen, union leaders, and (in some ways least important of all) racketeers. Who dominates the coalition varies from city to city and from time to time. In New York Lucky Luciano and Frank Costello may have been more powerful than anyone else in the city during their reign. But in Chicago and Gary, Indiana, it is politicians who for many years have had the ultimate and most important practical control of organized crime.

It is a mistake to look for a "godfather" in every crime network. A lesson to be learned from this study is that it is a network in which people come and go, dominant offices shift and change, roles vary and fluctuate, but the system goes on and on. The characteristics of the more colorful racketeers may make good newspaper copy but they do not help us understand how organized crime works, nor can they explain its continuance and its health.

This, then, is the story of Seattle's crime network. It was an unusually successful one as measured by its influence, its income, its duration, its freedom from legal sanctions, and its power over the life of the city and the state. The group that I found managing and profiting from organized crime in Seattle was like crime networks everywhere in that it was composed of some of the city's and state's leading citizens. Working for, and with, this group of respectable community members was a staff to coordinate the daily activities of prostitution, card games, lottery, bookmaking, pinball machines, the sale and distribution of drugs, usury, pornography, and even systematic robbery and burglary. Representatives from each of the groups engaged in organized crime made up the political and economic power centers of the community, met regularly to distribute profits, discussed problems, and made the necessary organization and policy decisions essential to the maintenance of a profitable, trouble-free business.

The study began in 1962. For the next five years (1962-67) I spent a large amount of time observing and interviewing people involved with Seattle's criminal networks. My research took me into the backrooms of cabarets, cardrooms, jails, executive suites, and politicians' chambers. In 1967 I left Seattle but the research was continued. I went back for three months one summer and for several shorter visits. In 1971 David Keown and I visited Seattle twice and he stayed for several months gathering data for his master's thesis. Through contacts with friends and informants the research has continued to the present day though most of the findings reported in this book deal with the time period from 1962 to 1973. But the situation that is described could as well be a description of 1978.

In what follows I have used a combination of real and fictitious names. In some cases fictitious names are necessitated by my obligation to protect those who provided the information that made this book possible. Where pseudonyms appear I have indicated this by the letter (P) following the name used.

Whether or not the names used are fictitious, the events described are real. It is not my intention to dwell on the scandals and personalities of the people involved in what I found in my research. Rather, my intention is to show how and why these relationships occurred in Seattle and why and how they occur elsewhere as well. As this book is going to the printer, a group of journalists have recently published materials detailing illegal businesses and crime networks in Arizona that implicate some of the most prominent political and business figures in the United States. With a few changes of names and political affiliations the Arizona materials could be piped into the findings from Seattle, Chicago, Newark, or anywhere else.

CHAPTER ONE

You Can Get Anything You Want if You've Got the Bread

I N A VERY real, if surprising, way my work on the crime network began with an observation of Mark Twain's. He noted that "science is a fascinating thing: we get such wholesale returns of conjecture out of such trifling investments in fact." The trifling investment in fact that characterized the study of crime in the 1960s was a major impetus for me to shed my academic stance long enough to go into the streets of the city—more precisely, down to skid row and the black ghetto—to see what was taking place.

I chose this area of the city for a good reason: 80 to 90 percent of all the arrests in every city in the United States take place in the skid-row, lower-class, slum areas. I wanted to know why the police made most of their arrests in this rather small geographical area and, more precisely, how the working policeman decided to arrest some people and not others.

In 1962 a change in the sociological weather was taking place that was affecting us all, and it made us look again at what had often been taken for granted. Sociologists began to look through the windows of police cars and behind the bars of jail cells to discover "the law in action." I was skeptical that such a practice would yield reliable results. I decided, therefore, to watch the law work from the vantage point of those it worked on.

In an earlier time I had passed through skid rows in various cities while bumming around the country and working as a migratory laborer. I felt, therefore, that I could pass as a resident if I dressed and acted as I remembered others in those areas dressing and acting.

With two days' growth of beard, a pair of khaki pants, and an old shirt, I drove down to the edge of that magical ring that circumscribes and, in fact, effectively hides skid row from the eyes of those who do not care to see it. I walked the two blocks between the commercial center and skid row, turned a corner, and found myself *there*: incognito— almost. One block later two large black men stepped from doorways and moved toward me. Whoosh went my adrenalin.

"Got a buck, buddy?" It used to be a quarter, I thought.

"No, sorry." I was unnerved by the realization that they knew I was enough of an outsider to try to put the bite on me for a dollar.

It was raining this day, in that ubiquitous rain that is the hallmark of Seattle's climate. So I looked for shelter and found a seat in Tip's Amusement Parlor (P),* where I had a cup of coffee. I didn't like coffee and would have preferred tea, but coffee, I calculated, was essential for the image.

Pinball machines stood against the wall at Tip's. After my coffee I played one, and the waitress gave me a strange look

*The letter (P) indicates a pseudonym.

when I walked away from the machine with four unplayed "free games."

"Hey, don't you want the money for them games you won?"

"Oh. Oh, yeah." She went to the cash register and gave me forty cents. Then she went to the machine and rang off the games I had won.

Out in the rain I wondered about the meaning of all that. My thoughts were interrupted, however, by the sight of a patrol car moving slowly down the street. I walked in the same direction. The car, with two policemen inside, stopped at the curb and motioned to a man standing in a doorway. The man went to the car. They talked for a minute. The patrol car pulled away and the man went back to the doorway.

For the next several days I observed numerous incidents of this kind. They made little sense at first: foot patrolmen would, apparently at random, walk up and shake the handle of some closed businesses while completely ignoring many others. I saw people who appeared to be only slightly intoxicated arrested while others who were barely able to walk were either ignored or told to go home.

Once in the middle of a sunny (for a change) Friday afternoon a very large Spanish-looking woman ran onto the street from a small hotel entrance. She was screaming, "He's gonna kill me."

She saw a footpatrolman walking by and anxiously ran up to him. He waved his hand impatiently to ward her off and continued his walk down the street. A patrol car turned the corner in the next moment and moved slowly down the street. The woman ran up to the window of the car and said, "He's gonna kill me." The patrol car pulled away from her, turned the next corner, and was gone.

After a week of observation, my only conclusion was that

the arrest–nonarrest, action–nonaction decision of a policeman was totally random and irrational.

Sitting in Tip's Amusement Parlor one afternoon, I was joined by a patrolman whom I had seen several times. I started a conversation. He asked me what I did and I said, "I drive a truck." In the middle of his lunch I said, "You know something, I have always wondered how you guys decide who to pick up and who to ignore—where to look for things and where not to."

He replied, "Look, when you know a place as well as I know this one—I been on this beat for fifteen years—you just naturally know where to look, who's okay, and who needs to be watched. If a light's on when it should be off, I go see. If a broad's on this corner when she usually works uptown, I check her out. It's like when my old lady don't cook dinner, I know something is wrong."

This made sense to me so I accepted it as the start of an explanation.

Tip's was only a few minutes from the downtown business section. It stood behind an invisible wall that separated the city's skid row area of flophouses, Salvation Army relief centers, drunks, occasional workers, and amusement parlors from the rest of the city. It was a simple thing to cross the imaginary line and pass out of the respectable community. But despite the ease of access, only those with special interest in the pleasures, pains, and profits to be had behind the wall ever ventured there.

Behind the façade of banks, office buildings, and department stores, a different life pounded out a heartbeat distinct from that of the neighboring commercial district. Tip's, along with half a hundred similar establishments, was very much a part of this invisible world hidden within the city.

The outside of Tip's had the appearance of a run-down

bowling alley. Two of the bulbs in the neon sign were burned out; the paint was peeling and the door was painted an offensive green that was purchased because it was out-dated and therefore inexpensive. Only the large plate-glass window which provided a panoramic view of the street was new and well kept.

Inside Tip's was a long lunch counter where Millie (P), an over-the-hill ex-prostitute and sometime junkie, served coffee hot enough to take away the chill of a night spent in a cold, wet alley. Other than the long lunch counter and chair behind the cigar case beside the cash register there were no seats in Tip's. A row of pinball machines stood where booths might have been. The uninitiated played pinball for the sheer joy of watching the flashing lights and the meaningless numbers hop around the face of the machine. The initiated played for pay—or so they hoped. These machines were part of a relatively recent innovation in pinballs; they were "multiple coin" machines. The principle is simple enough: instead of inserting one dime and playing the game, you can insert as many dimes as you can shove into the slot. The more dimes you insert the higher the odds go and the more you stand to win—or, more likely, to lose.

Naturally the odds do not increase as a straight increment of how many dimes you put in. The machines are set to make the increase in odds something less than the increase one might expect mathematically to occur with every additional dime. Some of the players no doubt were aware of this but played anyway. Others—one suspects the majority—were really taken in by the assumption that underlies all gambling: that the "house" is in fact gambling and can be beaten. In reality the house never gambles: it only takes advantage of some well-known and clear mathematical principles of chance. The house cannot go broke and gamblers cannot beat the house no matter how much an individual may win. In the end the laws of chance are more powerful than the laws of luck.

On cold winter or rainy days, the area around the pinball machines and between the machines and the window are filled with men standing around. Since it rains more often than not, business was usually brisk. Most of the customers were unemployed, unattached men for whom the inside of Tip's offered some relief not only from the incessant drizzle but from the boredom of their cheap hotel rooms or the bad coffee of the "social clubs" set up by various charities.

One afternoon while I was having coffee at Tip's I noticed people going in and out of a back room. I asked Millie, who had become my friend, where these people were going.

Millie: "To play cards."

Me: "Back there?"

Millie: "Yes, that's where the poker games are."

Me: "Can I play?"

Millie: "Sure, just go in. But watch your wallet."

So I go, hesitantly, through the back door and into a large room which has seven octagonal, green felt-covered tables. People are playing five-card stud at five of the tables. I am immediately offered a seat by a hand gesture from the cardroom manager. I play—all the time watching my wallet, as I had been advised.

There is no money on the table, only small poker chips. The chips, however, are purchased from the cardroom manager. The limit on the bet varies but ranges between three and five dollars at these tables. The players are an interesting assortment of men most of whom seem to be "down on their luck." They are mainly middle-aged men playing conservative cards with what appears to be a group of friends. Most of them are acquaintances, a few are friends. The daytime game tends to draw the same group of people together day after day barring illness or recovery from a drunk. The players are amazingly patient and remain in their chairs hour after hour watching the cards come and go and the chips move around.

Occasionally a stranger—a sociologist dressed like a truck driver or an honest-to-God truck driver who comes by on his route to play for a half an hour—enters and leaves the game. The rhythm is only slightly jarred by these outside intrusions. Otherwise the scene has the distinct aura of a well-rehearsed play.

At noon the tables fill to capacity as shopkeepers and workers from nearby offices step across the line into skid row and play a few fast hands of poker or rummy.

Other than the players there are only the waitress and the cardroom manager present. The waitress is a marvelous contrast to Millie; if Millie gives the appearance of an over-the-hill prostitute, Margaret (P) gives the distinct impression that she is *not* over the hill. The manager is casual and friendly without being exuberant. The atmosphere is like that found in truck stop cafes, where conversation is limited and pointed but with an undertone of easy humor focused on making fun of one another's weaknesses or strengths.

Across from the cardroom, somewhat closer to the toilets on the other side of the hall, was a small door that led to a room with a sign (in yellow and red letters) announcing PANORAMA. Tip's' panorama was filled with machines which, for only ten cents, played two-minute reels of film showing women undressing and couples copulating. There are usually two distinct groups of people at panorama. First and most obvious is a counterpart to the men standing out front by the pinball machines: a row of sleepy-looking males leaning against the back wall of the room. Second are those who come in with something specific on their minds: men in business suits with neatly trimmed hair and boys of sixteen or so who are getting some sort of education. Like the difference between the initiated and uninitiated at the pinball counter, there are the "fish" and the "insiders" of panorama as well. The businessmen and the boys are mostly fish. The men leaning against the wall are insiders.

For the uninitiated the ten cents spent on the reel brings two minutes of viewing interest. However, what the initiated know is that the film becomes more and more explicit in its sexuality as each dime is inserted. What starts off as a film of a woman undressing ends as a film of a man and woman engaged in oral intercourse. The men leaning against the wall know that it takes five dimes to move from undressing to finale; they wait patiently for the boys to come and go with their dimes until the last reel is due, then they invest *their* money.

For the next several weeks I played poker in Tip's every day. In conversations with the cardroom manager, the waitresses, and the other poker players, I learned the truth of what a taxi driver had told me the second day of my research: "You can get anything you want in Seattle if you've got the bread." Gambling, bookmaking, stud-poker games, prostitution, drugs, pornographic literature and devices, high-interest loans, stolen property, bingo parlors, and pinball machines that pay off were available on practically every street corner of the hidden city.

Bingo began at ten in the morning and went until eleven at night inside the Alpha Bingo Club, one of eleven bingo clubs operating in the city. Here you found older people, many with shopping bags beside them, whiling away a few hours. Some played an amazing number of cards all at once: as many as fifteen or twenty at a time. The room was barren, with an invisible sign that said "strictly for profit." The players were intent on the game. My field notes on one of my visits to the Alpha Club report: "At the front of the room on a slightly elevated platform an attractive woman moves a basketful of ping-pong balls with numbers on them. She reaches in and calls out 'B 43.' The players quickly search their cards for that number. Each card costs ten cents. Cash and prizes go to the winners, though mostly the cash goes from the players to the bingo parlor." Enough cash goes that way to make the bingo parlor owners wealthy men. The secretary to one bingo operator explained that "normal" profits were not high enough, however, to keep the owners from cheating the customers. One of the games played is called Blackout. The idea is simple: the house pays off an extraordinarily high prize to the lucky winner, but each time a round goes by with no winner the size of the prize dwindles. When Blackout is called, there is a discernible quickening in the atmosphere.

Most often so many rounds go by without a winner that the prize slides from five hundred to twenty-five dollars. The bingo card manufacturer informed the purchaser that there is one number which appears on all the cards and without which none will ever yield the complete line across, down, or vertically necessary for a "bingo." Thus, the lady on the elevated platform, who juggled and picked the balls, needed only palm the one ball with the number necessary to win, and see that it did not get called until the prize had dwindled from five hundred to twenty-five dollars.

Occasionally, however, someone was allowed to win the big prize. This was done to keep the rumor around that huge payoffs were possible. Unfortunately for the customers the "huge winner" was, more often than not, a plant: someone hired by the owners to spend an afternoon (at two dollars an hour) playing bingo and to return the five-hundred-dollar prize as soon as he or she left the room with a big smile and a satisfied air.

The stories I heard led me to visit innumerable bars, cafes, cardrooms, and bingo parlors in the area. There were some variations in clientele, some variation in games played, but the fact that gambling was conducted openly and rampantly throughout this part of the city could be observed by anyone who cared to look. The police did not *seem* to be looking. It became my self-appointed task to find out why.

At the end of the month, as I sat talking to Millie, a partial answer to some of my questions was suggested. A man dressed in civilian clothes but whom I knew to be a sergeant on the vice squad came in and went into the manager's office.

Me: "Who is that?"

Millie: "He's the bagman."

Me: "The what?"

Millie: "The bagman. He collects the payoff for the people downtown."

Me: "Oh."

Nightfall brings many more people to the area. The cardrooms fill up, the panorama and pinballs get busier, and often there are lines of people waiting for their turn. On the street other activities come to life. Bingo parlors that have played most of the day to "little old ladies with shopping bags" now fill up with middle-aged men and women who play three, four, or five cards at a time. The small shops specializing in pornography and sexual mechanics light their neon signs and prepare for the rush of the evening.

Now on the street are more of the same people who played cards in the day. Those who live in the area are more numerous after dark. There are the drunks, the occasionally employed, the disabled, and the retired poor who live on skid row because of its cheap housing and food. But added to this nucleus of residents is an equal, perhaps even greater, number of nocturnal visitors who steadfastly avoid the area by day. These are "square johns," whose money makes the place live and die. These are the people who come at night for the gambling, the sex, the drugs, and the liquor that may be found elsewhere but are concentrated here and brought conveniently together.

Prostitutes, who during the day are occasionally drinking coffee in cafes or hanging around bars in the late afternoon, become more visible and more aggressive with nightfall. Some walk the streets, stand on streetcorners, or saunter along in front of cheap hotels. Others frequent bars and amusement parlors looking for customers. I met Judy (P) in front of a hotel. It was a slow evening and she was cold. So she accepted my invitation to go have a drink. We talked: not about her but about life, drugs, and women. Women, it developed, was a subject about which Judy had done a great deal of thinking.

"In this society women are nothing but a commodity. You buy and sell them for their sex and discard them when their sex runs out. I sell my sex openly. Most women hide the sale behind a marriage license."

The really profitable prostitution did not take place on the streets or in front of hotels. "The better girls work in houses or apartment buildings. When I'm clean [not on drugs] I can work in those places too, but lately I've been too strung out to make my way up the hill."

Prostitution is widespread and comes in an array of packages. Streetwalkers concentrate near the pockets of vice. Higher-class prostitution is located in whorehouses "up on the hill" and in apartment houses located in more respectable parts of the city where call girls live and work. In recent years body-paint and massage parlors have emerged as fronts for prostitution. Judging from the ever-increasing number of prostitutes and customers, apparently it is a myth that with the liberalized sexual mores of the time, "amateur competition" is driving the professionals from the job.

In Seattle of the 1960s there were at least ten whorehouses in the tradition of New Orleans, at least one of which had a madam that would make Sam Goldwyn envious. She was large, full-breasted, aristocratic in bearing, with a voice soft and cultured. The house was red-carpeted. At one time the madam was protected by a high-ranking police officer who was one of her closest friends and came to see her through a back door that no one else used.

Another part of the night scene were the high-stakes poker games that began around midnight. These games were not so visible as the small-stakes games in the back-rooms of the amusement houses. A few dollars of illegal gambling money across a table is one thing, but when fifty to a hundred thousand dollars changes hands every night, players and managers become more discreet. To play high stakes necessitates making contact with someone who can get you in. Out-of-town businessmen staying in expensive hotels can find the games through hotel porters, desk clerks, or taxi-cab drivers, all of whom receive a small compensation (ten or twenty dollars) for steering customers to the games. Others must make contact with the right connections.

After hearing of the high-stakes games and gaining confidence that I could play stud poker without losing my shirt, I asked the cardroom manager, with whom I had often talked, if he could get me into a "bigger game." One night as I was leaving he suggested that I stay a while longer. At 1:00 A.M. he closed up. I waited for him to count the money in the cash register and lock it in the safe. We then went up the street to an office building which was kitty-corner from the police station. There, on the second floor in an otherwise empty room, was a card table. Soon there were six players (including myself) sitting at the table playing a pot-limit game. It was "a sweaty experience," as the cardroom manager would say. Most bets were for more money than I was carrying and every bet was more than I could afford. We played five-card stud.

On the first hand I was dealt cards that were both lower than the card showing in the hand of the player immediately to my right. I had to play very cautiously because the pot and each bet could skyrocket. If it went too high too fast, I would have to drop simply because I would not have enough cash to cover the bet. With pot-limit poker each bet can be as high as the total amount of money in the pot. Since there were six players, and we were anteing five dollars each, the first bet could be as high as thirty dollars. If everyone stayed, then the next bet (on the third of five cards) could go to $30 + (6 × $30), or $210.

Being lower than the other players, I dropped. This round of betting did not get too high so I was encouraged. In the next round of cards I again had a low pair to begin, so I dropped again. The next round was critical for me. I had come with limited cash. I could neither afford to continue dropping (at five dollars each time) nor afford to play in a hand where the betting was extremely high. I had to calculate both the chance of winning and the chance of betting when others would not.

On the third hand I was dealt a pair of aces. This meant that I was probably going to win the pot if I could keep others from betting too high. I bet high with the ace of hearts showing, and, as I hoped it would, this scared away three of the other players. On the next card I bet high again and the other two dropped out. This gave me a small cushion for playing. The gods of sociology were smiling on me.

The rest of the evening I won and lost various pots; I selected those that I thought would not attract the high rollers and played cautiously. By the end of the evening I was a winner; and, in fact, I was able to finance other poker playing with the winnings from that first night.

The game broke up early—five-thirty in the morning. I had left a few minutes earlier and stood on the corner when the other players drifted downstairs. The man who ran the game and who took the cut for the house told me it had been a bad night, with only a thousand dollars for the house.

Tip's, its customers, managers, and waitresses are bland compared to the more intrigue-, violence-, and profit-infested cardrooms and gambling dens. At 608½ Union Street, above Bob's Chili Parlor (P), was the Caledonia Bridge Club (P). The front of this operation was a social club where people could gather to play bridge. Some people actually did play bridge—for money, with the owner taking a share of the stakes. Others played poker, and pan, and some shot dice. During a dice game on April 2, 1968, Robert Kevo, a well-known local gambler, was shot and killed. The person who shot him was agitated, according to observers, because he had been waiting too long for a seat at the table and Kevo refused to give up his seat.

Six-eleven Park Avenue was the home of a cardroom and high-stakes poker games. It was rumored that the man who ran this cardroom also worked as an enforcer when someone who owed some of the gamblers or loan sharks money needed persuading. It was said he could break a man's legs more efficiently than he could cut a deck of cards. And he was very adept at card cutting.

Cardrooms, bridge clubs, chili parlors, and restaurants were also the scene of other illegal enterprises: the distribution of drugs, the handling of stolen merchandise, the acquisition of illegal liquor (where taxes had been circumvented, for example), and the arranging of illegal, highinterest loans. People who ran some of these establishments were also called upon from time to time to serve as collecting agents for outstanding loans; steerers to put people in touch with gambling, prostitution, and drugs; and, last but not least, handmaidens to those above them who needed special jobs done.

During my night sojourns I saw the skid-row scene repeated over and over again in various pockets of the city. The black ghetto had its own versions, while the Japanese, Chinese, and Filipino communities had theirs. The management shifts, the games vary, and the sex differs, but the formula is the same: money for crime.

On Capitol Hill in the black ghetto, one of the oldest established whorehouses in the country was still flourishing in the mid 1970s. The owner and manager had been arrested for procuring, dealing in drugs, having gambling on his premises, white slavery, and a host of other offenses. He has yet to be convicted of anything.

In the Filipino community a prominent man in the rackets is a good old American success story. He came to Seattle in the 1930s when, I am told, police had an undeclared racist war against the Filipinos.

"If you were a Filipino youth it was worth a night in jail to simply be standing on the corner or walking slowly down the street."

Shortly after arriving in Seattle, he saw an opportunity to help his fellow Filipinos and, incidentally, to make a profit from benevolence. He established the Filipino Community Club (P). The club provided a place for Filipino men to come in out of the rain. It kept them from the visibility of police and the arrests that attended that visibility. It gave them a place to while away the endless hours of unem-

ployment in a community which, because of its historical
roots in the importation of male-only labor immigrants, was
populated by few women. The owner installed card games
and served as the community's principal informal and illegal moneylender. The card games were supplemented by
various forms of lottery and numbers rackets modified to
resemble similar games from the Filipinos' homeland.

All of these innovations pleased not only the owner and
his customers but the police as well. Having Filipinos off
the street meant less trouble for the police. Having a reliable associate who would, if need be, provide the police
with information about troublemakers or, more specifically, someone who had committed an unsolved crime
made their work easier and more efficient. Furthermore,
the police shared the profits from The Community Club,
which paid them off regularly and handsomely for the
privilege of remaining open and doing business.

The Filipino Community Club thrived; the police payments increased. In time, dealing in drugs and women
augmented everyone's income. In addition there were contributions to various politicians' campaign expenses and
some influence over the Filipino vote.

People working out of the club ran a nice little usury
business on the side. Filipino immigrants arrived im-
poverished. They were provided room and board for a few
weeks and given enough cash to get started. When seasonal
work came, the loan sharks would be paid back at eighty-
and ninety-percent interest. The same system could be
used, with carefully chosen customers, to enable people
out of cash to gamble in the social club—with loans made
at high illegal interest rates.

Many of the men in the Filipino community work sum-
mers in the canneries of Alaska and are unemployed the
remainder of the year. With an accumulation of surplus

capital some enterprising capitalists came to invest in usury. Seasonal workers were loaned money in the spring,
when last summer's earnings were running out. They paid
back the loans with their first month's pay. These were
high-risk loans which led to the creation of a "collection
agency" which employed people to convince debtors it was
time to repay the loan or have their legs broken.

There are large profits to be had from the poor and the
occasionally employed, but the lifeblood of high-stakes
gambling and usury is the money spent by members of
"respectable" society, particularly people whose incomes
can be concealed from the Internal Revenue Service: medical doctors, dentists, and lawyers, whose fees can be
readily hidden. For them, gambling with money they do
not have to claim on their income-tax return is gambling
with money most of which they would otherwise have to
pay in taxes.

A frequent participant in the high-stakes games whom I
had noticed losing substantial sums of money on several
occasions explained it to me this way: "I can afford these
games because I'm only betting ten or fifteen percent of
what I actually wager. I have a large income but one which
I can hide from the Revenue people by taking my fees in
cash or in personal checks. If I report all my income I
would have to pay eighty to ninety percent in taxes of everything I earn over sixty thousand dollars. So, say I end
the year with twenty-five thousand dollars in unreported
income. If I spend it on houses or vacations, they could
establish that I was living better than my reported income
would allow and thus hold me liable. But if I gamble with it
there's none to know. So when I bet a thousand dollars I'm
really only betting one or two hundred. If I should win a
large sum in a year, then I could even report that as income, pay the eighty to ninety percent and still come out

ahead. Meanwhile I have a really good trip because I love to play poker for high stakes. And I can always tell my wife I'm on night duty at the hospital. She stopped checking on me years ago."

Another frequent player supported this viewpoint. A lawyer who lost and won large sums said succinctly: "There may be better tax dodges than gambling, but no other way is half so much fun."

Poker games go on all over the city in hotel rooms, office buildings, and fraternal organizations. In the middle-class neighborhoods, card games flourish at the Elks Club, the American Legion, the Moose lodge and the city's leading country clubs. These games are organized by some of the same people who own and run the cardrooms in skid row. They are different in significant ways, however; the players are mostly upper-middle and upper class; and the amount of money bet is infinitely greater than what can be seen at Tip's' open tables.

Recently a national survey on gambling showed that the average amount of money spent gambling in the United States by a representative group of people was thirty dollars a year. Although this figure may be an accurate estimate of the average, it clearly does not tap the amount spent by those who seek and find gambling. For not only were these high-stakes games well attended, but the local fraternal organizations all contracted out to the high-stakes games for them to provide "fun nights" for club members.

Fun nights were ostensibly limited to members only, but in most instances one could obtain a temporary membership, good for the one night, by paying two dollars at the door. On such nights the club or house where the event was held looked startlingly like a Las Vegas casino. There were roulette, dice, cards of all kinds, blackjack, cocktail waitresses, and, in adjoining rooms, skinflicks and live strip-tease.

For the really wealthy who are reluctant or unable to venture to skid row, high-stakes games were available in surroundings more amenable. In the better hotels the bellboys and desk clerks served as steerers to get wealthy, out-of-town people into high-stakes games that were often located in the hotel where they were registered.

Or, for those who knew the city there were amusement parlors and there were *amusement* parlors. The two most famous clubs in the downtown area, The Ram and The Turf, were scenes of high-class games where lovely women entertained customers with smiles and promises. There were games where contact could be made for sex, drugs, or whatever the customer wanted. And in the backrooms telephones rang often but the conversations were short. Bookmaking operations of considerable magnitude were conducted in these high-class amusement centers.

Here the customers all wore business suits or flashy sportcoats. Many were from out of town. Conventions that bring thousands of people a year to the city bring millions of dollars to the gambling tables, thousands of dollars to prostitution, and an inestimable amount of money for drugs, liquor, usury, and other illegal businesses.

Winter set in. Tourism declined, and the size of the pots in the high-stakes games grew smaller. It was a good time to spend talking instead of observing. It was also time to find some people who were deeply involved in the rackets. These people could tell me how it all worked so smoothly with so many different facets apparently coordinated into a workable enterprise. Thus I began searching for those in the know who were willing to talk.

CHAPTER TWO

Being in the
Business of Vice

THE MAJOR customers of both legitimate and illegiti-
mate businesses are people whose incomes come
from the other. That is why it is not so difficult to discover
the business of vice in a city.If it were too well hidden, the
customers would not be able to find it. But what can be
observed and played is only a fragment of the picture.
Understanding requires getting behind the scenes, into the
boardrooms of management. That is not quite so easy.

Drinking beer, playing poker, buying meals, and sharing
bottles of wine with cardroom managers, bartenders, professional thieves, prostitutes, and others involved in the
rackets gave me valuable insight into the day-to-day workings of vice. The mysteries were, however, greater than the
discoveries at this point. For I knew that somewhere there
had to be people who coordinated the various activities.
People who skimmed the profits and provided protection
from law enforcement. Somehow the machines had to be
manufactured, serviced, distributed, and the profits

counted. There had to be some sort of an organization and the police had to be cooperating by not enforcing the law.

The puzzle only became more complex as the extent of vice in the city became more apparent. I learned of huge drug transactions and rings of professional thieves and cooperation between union officials and state politicians to sell truckloads of stolen liquor to the state liquor board. I was consistently met with stories about police payoffs and corrupt politicians who reaped huge profits from various rackets in Seattle.

For several months I interviewed everyone I could in an informal, casual way. I had hints and inferences but nothing substantial enough to answer my question. I decided that a new strategy was called for. I had to break the logjam of an endless amount of information on particular games and types of criminality but nothing substantial on how it was organized and by whom, if in fact it was.

I decided to play my trump card.

I asked the manager of the cardroom where I usually played to go to lunch with me. I took him to the faculty club at the University of Washington. This time when he saw me I was shaven and wore a shirt and tie. I told him of my "purely scientific" interests and experience and, as best I could, why I had deceived him earlier. He agreed to help and began by putting me in touch with Charlie MacDaniel (P), an energetic, fast-talking, overly curt, ex-professional boxer.

Charlie MacDaniel once owned a restaurant in the downtown section of the city. The restaurant had a cardroom attached to it and was, before Charlie bought it, the location of one of the oldest established bookmaking operations in the city. His experience with the business he purchased is an excellent example of how the vices are organized.

Before moving to Seattle, Charlie had accumulated considerable capital from selling a restaurant he had operated in a small town just north of the city. The restaurant was a converted sailing vessel in the harbor, and for a fairly high price people had the privilege of eating their meals on the deck of what once was a ship that carried merchandise from China to the United States in the 1800s.

It was a very profitable venture for Charlie. And when a group of businessmen offered to buy him out for a price substantially above what he had invested in the enterprise, Charlie decided it was time to sell. With over eighty thousand dollars in the bank Charlie began looking around for an opportunity to invest his money elsewhere. He was attracted by an advertisement in Seattle's leading newspaper: "Excellent investment opportunity for someone with $30,000 cash to purchase the good will and equipment of a long established restaurant in downtown area. . . . "

Charlie made the necessary inquiries, checked the books with an accountant, and decided to purchase the business. He thought he was buying the business from a Robert Battaglia. In fact, Battaglia was only the front man for a group of people who owned a number of businesses specializing in high-stakes poker games, prostitution, and bookmaking. These people, the real owners of the building and restaurant Charlie had purchased, had had to sell their business when they were indicted in Oregon by a grand jury investigating organized crime.

These things Charlie did not know when he purchased the business. He began very soon, however, to realize that the business carried with it more complications than he had anticipated. Shortly after the purchase Battaglia called on him. Charlie recalled, "We had just completed taking the inventory of [the restaurant]. I was then handed the thirty-thousand-dollar keys of the premises by Mr. Battaglia, and he approached me and said, 'Up until now, I have never discussed with you the fact that we run a bookmaking operation here, and that we did not sell this to you; however, if you wish to have this operation continue here, you must place another five thousand dollars with us, and we will count you in. Now, if you do not buy it, we will put out the bookmaking operation, and you will go broke.' 'In other words,' Mr. Battaglia continued, 'we will use you, and you need us.' I told Mr. Battaglia that I did not come to this town to bookmake or to operate any form of rackets, and I assumed that I had purchased a legitimate business. Mr. Battaglia said, 'You have purchased a legitimate business; however, you must have the bookmaking operation in order to survive.' I promptly kicked him out of the place."

The question of how "legitimate" the business was that MacDaniel had purchased was not as simple as he thought. It was, to be sure, a licensed operation. There was a license to operate the restaurant, and a license to operate the cigar stand (where a bookmaking operation had taken place before MacDaniel bought the place). Although providing a "legitimate business," these licenses had the effect of making the owner of the business constantly in violation of the law, for the laws were so constructed that no one could possibly operate a legitimate business legally. Thus, Charlie MacDaniel had unknowingly purchased an enterprise that was inevitably vulnerable to harassment and even closure by the authorities if he failed to cooperate with the law.

The cardroom attached to the restaurant was the most flagrant example of a licensed operation that was of necessity run illegally. The city of Seattle had adopted by administrative fiat a "tolerance policy" toward gambling. This tolerance policy consisted of permitting cardrooms such as Charlie's, pinball machines, bingo and panorama shows to be licensed by the city. The policy allowed a maximum one-dollar bet at the card table in rooms such as those in MacDaniel's restaurant.

The tolerance policy was in clear and open violation of state law. Section 9.47.010 explicitly states:

> **Conducting gambling.** Every person who shall open, conduct, carry on or operate, whether as owner, manager, agent, dealer, clerk, or employee, and whether for hire or not, any gambling game or game of chance, played with cards, dice, or any other device, or any scheme or device whereby any money or property or any representative of either, may be bet, wagered or hazarded upon any chance, or any uncertain or contingent event, shall be a common gambler, and shall be punished by imprisonment in the state penitentiary for not more than five years.

This general illegality of the cardroom was not, however, easily enforceable against any one person running a cardroom without enforcement against all persons running cardrooms. There were wrinkles in the tolerance policy which made it possible discriminately to close down one cardroom without being forced to take action against all of them. This was accomplished in part by the limit of one dollar on a bet. The cardroom was allowed to take a certain percentage of the pot from each game, but the number of people playing and the percentage permitted did not allow one to make a profit if the table limit remained at one dollar on a bet. Furthermore, since most people gambling wanted to bet more, they would not patronize a cardroom that insisted on the one-dollar limit. MacDaniel, like all other cardroom operators, allowed a two-to-five-dollar limit. Thus the policy was such that in reality everyone would be in violation of it. It was, therefore, possible for the police to harass or close down whatever cardrooms they chose.

The health and fire regulations of the city were also written in such a way that no one could comply with all the ordinances. It was impossible to serve meals and avoid violation of the health standards. Thus, when the health and fire departments chose to enforce the rules, they could do so selectively against whatever business they chose.

The same set of circumstances governed the cabaret licenses in the city. The city ordinances required that every cabaret have a restaurant attached; the restaurant, the ordinance stated, had to constitute at least 75 percent of the total floor space of the cabaret and restaurant combined. Since there was a much higher demand for cabarets than restaurants in the central section of the city, cabaret owners were bound by law to have restaurants attached, some of which would necessarily lose money. Moreover, these restaurants had to be extremely large in order to constitute 75 percent of the total floor space. For a one-hundred-square-foot cabaret, an attached three-hundred-square-foot restaurant was required. The cabaret owners' burden was further increased by an ordinance governing the use of entertainers in the cabaret. It required that any entertainer be at least twenty-five feet from the nearest customer during her act. Plainly, the cabaret had to be absolutely gigantic to accommodate any customers after a twenty-five-foot buffer zone encircled the entertainer. Combined with the requirement that this now very large cabaret had to have attached to it a restaurant three times larger, the regulatory scheme simply made it impossible to run a cabaret legally.

In effect, such ordinances gave the police and the prosecuting attorney complete discretion to choose who should operate gambling rooms, cabarets, and restaurants. This discretion was used to force payoffs to the police.

MacDaniel discovered the payoff system fairly early in his venture.

I found shortages that were occurring in the bar and asked an employee to explain them, which he did. "The money is saved to pay the 'juice' of the place." I asked him about the "juice." He said in this city you must "pay to stay." Mr. Davis said, "You pay for the bagman (from the police department) two hundred and fifty dollars per month. That takes care of the various shifts, and you must pay the upper brass also two hundred dollars each month. A bagman collects around the first of each month, and another man collects for the upper brass. You get the privilege to stay in business, that is true. However, you must remember that it is not what they will do for you, but what they will do *to* you, if you don't make these payoffs as are ordered. "If I refuse, what then?" I asked. "The *least* that could happen to you is you will lose your business."

During the next three months Charlie made the payoffs required. He refused, however, to allow the bookmaking operation back in the building or to hire persons to run the cardroom and bar recommended to him by the police or by the people from whom Charlie had purchased the business. He also fired one employee whom he found taking bets while tending bar.

In April of the same year a man Charlie had known before buying the restaurant came to Charlie's office:

Mr. O'Keefe met with me in my office and he came prepared to offer me five hundred dollars per month—in cash deductions—of my remaining balance of the contract owing against (the restaurant) if I would give him the bookmaking operation, and he would guarantee me another eight hundred dollars a month more business. He warned me that if he wanted to give my establishment trouble, he would go to a certain faction of the police department; if he wanted me open, he would go to another faction. "Do some thinking on the subject, and I will be in on Monday for your answer." Monday I gave Mr. O'Keefe his answer. The answer was, "No."

In June of nineteen hundred and sixty, a man by the name of Joe (Gaspipe) Gasparovich, who I found later was a second-string gang member of Mr. Battaglia's, made application to me to operate my cardroom. I did give him the opportunity to operate the cardroom because I had known him some twenty years ago when he was attending the same high school that I was. After I had refused the offer of Mr. O'Keefe, Mr. Joe Gasparovich had received orders from Mr. O'Keefe and Mr. Battaglia to run my customers out and, in any way he could, cripple my operation to bring me to terms. I terminated Mr. Gasparovich on November sixth, nineteen hundred and sixty, and shortly after, after I had removed Mr. Gasparovich, Police Officer Lyle J. LaPointe said that I had better reappoint Mr. Gasparovich in my cardroom, that his superiors were not happy with me. If I did not return Mr. Gasparovich to his former position, then it would be necessary to clear anyone that I wanted to replace Mr. Gasparovich with. Officer LaPointe felt that no one else would be acceptable. He further stated I had better make a decision soon, because he would not allow the cardroom to run without an approved boss. I informed Officer LaPointe that I would employ anyone I chose in my cardroom or in any other department. Officer LaPointe said, "Mr. MacDaniel, I think you do not realize how powerful a force you will be fighting or how deep in City Hall the money goes." I did not return Mr. Gasparovich, as I was ordered by Officer LaPointe, and I did select my own cardroom bosses.

On November seventh, nineteen hundred and sixty, I received a phone call stating that I soon would have a visitor who was going to shoot me between the eyes if I did not comply with the demands to return Mr. Gasparovich to his former position. . . .

No one shot Charlie between the eyes. However, the state liquor inspector came and found Charlie in violation of the liquor laws for serving alcohol to someone who was inebriated. The liquor board asked the city council to revoke his license. The city council licensing committee unanimously voted to comply with the board's request. Charlie appealed to the city council through an attorney. His license was reinstated, but for a month he was out of the liquor business and losing money.

Subsequently MacDaniel had a string of visitors. First came a teamster who intimidated the customers in Charlie's bar and tried to pick a fight with him.

"I've got a quick temper," Charlie said, "and I came out from behind the bar, and, even though he was twice my size—I used to be a professional boxer when I was young and I'm still pretty strong—I threw him out of the bar." The next morning when Charlie opened his restaurant he was welcomed by gaping holes in the front windows of his building. "Vandals" had attacked. A police department memo dated October 18, 1960, said this about the event:

Intra-Department Communication
Seattle Police Department

From: D. B. Packard
To: Capt. E. T. Corning
Subject: Vandalism at "Bats" on 1st Avenue

This is a copy of the notice which has been posted in the window of "Bats." Officer Wenger reports that the window was broken this A.M. when he came to work and that other acts of vandalism have been committed at this address as, (he believes) a result of said notice being posted. He is making a major. Inspector Porter* is acquainted with this case also.

*Inspector Porter later became King County sheriff.

The "notice" referred to in this police department memo was a statement Charlie posted in his window telling of police harassment and shakedowns that were damaging his business and his "good reputation."

Following the broken windows and other acts of vandalism, Charlie was visited almost daily by inspectors from the fire department, the health department, and the state liquor board. Fire inspectors came to inspect all his equipment: stoves, fire extinguishers, gas and electrical outlets—at exactly twelve noon when the restaurant was full of customers. The inspections lasted "a good hour" and made it impossible for his customers to be served in a reasonable amount of time. Health inspectors chose the dinner rush hour to arrive for their inspection. They insisted that all the pots and pans in the kitchen be emptied so they could inspect them. Stoves had to be moved to check for dirt and uncleanliness. This too had the effect of running customers away.

Members of the Teamsters Union as well as other people Charlie identified as being associated with gambling and other rackets in the city came into his restaurant, bar, and cardrooms and began starting fights. Meanwhile shortages from the bar and restaurant were increasing. Finally, as if to punctuate the last gasp of the dying business, policemen, like pallbearers, came and stood around the cardroom and bar. The net effect, as Charlie put it, was: "No one likes to play poker with a cop standing over his shoulder. And, of course, if I enforced the one-dollar limit the customers would simply disappear."

Disappear they did.

Ready for a compromise after losing substantial sums of money during the six months in which he was subjected to this pressure, Charlie called and offered to sell the place to Battaglia for the price he had offered six months earlier.

Battaglia informed him that the price had changed. Now he would pay twenty thousand dollars for the entire business and equipment. This was forty thousand dollars less than Charlie had paid originally. Charlie held out for six months, then finally sold at a loss of all his capital. On selling, he placed the following notice in the window of his business:

NOTICE

DEAR PATRONS:

THANK YOU FOR YOUR PATRONAGE FOR THE PAST 3 YEARS:

THIS RESTAURANT HAS BEEN FORCED TO CLOSE BECAUSE I REFUSED TO JOIN THE GAMBLING SYNDICATE AND I REFUSED TO BE FORCED INTO FURTHER PAYMENTS OF EXTORTION MONIES TO THE PROTECTION RACKET WHOSE ENFORCERS ARE CERTAIN MEMBERS OF THE POLICE FORCE.

I HAVE ISSUED A PUBLIC CHALLENGE TO THOSE WHOM I HAVE ACCUSED OF THESE ATROCITIES—TO A TEST OF TRUTH—A TEST THEY DARE NOT TAKE—A LIE DETECTOR TEST. I HAVE AGREED TO TAKE SUCH A TEST, THE GREAT WHITE CHIEF AND THE LORD HIGH MAYOR HAVE NOT ACCEPTED, THEY DARE NOT ACCEPT.

SINCERELY YOURS

Charlie decided to spend some of his remaining money and much of his energy exposing the corruption. He hired an attorney and spent many hours gathering information and affidavits from people. He also held a news conference in which he harangued the media, politicians, and police. The official response of the police and politicians was to classify him as a "paranoid" who had lost contact with the world. This depiction worked fairly well: the newspapers stayed away from his press conference and no one printed what he had to say. Even the affidavits were dismissed as being irrelevant.

After selling his restaurant Charlie returned to his former home and began developing some land he owned there. He sold lots to people for houses and cottages. He also built a water system for the area and provided water and sewage for a monthly charge.

In the spring of 1962 a man came and bought some of Charlie's lots. The man claimed to be a lathe contractor but he never worked. He built a forty-five thousand dollar house and spent all his time wandering around the neighborhood talking to people who lived in the area. He systematically went to the other landowners and told them that MacDaniel was robbing them blind by overcharging them for the water and sewage system. In time the people in the community organized to force Charlie to relinquish his ownership of the utilities. Charlie reported that "since this was my only source of profit from the enterprise, I couldn't let this happen."

A lengthy court battle ensued, with Stanley (P), the unemployed "lathe contractor," supplying most of the funds and spearheading the attack.

There were harsh words between Stanley and MacDaniel on several occasions. One day Charlie went to his land and found that an expensive piece of bulldozing machinery had been driven off a cliff. He was told that evening by Stanley that "accidents happen to people who push the wrong people around," though at that point, according to Charlie, no one in the area except the police should have known about the equipment being damaged.

Several weeks later Charlie was working at the marina

adjoining his property when Stanley and his son came to the top of the cliff overlooking the marina:

He came down to where I was working in the marina and it was he and his boy. This is to make it short. There was more to it than this. He was throwing rocks down on me, see, he and his boy. He had a baseball bat and he was hitting some and he was throwing others and I was getting out of there and I went up to get in my truck to get out of there and he met me at the back of the truck and said he was going to bash my head in with the bat. He had a boy about seventeen. So, then I was scared. I don't care what anybody said. I had no witness; I had nothing there. But a car had just drove up about that time and it happened to be two friends of his. I think this was not planned, just something that accidentally happened. It's the little things that throw us off, not the big things. And I could see that he was going to set up the thing to try to kill me. Well, when these people drove up, they said, "Come on, let's go up to the house." I hadn't said any words at all to this fellow at this time. I hadn't said nothing at all; just watching them. Every time you are in a fight you watch the other fellow's eyes, you know. I always do, anyway, to see what kind of move he's going to make. He said, "Just a minute. I'm gonna bash this son of a bitch's head in." And he turned around and poked me with his bat and at the same time his boy said, "I want to get in on this, too." So when he poked me with this bat, I shot him. I had a little Derringer twenty-two, you know, and I didn't think I even hit him, you know, 'cause he just stood there with very little expression; but I hit right, just through the meat up here. I didn't hit his heart. It was just lucky. I didn't want to kill him anyway. I just wanted to stop him. And so he backed up about six or seven paces and he turned to those people and he says, "I want you to witness he shot first," and he pulls out a thirty-eight and he shot at me. I dove in back of the truck and moved up around the truck and he shot through the fender and the next shot, he shot through the windshield. And here I was. They say I laid down on the ground, you know, and they grabbed me and of course, I spent four days in the klunk while the sheriff was investigating but they didn't put him in the klunk, the klink you know. But this I couldn't understand. I had been out there for twenty years, you know. It has been my residence for twenty years and never been arrested for anything like this at all, speeding, you know. But nothing else. No thefts, no assaults, you know, nothing like that. And so then they let me out on bail, one thousand, five hundred dollars' bail. They indicted him and me on a second-degree assault charge, but he didn't have to go to jail. He was free all the time, and they let him know ahead of time what his bail was going to be so he had all the privileges that are afforded to a visiting king. So I got started on this thing because they don't usually do that. As a rule, the sheriff will take both parties in, put them in jail and sift the facts. They will say, "Well what happened here?" But they didn't do it in this case, and of course, this is very irritating and very aggravating. So this is the first of the tourist season and I didn't have any time to do any investigation. The attorney was out of town at this particular time, when they set the bail. During the summertime they sneaked a hearing for him, and he was absolved of these second degree charges. Now my attorney didn't know anything about this. I called him up when I heard a rumble. I got people who come around and tell me these things when they find out something. Now, I says, "The fellow says there was some sort of justice court action pertaining to the case up there." He didn't know what it was: it was all silent. There hadn't been one word out, nothing and so I called him up and said, "I want some information." He said, "There's nothing: nothing has happened at all." So I started my investigation a week after, pertaining to the whole case in general about these people, and I went up to the area they were from just before they came down here, and I found that he was working with Twitchell in the south end patrol group. Twitchell was the one who was indicted, convicted, of the prostitution ring.

. . .

Eventually Charlie was acquitted and the case dropped. However, he continued to receive phone calls telling him that he would be killed if he didn't move out of the state. He "ran scared for about a year," then decided he had had enough. Charlie MacDaniel moved to a small town out of state and purchased a small cafe. Several years later I spent a weekend with him there. He was living on an income that was only a small percentage of what he had when he purchased the restaurant with the cardroom; he was a man broken economically and spiritually. At night he locked his doors and would not venture out into the street. He thought he might have to move again because he was convinced that "they" had traced him to Arizona. When some youths broke his windows one night, he thought it was "them" trying to intimidate him.

The half a hundred other restaurant operators who had cardrooms, pinballs, and bookmaking operations in Seattle were more cooperative. They hired the cardroom managers recommended by the police or by "the syndicate." They permitted the bookmaking operations, and they settled for a small profit from the pinballs. They also paid off the right people.

Charlie's payoff, probably because he was difficult to deal with, was less than what most operators would have had to pay for such a prime location. His payoff totaled four hundred and fifty dollars a month. Similar establishments with comparable business were paying as high as eight hundred a month, in two separate payments.

In 1968 there were fifty-one licensed cardrooms in Seattle. Federal records showed that Seattle had more gambling licenses issued than any city in the United States outside of Nevada. The fifty-one cardrooms were twenty-five fewer than, the city records showed, had existed at the peak of the cardroom craze four years earlier. These fifty-one cardrooms were owned mainly by independent businessmen, most of whom were first and foremost *not* gamblers but restaurant-owners like Charlie. Some of the cardrooms, in fact the largest ones, were owned and run by professional gamblers or by a group specializing in illegal businesses. But for most cardroom owners the cardrooms, panorama, pinball, and bookmaking operations were sidelines whose profits went mainly to other people. A restaurant with ten pinball machines which grossed over one hundred thousand dollars from the machines received less than 5 percent from this gross. Similar reimbursements came from panorama, and only a slightly higher net profit went to the owner from cardrooms. From the businessman's point of view, the illegal games and enterprises were an attraction that brought in customers for the restaurant business. In some cases the illegal enterprises were merely tolerated to keep police and fire and health inspectors from harassing him. This was in reality a highly sophisticated protection system.

Charlie's story and his experiences opened up a new perspective on vice in Seattle. For the first time it became clear that the best way to view the rackets was not as "crime" in a conventional way but as an industry. But who ran the industry? If not the cardroom owners, then who reaped the profits?

To answer these questions, I let it be known to everyone I could that I was interested in studying the entire system of payoffs and political intrigue connected with the rackets. I asked Charlie, as well as all of the other contacts I had previously made, to have anyone and everyone who was interested in talking about such matters to get in touch with me.

Soon I began receiving telephone calls: "I understand you are interested in the police. Did you ever think to look into ——'s investments in Mexico?"

A surprisingly large number of people called and asked

to meet me. One caller insisted that we meet in an abandoned warehouse down at the docks. It was a scary experience, but one that proved invaluable. This man had been part of the police payoff system for over twenty years. Not only was he able to tell me what was happening in the 1960s, he also provided insight into the political history of the rackets in Seattle.

The next several months were taken up with meetings and interviews with people "in the know." At first I asked if I could record the interviews on a tape recorder I carried with me. Although I was usually told that this would be all right, I realized that it stifled spontaneity and so I stopped. Still, I was losing a great deal of detail, and detail was what I needed most. My sources of information now were people who to a greater or lesser degree were aware of the support systems in the city that were perpetrating and maintaining illegal businesses. It was my aim to piece together from their information the organization of the vice industry. What became increasingly clear, as I developed more and more information, was the fact that, while some people were incredibly knowledgeable about certain aspects of the rackets, no one really understood how it all fit together. Not even those who sat at the very top as major financiers, profiteers, and manipulators in the enterprise knew.

To piece it together, however, required an almost endless amount of sifting through interviews. It was a formidable task and one made more difficult by my having to rely solely on notes usually taken after the interview had terminated. I decided to tape the interviews without the interviewees' knowledge. This was obviously dangerous and ethically offensive. The tape recorder I used was a brief case, but there was danger that it might break or develop a mechanical problem that would reveal that the interview was being taped. Some of the people being interviewed would have gotten violent had this happened. I decided to take the risk and hoped I could fast talk my way out of any difficulty if worse came to worst. The ethical problem was more difficult. I resolved it, to my satisfaction, this way: At the end of every interview I informed the person to whom I had been talking that I had taped our conversation. I removed the tape from the recorder and handed it to him or her. I explained that I would use the tape only for scientific research. No one but me would ever hear the tapes or see the transcripts. In anything I wrote I would do everything possible to conceal their identity. But if they wanted to take the tape and destroy it they were free to do so. In all but one instance the tape was handed back to me, and I was able to use it. In the one case where I could not have the tape back, a man had described a murder he had committed.

The central question that emerged from the interviews and conversations that occupied the next several years was exactly who was supporting, financing, and profiting from the business of vice.

CHAPTER THREE

Profits and Payoffs

BOB WILLIAMS (P) was only nineteen years old when he was arrested in the black neighborhood that was his turf. He was only nineteen when he was beaten to death in a jail while in the custody of the police. Like many other nineteen-year-old black youths, Bob Williams, judged by white middle-class standards, was sophisticated beyond his years. He knew how to turn a honky around, how to survive in what he called "the jungle," and how to buy cheap, sell dear, especially when he was buying and selling dope.

"I'm an independent. Some of these guys have all kinds of strings on 'em. Not me, man. I'm my own boss. Ain't nobody gonna pull me around by the nose."

According to a police sergeant on duty the night Bob Williams was taken in, "We had been watching Williams for some time. We knew he was heavily implicated in the narcotics traffic and we were just waiting for our chance. An informant told us he would have a lot of the shit on him that Friday so we picked him up."

Williams was arrested "on suspicion." At the time of his arrest he had over fifteen hundred dollars worth of heroin in his possession. The heroin, like whoever beat him to death, disappeared.

According to the policemen who arrested him, Bob called them names and tried to jump out of the car. I do not know what happened between eight P.M. and midnight, but shortly after midnight Bob was brought into the emergency ward of General Hospital badly beaten and unconscious. He was released back to the police the next day at twelve noon. The same intern who had patched him up Friday evening was still on duty Saturday about four P.M. when Bob was returned to the hospital again badly beaten, this time with a concussion. The police told the intern that "inmates in the cell keep beating him up." Bob Williams died at three A.M. Monday from a brain hemorrhage caused by blows to the head.

The intern told me he believed the police had beaten him to death. The coroner listed the cause of death as "accidental." No one was ever charged with any criminal offense in connection with Bob's death.

Friday night, while Bob was in jail, a white physician who had lived in the city for a number of years drove through the black ghetto. His car weaved down the street and stopped near a corner. He took a .38 caliber revolver out of his glove compartment and began shooting into the night air. The police came, stopped him, and took him to jail. The police called his wife and she came to the jail. The doctor was released to his wife's custody. He had spent a total of forty-five minutes in custody.

On Saturday night, as Bob Williams lay dying, I played poker in a high-stakes poker game where thousands of dollars were illegally bet. A sergeant from the vice squad of the police department participated in that poker game.

Bob Williams paid a heavy price for his involvement in

the drug business. Others who made all or part of their livelihood from the drug business were more fortunate. The informant who told the police when to pick up Williams was generously supplied with heroin by the police.

Behind this tragic case lies a fundamental truth about policing in America: the small, unprotected, unconnected entrepreneur furnishes the arrests and the "crime problem" that provide a smoke screen behind which profitable, organized, politically connected groups commit more serious, more profitable, and more common crimes.

Why the enforcement of the criminal law takes this shape is quite complicated in some ways. In one sense, however, it is very simple because it all reduces to money and profits. The money flowing through the rackets is large, and the profits are doubtless the highest of any industry in the world.

Item: From 1956 to 1970 each of eleven bingo parlors grossed over $300,000 a year. The owner of one bingo parlor netted $240,000 a year *after* all expenses, including payoffs to police and politicians, were paid.

Item: From 1960 to 1970 there were over 3,500 pinball machines licensed in the state. These machines grossed over 7 million dollars a year. The investment necessary for purchasing and servicing the machines was miniscule. The taxes were nonexistent since all returns were in cash and could be hidden. There was one "master license" for the county. It gave one organization the right to place pinball machines in the amusement parlors, cabarets, and restaurants. This small group of businessmen, closely tied to political and law-enforcement people, had a monopoly on one of the most profitable businesses in the state.

Item: In 1968 Seattle had the highest number of federal gambling stamps issued in any state in the U.S. except Nevada.

Item: A jeweler in Seattle was a major source of short-term loans to people in the drug business. Typically he would loan large sums of cash for a short period of time and receive in return a very high interest on the money. One transaction alone involved the loan of $220,000, with the understanding that the jeweler would receive back $350,000 "within thirty days."

Item: A consortium of businessmen, bankers, politicians, and racketeers invested in an "amusement center" which fraudulently issued stocks and netted the six investors over $100,000 apiece in six months on a $10,000 investment.

Item: High-stakes poker games that went on each night in dozens of locations throughout the city had stakes bet in an evening that often exceeded $100,000. Seven nights a week, 350 days a year, the people who organized and managed these games took away 10 percent of the pot. On a bad night for the house the management took home only $1,000, but on good nights management grossed $10,000, which was the rule rather than the exception.

The list could be expanded.

One of the reasons we fail to understand crime is because we put crime into a category that is separate and distinct from normal business. Much crime does not fit into a separate category. It is primarily a business activity. The fact that it is an illegal business activity is an historical accident beyond the control of those who engage in the business. But the mere fact of this historical accident does not change the basic character of the enterprise. The place to start the analysis is with the profit structure and with the business expenses required to keep the profits coming in.

In Seattle the rackets constituted one of the largest industries in the state. Gross profits from gambling alone amounted to more than fifty million dollars a year. Of course, this is only a rough estimate pieced together from information supplied by people who ran various gambling enterprises. It is, however, consistent with an intriguing variety of information I gathered from diverse sources. The following fact should give more than casual confidence in the reliability of this figure. A recent national survey shows the U.S. adult spends an average of thirty dollars a year on gambling. Over a million people live in Seattle, and if everyone spent the average on gambling, the total would be close to forty million dollars a year. Seattle is a favorite convention and tourist city and could easily run the total amount spent on gambling up to the estimate of fifty million dollars a year.

The profits are for the most part tax free. A pinball operator told me: "At the outside, our reported income is only one-third of what we actually take in. There isn't a federal agent in the world who can tell how much I skim off the top of a pinball machine once I've gotten to the counters."

"Fun nights" at the fraternal clubs, high-stakes poker games, cardrooms, etc. contributed huge sums. Not counted were all the other illegal businesses associated with some of the same people who ran, owned, financed, or profited from gambling. They include drugs, prostitution, cabarets run illegally, real-estate transactions, illegal stock and bond transactions, and stolen liquor.

The total profits of these various illegal businesses exceeded a hundred million dollars a year in Seattle, and this placed gambling, narcotics, fraud, usury, and organized theft among the state's two or three largest industries.

Legitimate business relies on the support of the law and the courts to ensure predictability and adherence to contracts. Illegal business cannot openly "go to court" if a debtor refuses to pay a gambling debt or to make good on an agreement to purchase a large supply of narcotics. But illegal business must be able to accomplish the same end or else the risk to the capital investment will be too great. The simplest, most direct way to ensure that the investment will return its potential profits is to include as partners those whose job it is to see that the illegal acts are punished by law. That is what happened in Seattle and what happens everywhere. Politicians, law-enforcement officials, professionals (especially lawyers, accountants, bankers, and realtors), and "legitimate" businessmen become partners in the illegal industry.

If I asked any of the dozens of people who practised the arts and crafts of gambling why the police did not enforce the laws prohibiting such acts, they gave the same answer: payoffs. Payoffs gave the police "a piece of the action," a part of the profits. And even a part of the profits was a lot of money.

At the operational level the cooperation of politicians and law enforcers takes place through the payoff. A bagman collects an established payment from every enterprise engaged in illegal business. Cardroom operators were surprisingly consistent in their reports of how much they paid off. The large operators paid $350 a month to the police and $300 a month to "the syndicate." Smaller operators paid $250 a month. Bingo parlor operators, "social club" owners, and gamblers in the Chinese, Japanese, and black ghettos paid less. The amount depended on the size of the operation and the amount of protection received.

Fred Lindesmith (P), a seventy-two-year-old man dying of arterial sclerosis, was on the police force in Seattle for twenty years. He participated in the payoff system and retired financially secure at age sixty-five. Fred had earned enough "extra money" as a partner in illegal business to send his two children to college with all their expenses paid. By the time he was seventy years old, however, he had grown disillusioned with the bastardization of police work he had helped to create. He was, he said, wanting to "set the record straight."

Q: Can you describe the payoff system?

A: Whoever was acting as official or unofficial treasurer would have the responsibility to see to it that the right people got their share. Skip Tower (P) did it for a while. Then Bob Furman (P) took his turn. Everyone involved got their share. When Ben Cichy was killed they sent someone out from downtown to burglarize his place. Three black dudes went out and tore up the floor looking for where he kept the monthly payoff money hidden. They left twenty thousand dollars worth of jewelry just sitting on the table. They were obviously not burglars, but people sent out from downtown. They terrorized Cichy's wife to death.

Q: Who got the money?

A: Everyone. The beat cop, the vice-squad captain, the prosecutor. Everyone. It depended on the gig. Narcotics payoffs went through the vice squad and the patrol division. Sooner or later it all went up to the top.

Q: Anyone else?

A: Of course the city council had its people with their hands out also.

Q: But how exactly . . . ?

A: Okay. It's like this. There's a bagman who collects the money from tavern owners, the cardrooms, or the whorehouses. He brings it in. He takes a small cut. Then the sergeant in charge of the division, say the vice squad, takes his cut and passes it on to the police department's bagman, who takes it on up—a piece here, a piece there. Then it goes to the assistant chief, and he takes it on to people in the prosecutor's office and sends some over to the city council. The patrol division had their own payoff system. The patrol division was required to make its payoff to the mayor's office depending on whether the particular mayor was cooperating, and they all have, *except one* in recent years. . . . And there was a separate payoff system for burglary and narcotics. Burglary was probably as big as gambling. And individual narcotics ripoffs, sporadic but very lucrative payoffs in major narcotics transactions. Thousands of dollars in a single payoff.

Q: Who to?

A: To the narcotics dicks, then to be divided right up through the chain of command to the majors and lieutenants, and the assistant chief and the city councilmen.

Q: All on the local level?

A: Yes and no. There was another line that went to the state, and the state had its own gigs. Liquor licenses and payoffs for illegal booze, stolen whiskey from the state warehouses, watered-down whiskey and all that stuff went straight to the state. Frank Schneider (P) has for years been going between the governor's office and local payoff systems. People in the House of Representatives got theirs as well. In fact the guy who flies the payoff money to San Francisco every week is in the House of Representatives.

Q: What about different counties?

A: I'm not too sure about that setup, but it figures that they cooperated with one another—talked about how much profit there was and what each got from it. You should talk to ____ about that.

Q: You mentioned narcotics ripoffs. . . .

A: Yeah. Narcotics was really big. Even bigger than pinballs or cardrooms. It's kind of long and involved. The police would use this guy ____ to set up narcotics dealers.

Q: Like Bob Williams?

A: Yeah. Like Bob Williams. You know what happened to him?

Q: Yeah.

A: Well, they'd set up a narc dealer and make the arrest. Then they'd confiscate his stuff and turn it over to ____, who'd sell it, and the police would get a big share of the profit. The police would also have a fat narcotics arrest record, but the heroin and pills and stuff would still get to the street. I know the names of all those guys. I'm particularly close to the latest one who managed this operation, former lieutenant of the narcotics squad.

Q: At the state level, who do they work out of?

A: The state patrol; State Highway Patrol.

An item in the daily paper gave an indication of what happened to some of the profits. Lt. T. Ryther (P), who had been a police officer for thirteen years, died suddenly of a heart attack at age forty-one. At the time of his death he left an estate valued at $241,786. During his thirteen years as a police officer, Ryther had lived in a large, seventy-five-thousand-dollar home, owned two fully paid for expensive automobiles, and taken vacations in Hawaii. He had never earned over twelve thousand a year in salary from the city. He had, however, earned more than twice that amount in payoffs from illegal businesses in return for the protection and cooperation he gave them.

Both the King County prosecutor and the sheriff owned expensive homes in the city's most prestigious neighborhoods. The prosecutor also owned a fifty-foot ocean-going yacht. The assistant chief of police lived in an expensive house and built another for his son in an even more expensive neighborhood. The county prosecutor also directed unknown sums of money to state and local politicians who supported his kind of politics and his kind of criminality.

Policemen told a standard joke in the department: "If you cleaned this city up, we'd all have to go on welfare 'cause none of us could live on our salary." Some of the policemen, ironically, lost a good percentage of their illegal earnings to the gamblers who were paying them off or to other police officers. Others spent large sums on whiskey and nights in cabarets. Still others invested in businesses and left the force. One ambitious and clever young officer saved enough money in three years working on the narcotics squad to purchase a large retail store in the downtown section of the city.

In a sense the illegal businesses *were* paying taxes in the form of monthly and annual payoffs to people at all levels of law enforcement and government. It is, however, misleading to see this network of money-flow as involving only profits and payoffs. In fact, what took place was a complicated set of illegal and legal business relationships which were the flesh and bones of a network of people engaged in the systematic reaping of profits from illegal businesses.

This cartel constituted a crime network that was a subterranean organization which greatly affected, as surely as it undermined, the political economy of Seattle.

CHAPTER FOUR

The Crime Network

THERE WERE over a thousand people in Seattle who profited directly from the rackets, bootleg whiskey, organized theft and robbery, drug traffic, abortion rings, gambling, prostitution, land transactions, arson, phony stock sales, and usury. Everyone who successfully engages in these criminal activities must share the profits with *someone* or some group of people. The more regulated the criminal activities and the more successful the participants, the more systematized the profit sharing. The entire system is simply a collection of independent operators who cooperate and compete according to their ability, their power, and their interests.

Disparate as it is, widely distributed among people in different walks of life, and changing all the time, there is nonetheless a hierarchy. Some people are more important than others. In times of crisis some people have the power to make critical decisions while others do not. Not surprisingly, those who profit the most from the rackets and who also have the power to take action are the most likely to meet and discuss problems and prospects. In Seattle the group of power-holders who controlled and set policy for the illegal business enterprises varied. Over the years the more active participants included a King County prosecutor, a Seattle city council president, an assistant chief of police, city police captains, the King County sheriff, the King County jail chief, undersheriffs, the president of the Amusement Association of Washington (who had the only master's license for pinball machines in the county), a Seattle police major, and an official of the Teamsters Union. In addition there were persons from the business and professional community who were members of the network and who in a quiet, less conspicious way were as influential over illegal business activities as were the more visible operatives listed above. They included a leading attorney who defended network members and joined them in investments in illegal enterprises, a realtor who arranged real-estate transactions and shared investments, an officer of one of the state's leading banks, a board member of a finance company that loaned money exclusively to businesses or individuals who were either members of or under the control of the network, and various labor union officials—mostly in the Teamsters Union, but high-level officials of other labor unions were also involved from time to time.

One of the problems with determining the real power sources in an enterprise as inherently secretive and variable as a crime cartel is of course the line between active participant (or policymaker) and compliant benefactor. For example, a prosperous retail store-owner in the city often invested in and profited from illegal enterprises ranging from real-estate frauds to drug traffic. He also financed and arranged for the transportation of stolen jewelry out of the United States to Europe, where it could be recut and sold on the European market. He never set policy, never became involved in the day-to-day decisions, never allowed himself even to be consulted about the handling of a particular problem within the ongoing enterprises. Yet he knew of most of the problems and could well have been influential had he cared to make his wishes known. He preferred to remain silent. His decision, he told me, was based on the "good old American tradition of self-preservation." He felt that the less he was involved in "administration," the more likely he was to remain unconnected publicly with the "seamy side of business." He acknowledged, however, that when a newspaper reported the death of a member of the network due to "accidental drowning," he knew it was no accident.

A further problem is to decide the point at which one has enough information to feel confident that the rumors and allegations being put forward as "facts" by informants match sufficiently with other data to be acceptable. The people mentioned so far were all well established in the minds of all my informants in a position to know. These people also exhibited life-styles which clearly showed incomes in excess of anything they could have had from their legal incomes. (The county prosecutor claimed publicly that his standard of living exceeded that which his salary could support because of monies his wife had inherited.)

But it was also alleged by some informants, who should have known, that the real power in the illegal business enterprises lay with high-ranking officials in state politics, a close associate in Seattle, and a former Seattle city council member. I was unable to establish the validity of these claims. In the end the consistency of informant reports convinced me that the governor was indeed a beneficiary of heavy political campaign contributions from network principals. He, like many others, benefited from the profits and left the management to others.

At one time (1963-65) it was fairly easy to identify seven people who constituted the backbone of the network. This group shifted, however, and some of the seven became less involved while some new people emerged as principals. Both composition and leadership are variable; success is determined by connections and profits. When drug trading becomes more precarious, the people involved may lose considerable influence; when cardrooms come under fire, those people whose profits or payoffs are principally in cardrooms lose their influence.

Whatever the composition, this coalition of shifting membership (but fairly constant leadership) persisted and had more to say about how the rackets were run than anyone else. It also met more or less regularly, but here too the pattern was not akin to a monthly board of directors' meeting but was more a series of meetings between key players from different walks of life. Politicians who were deeply involved in the network met regularly at their "businessmen's club" with members of the city council, the county board of supervisors, and several key businessmen who were profiting from the rackets. Law-enforcement officers met monthly with a pinball operator who was the head of the Amusement Association, an association of pinball operators which was the official lobby for the pinball machine owners. The head of the Amusement Association in turn met with other businessmen, at least one of whom was reputed to be the bagman for state politicians.

Some sense of the organized–disorganized nature of the rackets can be gleaned from a series of incidents in the mid 1960s which involved an attempt by Bill Bennett (P) to take over part of the pinball operation in the city. Bill's brother Frank was one of the prominent racketeers in town, a man generally believed to be involved in prostitution and the collection of payoffs for state officials (including the governor) as well as the police. Bill decided that he wanted a piece of the action in the pinball business. He tried at first to demand a territory but he met with resistance. Pinballs were at the time concentrated pretty much in the hands of several people. The only master license in the county was held by the Amusement Association. As president, Ben Cichy represented not only his own interests as the major pinball operator in the state, but also the interests of other pinball operators. Ben Cichy was well protected in his position. As president of the association that looked out for the pinball interests, he met regularly with and allegedly paid substantial sums of money to politicians, to Frank Bennett (P), and to members of the police department. In addition, the Amusement Association collected from all pinball operators a monthly fee that was used to ply state and local politicians with liquor, parties, and women for favors, not the least of which were large campaign contributions to politicians who worked in the interests of pinball owners. Thus Bill Bennett was taking on some formidable opponents when he tried to muscle into the pinball business. On the other hand, Bill and his brother Frank were well connected in political and business circles. Among others, Frank was closely allied with politicians who were the political and personal enemies of the county prosecutor and might well have been favorably disposed toward an attempt to undermine part of his political base.

When Bill's efforts to gain part of the pinball operation were turned down by Cichy and the other owners, he filed what is referred to as an "underworld anti-trust suit." He and some of his men began throwing Molotov cocktails through the windows of places containing Cichy's machines. Some restaurant owners were roughed up. This caused some attention in the press, so people were getting

nervous. To ralm things down, the pinball operators offered to let Bill in if he would agree to pay them twenty
thousand dollars for the loss of their territory plus a fee of
two dollars a month for each machine over and above the
fifty cents per machine that went to the Amusement Association for lobbying.

The agreement reached by the other pinball operators
was, however, not satisfactory to the chief of police, who
saw Bill as a "hoodlum." This was one of the few occasions
when the chief put his foot down. An informant in the
police department said that "in all likelihood" the chief ve-
toed the agreement as a result of support and instructions
from the county prosecutor. Because of the trouble Bill had
caused, the chief insisted that he leave the state, which he
did.

Several features of this event are important. First, it un-
derlines the competition between different persons acting
primarily as individuals out to increase the size of their
business and their profits. It also illustrates, however, that
when the entire enterprise is threatened, it is possible for a
coalition of the more powerful members of the rackets to
force less powerful members to acquiesce. The incident
also indicates an important element in the way any network
protects itself. The two-fifty a month which Bill would have
to pay for each machine was divided between protection
(two dollars a month) and lobbying (fifty cents a month).
The one activity is presumably criminal (by statute), the
other legal.

Was This Crime Network, Then, the Local Mafia?

I talked with many people about the possibility that this
network was a local branch of the Mafia. A professional
thief who had also worked in the rackets (gambling, prostitution, drugs, etc.) told me, "You can forget that Mafia

stuff. We are Hoosiers out here. There is no organized crime like they have back east, like in Kansas City and Cleveland. We're too independent out here."

This same feeling was expressed time and again by people at all levels. Virtually everyone in a position to know anything about the rackets in Seattle echoed these sentiments: "Every time you check the Congressional Record and you see the FBI diagramming the Mafia families in San Francisco, you can tell them to shove it up their ass, because you can't diagram this. If you do diagram it, you can't read your diagram when you're done. It's all squiggly lines: the chain of command and who's in charge of any operation and who's entitled to what cut of the graft, it's all very changeable."

Q: Is the police force more or less an independent thing, not controlled?

A: No, everybody has a part of the police department's ass. Really the police department is the biggest corporate hooker in the whole establishment. The Teamsters Union used them; Democrats at the time; the city council uses them; the license committee uses them; the prosecuting attorney also had an occasion to use the vice squad to make sure he is getting an honest count, if someone gives him trouble on pinballs. Police chief, or assistant chief, would use the department sometimes at cross-purposes to what the mayor or the prosecutor might like. The mayor or the prosecutor might not want trouble, let's say, from a bar operator, like Charlie MacDaniel. They really probably hated that, when that thing came to a head the way it did. The cops, however, went right in and hassled Charlie, because the cops were smarter. The cops know what's going on out in the street, and they knew better to make an example out of Charlie, even if it gets in the newspaper, than to lose control. The prosecutor is like any other crime boss. Something is wrong out there: he looks at a lieutenant, and he says, "Fix it." He might also add the admonition, "Don't be messy, fix it." And the henchman is a technician. Like any technician, he knows that sometimes you have to get your hands dirty when you fix the machinery. And the boss may not want any machine oil on the floor, but he may have to get some to get the machine fixed. So, beyond a certain point, if it gets messy, tough shit. Because the technician is responsible, and he doesn't want to be held responsible. And if somebody like Charlie MacDaniel gets too far out of line, you take whatever measures are necessary to cover your own ass. You worry about the boss later, see? Right now you're thinking about staying out of the newspapers, staying out of prison. So, on any given occasion, the loyalties of the policemen might be very divided; and this political structure that is controlling the rackets is very fractured. At times it is fractured along the straight Democratic against Republican lines. At times it is fractured along straight county bureaucracy against city bureaucracy. At times it was fractured along city lines, depending on who was contending for power and money. And that's why you can't chart it. It's not neat.

Q: And they're all dependent on each other.

A: And each one requires the silence of the other; no matter how ugly the fighting gets, they've got to keep it under and out of sight. This is one reason why I think there was very little killing, comparatively speaking. When people are killed, they were people within the apparatus, little people. Or people like Ben Cichy if he was, in fact, murdered, who admittedly are very visible, but for some reason somebody determined at that time that it was desperately important that he had to die.

But who exactly was it that could decide that so-and-so had to die?

I was advised by a telephone call from someone I had met in a high-stakes poker game that I should go to Vito's (P) Cafe on the second Thursday of each month and see who always ate lunch there at a table in an alcove.

For six months I went to the cafe as advised. It was indeed interesting to see, week after week, gathered at one table and talking low enough not to be heard by anyone else: the assistant chief of police, an assistant prosecuting attorney, an undersheriff, and an attorney from a firm of lawyers that specialized in criminal law.

These four people met regularly every other Thursday. Rarely, however, was the luncheon limited to just the four. A local contractor, a realtor, a businessman whose firm specialized in "investments," the head of the Far West Novelty Company and president of the Amusement Association, a hotel owner, a member of the city council, a member of the county board of supervisors, an official of the local Teamsters Union, and once a newsman from one of the city's leading newspapers.

A friend told me that one of the regulars at the Thursday luncheon would like to talk to me. A meeting was arranged, and I met Von Bennett (P) at a bar. While we were drinking beer, I taped our conversation:

Q: __ said you would tell me about the Thursday lunch group.

A: That's the meeting of the local Mafia.

Q: What do you mean by that?

A: They're the boys that run the rackets: drugs, gambling, girls, bootleg whiskey, pinballs—all that stuff.

Q: Well, that doesn't make sense to me. I have heard that __ is the major person in the rackets—at least in some of the rackets—and he never goes there, does he? I at least haven't seen him.

A: Yeah, you're right, but that doesn't mean these guys don't run the rackets. It's like this: they work for guys with either political or police pull. They control those guys either because the big guys take a cut or because they have something on them. So this group kind of coordinates things. And they keep in touch with people in diverse fields, from bingo to booze.

Q: But how are they a Mafia?

A: Well, not like you read about a Mafia with a tightly knit organization, but these guys are as close as we come out here. They've got the most—a finger in every pie—but still, as you say, there's lots of others . . . all getting rich from the rackets. . . .

The people who are getting wealthy from the rackets are not the cafe, tavern, or cardroom owners. The people who are getting wealthy are the businessmen with capital to invest in an expanding, high-profit business, politicians and law-enforcement officers who can convert political or police power into wealth. It is an interesting, fascinating illustration of the two-faced nature of the adage that wealth is power. That is certainly true, but the other side is equally true: power makes wealth as well.

The network members who met regularly were more or less elected representatives of the business, political, and law-enforcement groups that profited most from the rackets. For a while Charlie MacDaniel was a problem for them when he was refusing to pay off and later when he tried (in vain) to publicize the existence of widespread corruption in the police department. The inner circle of the network, after consulting with their bosses and co-owners who stayed in the shadows, tried various strategies to deal with him.

The kind of publicity created by MacDaniel was extremely bad for some of the most important people in the network. Businessmen who thrived on the image of Seattle as a "clean city" and a "nice place to live" knew of the underlying life of crime, but they wanted to keep those realities from public inspection at all cost. Politicians knew of the potential careers ruined by public exposure of links to anything smacking of organized crime, so they wished to keep things quiet as well. But there were cross-pressures at work that were equally important to the smooth functioning of a crime network. A person who refused to pay his proper share (whether through the payment to the police or to the "syndicate") was a threat to the entire system. If Charlie MacDaniel didn't pay, there would be a lot more tavern, cafe, cardroom, and other business owners on the fringe of legality who would take Charlie as a model and refuse to pay as well. Thus, if someone caused trouble for the organization of vice in the city, a calculation had to be made as to how best to deal with the threat. In the case of Charlie MacDaniel the calculation that evolved out of deal-

ing with his periodic balking at "playing the game straight"
resulted in his being run out of business, out of the city,
and eventually out of the state.

Notice, however, that the acts which constituted a "policy" with respect to a "problem" were the result of a *process*,
not of a decision. True, someone decided what to do, but it
was a matter of a series of individual decisions made by
people who shared the same interests and views rather than
a ruling passed down by a boss. To the extent that there was
a boss, he may or may not have agreed with what finally
constituted the policy. But whether he agreed or not, the
policy resulted from the process of coping with a problem-
atic situation. And, of course, some of the different people
and groups involved in network activities had different
interests.

One feature of criminality that is almost always overlooked is the extent to which businessmen who operate a
presumably legitimate and wholly legal enterprise are involved either overtly or covertly in criminal activities. More
often than is ever acknowledged by law enforcers or investigators, businessmen are the financiers behind criminal
operations. In Seattle one of the city's leading jewelers
served simultaneously as a financier for large drug transactions and as a fence for stolen jewelry. Often businessmen
are co-opted by business and friendship ties to members of
the network. A vice-president of one of the city's leading
banks was a close associate of the county prosecutor,
lunched with him, contributed his personal endorsement
to the prosecutor's political campaigns, invested in things
the prosecutor recommended, supplied links to other businessmen for the prosecutor, arranged loans, and so forth.
Both the vice-president of the bank and a jeweler were key
members of the network. Their money financed criminal
activities and they reaped huge profits from them.

Newsmen on the city's leading newspapers were also implicated. In one case it was principally through receiving gifts from various members of the network. There were also rumors that an editor received a monthly income from the network. This seems unlikely, for the editor was not only co-opted by friendship and small favors, but the newspaper was opposed to exposing any graft or corruption lest the city reassess the value of the newspaper's property. A local politician and one-time candidate for sheriff possessed information linking an editor of one of the newspapers with a national wire service that reported racing results. The police were also aware of these links. This information was never made public, perhaps because the keepers of the news are in the end the safest possible mediums for conducting illegal business activities.

There is clearly no "godfather" in the crime network, no single man or group of men whose word is law and who control all the various levels and kinds of criminal activities. There is, nonetheless, a coalition of businessmen, politicians, law enforcers and racketeers (see diagram) who have a greater interest in the rackets than anyone else, who stand to lose the most if the operation is exposed, and who also have the power to do something when it is called for. These men do not have unlimited power, to be sure, and they must assess their power in each incident to see what is the best strategy to follow. Thus, when someone firebombed competitors, there were some in the network who wanted to acquiesce to his demands, some who wanted to wait and see, and others who wanted to "kill that crazy son of a bitch." Killing him was a very dangerous alternative since it would surely create adverse publicity and hostility between various groups involved in the rackets. Letting him in might have the same effect. Eventually the head of the pinball operation agreed to let him in for a high price, with

Seattle's Crime Network

Financiers

Jewelers	Attorneys
Realtors	Businessmen
Contractors	Industrialists
Bankers	

Organizers

Politicians

City Councilmen
Mayors
Governors
State Legislators
Board of Supervisors Members
Licensing Bureau Chief

Law-Enforcement Officers

Chief of Police
Assistant Chief of Police
Sheriff
Undersheriff
County Prosecutor
Assistant Prosecutor
Patrol Division Commanders
Vice Squad Commanders
Narcotics Officers
Patrolmen
Police Lieutenants, Captains,
and Sergeants

Businessmen

Restaurant Owners
Cardroom Owners
Pinball Machine License Holders
Bingo Parlor Owners
Cabaret and Hotel Owners
Club Owners
Receivers of Stolen Property
Pawnshop Owners

Racketeers

Gamblers	Pimps	Prostitutes	Drug Distributors	Usurers	Bookmakers

the tacit agreement of the other pinball operators. But the chief of police resisted and was apparently able to force Bill out of the state.

Incidentally, a leading state politician who was also involved in the rackets arranged for Bill to obtain employment with a criminal syndicate in another state. Bill apparently decided that discretion was the better part of valor.

Bill's brother Frank owned a string of taverns and cabarets, a few hotels, and the major jukebox distribution company in the state; and he allegedly controlled most of the white prostitution rings in the city. After a visit to one of his cabarets I made this record:

> Frank plays with his keys constantly as he sits on the edge of his chair in his Starfire Room Cabaret. The naked women dancing on three stages simultaneously and the waitresses serving watered-down liquor stop by occasionally and ask him a question. He hands one of them the keys and gets up from time to time to do something in the back room. One of the women occasionally disappears upstairs with a customer. Frank looks totally bored by the scene. The money he's making, the naked women he's employing, the conversation about the rackets and his role in them are all old hat. What interests him is the possibility that once again, at age fifty-three, he may be going back to prison. This time it will be hard time. This time he does not have the promise of something big when he gets out. This time he will lose rather than gain.

Frank spent eighteen months in prison in 1942-43. Those months were "no picnic," but he was sustained that time by a promise given, the promise by a young politician that if Frank "took the fall" and served the sentence he would be "amply rewarded" when he was released. It was a fair deal, fair for the politician, fair for the others involved, and fair for Frank.

Frank was the son of a vegetable farmer in the county. His family was comfortable but neither notorious nor wealthy. He and some of his young friends were untouched by crime or rackets to any significant degree, but they were touched by the sin of many American men—womanizing. One of the women that Frank slept with regularly was only sixteen years old. She was also sleeping with several of Frank's friends. The young woman was arrested, and she confessed to the police that the older men had been having sex with her for some time. The police threatened all four of them with jail sentences. The four men denied the charge, and the police had only the uncorroborated testimony of the girl.

A young lawyer who was active in politics managed the business affairs of Frank's family. The four accused rapists fell to arguing among themselves as to how to get out of the predicament. They called in the family's lawyer to mediate. The lawyer contacted the police, who told him that someone had to stand trial. The police agreed, however, to drop charges on all but one of the defendants in return for a guilty plea. The lawyer took out a checklist and added up the pros and cons of having one of the four plead guilty to the charge. Some were married, some had businesses that would suffer; Frank was single and could afford the stigma. He was also only twenty-three, so the effect of having sex with a sixteen-year-old would look less awesome. The lawyer promised there would be no jail sentence, only probation or a suspended sentence. He also promised that when it was over the other men would put up the money to set Frank up in business.

The lawyer's power to negotiate a deal was less than he indicated it would be. He did get the charges dropped on everyone but Frank, but Frank had to spend eighteen months in the state reformatory. On release, however, the lawyer kept his promise and set Frank up with a liquor license, a tavern, and a going business, without Frank's having to invest any money.

While Frank was building his tavern business, the young lawyer was building a political career that led all the way to the state legislature. Frank and the lawyer-politician remained close and trusted friends. Frank, it was said, became the state politician's personal bagman. He went to the various rackets in the city and collected a monthly tithe. He collected, for example, a thousand dollars a month from the owners of bingo clubs. It was a substantial amount of money, but the profits from the bingo operation were sufficient to easily underwrite this and numerous other profit shares the owner made.

The next thirty years were good ones for Frank. He expanded his first club into the ownership of numerous other clubs, part ownership of the major jukebox distributorship in the area, partial control of some of the pinball operations, and he handled some of the organized prostitution in the city, especially the prostitution that ran out of taverns and nightclubs.

Frank also became a force to contend with. He was one of the people in the rackets who could stand up to county politicians and come away intact. On one occasion a leading politician called Frank in to put him in his place. According to someone who witnessed the encounter, when Frank entered the room, the politician said, "I understand you are the biggest pimp in the state." Frank replied, "Yeah, and I hear you like to play with little boys."

The politician had probably expected a humble racketeer to grovel at his feet. But Frank's own position in the rackets and his connections with state politicians plus some important influence in Washington, D.C., were sufficient to make it impossible for the local politico to squash him.

This did not elevate Frank to a position of omnipotence. Both he and the others would have eliminated their opponents in a moment if it could have been done without jeopardizing their own operations. But they could not. So an unappealing alliance prevailed year after year. Occasionally harsh words were spoken; threats and attempts to oust leading political supporters of each other's camps were made. But the détente persisted and indeed would persist today were it not for the fact that in time another faction emerged with the power to squash both parties to this alliance, but that gets us ahead of the story.

Two members of Seattle's leading families were also implicated through various business transactions with members of the network. The business transactions invariably came recommended by a leading local politician and brought the investors huge returns on small investments. They certainly should have realized that the enterprises were illegal, but in any case they participated and showed their appreciation by supporting the politician in the face of all sorts of opposition. When, for example, their political-business ally was threatened with exposure by a newly appointed U. S. attorney, these two businessmen flew to Washington, D.C., where they consulted with a personal friend who was an adviser to President Nixon. They asked him to have Nixon stop the inquiry. For reasons that will be taken up later their request was refused and the inquiry continued.

There were other positions (rather than individuals) that were crucial to the network's success. Two bear particular attention: the head of licensing for the county and the tax assessor. The people in these positions were never very powerful. Their careers were entirely in the hands of politicians. Nonetheless, what they did at their behest was of considerable importance to the network's continuance.

There were "considerate" assessments made on the taxable property of the two leading newspapers, the fact of which could then be used to keep them from publishing news the prosecutor did not want made public. There was also a payoff made to some politicians, a small part of which was sent down to the assessor through a firm in Portland, Oregon. This firm was hired by at least two of the state's largest industrial firms to keep the tax assessments on their corporation properties much lower than they should have been. Small wonder that the owners of these businesses always supported the cooperative politicians when they ran for office.

The head of the licensing division of the county also received a share of the profits, as well as some smaller payoffs he arranged by himself. To operate a tavern, a cabaret, a cardroom, a taxicab, or even a tow-truck company, it was necessary to have a license issued by the city's licensing division. These licenses were no less than a piece of very valuable property. They virtually guaranteed substantial profit from investment. The number of such licenses was kept to a level where anyone who had the license was certain to have his services heavily in demand. A tow-truck license cost ten thousand dollars "under the board." Depending on its location and potential, a tavern or a cabaret could cost fifty thousand dollars (plus monthly payments) to license. A cardroom might cost only one thousand dollars since there was not the certainty of profit accumulation from the cardroom. Monthly payments, however, would vary according to profits, as we have seen.

Liquor licenses were handled at the state level. The liquor board consisted of three men, all appointed by the governor for staggered nine-year terms. This board was the source of incredibly large sums for "campaign contributions" and outright graft for state politicians, especially those in positions influencing licensing and liquor policies.

At the root of the crime network's operation was the

money that got shuffled from the people who operated the rackets—the bookie, the numbers man, the whorehouse operator, the drug trafficker, the cardroom manager, tavern owner, or pinball operator—to the politicians, law enforcers, and businessmen who protected the network and its enterprises. The amount of money shuffled, as we have seen, was staggering.

The day-to-day decisions might have rested in the hands of seven, nine, or ten men who consulted regularly with the other principals in the network. But for such a widespread and profitable system to persist, a set of relations far more extensive than this and beyond mere payoffs had to develop, especially since the task of maintaining control over the various enterprises and the people involved was a task of major importance to everyone. As we shall see in the next chapter, the problem of maintaining control was much more complicated than first met the eye.

CHAPTER FIVE

Maintaining Control

S HARED INTERESTS are the root of the forces of social control that maintain silence and ensure mutual cooperation among the members of the network and those who work for it. The device by which all these people come to share an interest in maintaining corruption and widespread criminality is the payoff. Principally payoffs are in cash, the oil of capitalism's machinery. This money provides cash to meet monthly bills, to pay gambling debts, to finance political campaigns, to send children to private schools, to bribe officials for special favors, or simply to pay wages somewhat above those earned by comparable workers in "legitimate" employment.

There are gifts that supplement payoffs: a color television given to the newscaster, an antique automobile for a bank vice-president, a loan to a local businessman. And there is the use of public office to gather information that gives someone a special advantage in making a handsome profit from a small investment.

Those who cooperate and join the network are well rewarded. A routine and moderately paid government job can be turned into a source of wealth or at least considerable luxury. Seattle police captains received monthly stipends of five to eleven hundred dollars from the network. These, however, were the more blatant and in many respects less important techniques by which the network maintained control. More important by far were the people who moved from one position of power and influence in the government–business structures to another, all the time maintaining links with or control over important segments of crime enterprises. A few cases illustrate the interpenetration of different political and economic structures of network members.

1. A police officer and police inspector who worked directly under officers who coordinated payoffs within the police department was handpicked by a leading local politician to run for the office of sheriff when there was an opening. He was successful in his campaign. Afterward he received his salary as sheriff and large monthly sums as his share of network profits from the county.
2. A U.S. Coast Guard commander who was friendly with network members, upon retirement from the Coast Guard, was appointed to the state liquor board.
3. A fireman from the city cooperated with the crime interests by inspecting and harassing businesses or businessmen who refused to cooperate with the network. He also assisted in the destruction of some property network members wanted to burn in order to collect insurance. After five years as a fireman he joined the police force and was appointed to the vice squad, where he continued to work as a network member for seventeen years. With the support of leading people in the political power structure of the city, he was elected to the city council, where, along with

the president of the council, he worked diligently to protect the interests of network members. While on the city council he was appointed head of the licensing committee, from where he was able to control the licensing of both legitimate and illegal businesses.

4. Agents of the Federal Bureau of Investigation who either worked closely with network members or were suspiciously unconcerned about corruption were able to remain in the Seattle office for unusual lengths of time. On retirement they were offered attractive jobs in government and business. Contacts with network members were then used to bring in substantial business to their companies or law firms. The companies were of course pleased with the business and with the political contacts a former federal law officer brought to the business. For his part, the agent might be increasingly important in network policies and could direct several businesses central to network interests.

5. A former sheriff who worked closely (but not too wisely) with the network was appointed to the state parole board. In this position he was able to manipulate prison terms for network members as well as to punish persons who did not cooperate with them. He was also in a position to shorten prison sentences for people able to make payoffs to leading members, including, of course, himself. Most important, he could see that network members were able to "do a favor" for a politician or businessman who wanted to "help out a friend" by getting someone out of prison. Such mutual aid was a crucial ingredient in maintaining control.

This list of people who moved from position to position as the network solidified its control over local and state politics and law enforcement could be expanded to include judges, state legislators, and political officeholders at all levels. The examples selected are neither extreme nor unusual. They are, in fact, quite typical of how a crime network maintains control. They are typical of how American politics works. The fact that the profits that underlay the establishment of the network of crime were from business ventures that were illegal does not alter the fundamental fact that the process by which these interrelationships developed and persisted was no different from the process by which the same networks and interdependencies emerge and persist between enterprises that are legal and the political law-enforcement system.

For the system to work effectively there must be enough income to warrant mutually shared interests protecting and perpetuating illegal activities. Such a network would not arise to protect the interest of people devoted to the rehabilitation of derelict alcoholics.

The Business Community

People engaged in the manufacture, sale, or distribution of goods or services that are legal get involved with crime networks by pursuing profits in precisely the same way they pursue profits in legitimate business. The "decision" to join a network is often more an accident than a design:

> I met Jay (P) at the Rainier Club. We liked each other. We both had played sports in college and had a lot in common. We also like to drink and horse around. Then one day he called and told me he knew of a possibility for turning a nice profit if I had some unused cash lying around. It was a perfectly natural thing. Businessmen are always doing things like that. So I invested a good deal of money on Jay's recommendation. I guess I should have looked into it more

carefully, but I had no reason not to trust him. After all, he was a well known politician at the time. He told me it was to be used to import some things from Taiwan. I never saw a bill of lading though I see now I should have asked. Only later did I discover that I had purchased ten percent of a heroin shipment. I doubled my money in two months. Naturally, I didn't want to ask too many questions with that kind of profit. The next time Jay called I was ready to sell my wife to make the investment. We bought land together and some phony business connected with an amusement company, and Jay passed on tips to me about land deals. I liked the guy, and we agreed politically on most issues though he was a little too conservative for my blood. Still, in view of our friendship and everything I contributed heavily to his political campaigns and even supported him publicly. . . .

Similar patterns prevailed throughout the community. A realtor became involved by learning of an opportunity to invest in a hotel. The realtor was approached by a lawyer who did not identify his clients. The lawyer's clients, the realtor was told, were interested in purchasing an old hotel suitable for renovation. The location was not important, but the hotel did have to be in poor condition. The realtor found a suitable hotel, which the lawyer then authorized the realtor to buy for his clients. The realtor agreed to accept a share of the hotel as his commission.

The lawyer and his clients formed a corporation. They became a public corporation and sold stock. The proposed purpose of the stock was to raise capital to renovate the hotel. Few of those who invested over a million dollars ever saw the hotel. Nor were they ever aware of the caper in which they took part.

The corporation borrowed several million dollars (from the bank of which a member was vice-president) on the strength of the capital raised by selling stock. Contracts were granted for reconstruction. The principal contractor was a man who had moved to Seattle from Detroit, where he had been a member of a crime network that controlled much of the building industry in that city. The contractor agreed beforehand to kick back to the lawyer and his clients 50 percent of the value of the contract. When reconstruction of the hotel supposedly began, the insurance was increased commensurate with the construction that was allegedly taking place.

The insurance was prorated according to reports given to the insurance company by the contractor as to how far along construction had progressed. When the construction was supposedly nearly completed and insurance was close to its peak, the hotel burned down. In actuality, of course, the hotel had barely been touched. The money that was to have gone for reconstruction had mostly been skimmed off by those who formed the corporation and by the contractor. The insurance company paid the full amount. The stockholders were paid off, the company was liquidated, the state purchased the vacant lot on which the hotel had stood, and the stockholders profited a little. The criminal network profited a lot. Not only had they increased their capital by making a "shrewd investment," but they had along the way gained the friendship and allegiance of an important local realtor, who was most pleased that his commission had turned into such a handsome profit. The insurance company raised the price of next year's insurance by a fraction of a penny to cover the loss.

Property and the State

State, county, and municipal governments manage an enormous amount of property. They manage buildings that house government offices, municipal parking lots, jails, courts, roads, highways, and public buildings. They also manage and control licenses, franchises, and other forms of property that are the source of incredible profit to those who can acquire them.

Property, whether in the form of land, buildings, or franchises and licenses, is the cornerstone of capitalism. The property managed by the government for the most part (but not entirely) is "soft" property in the form of licenses, franchises, and information. The governor of the state, the county board of supervisors, the municipal governing board or mayor, the heads of licensing committees in the legislature or in the government control much of the soft property. It is used for a variety of purposes, of which the cementing of power and the conversion of power into wealth are the most important.

In 1964 a Republican replaced the incumbent Democrat who had been governor for two terms. One of the new governor's first official acts was to transfer over one million dollars in state insurance to the insurance company for which the governor had worked before his election.[5] The outgoing governor amassed a personal fortune while in office. In one instance he purchased a piece of land for $8,327 and sold it for $250,000.

There are good reasons in the legitimate business community for a crime network. Many of the city's legal businesses thrive or decline to the extent that goods and services provided by a crime network are available. One such industry is tourism. Hotels, restaurants, and taverns profit and thrive on vice.

An important ingredient in Seattle's economy is tourism. An important fact of tourism, in turn, is the attraction of conventions. Men who come to conventions are attracted to cities where gambling, prostitution, pornography, and various other "pleasures" are readily available. No one has to articulate this fact of life in order to have people in politics, business, and law enforcement adopt policies that conform to it:

> . . . everybody knew that a decent city that is growing has to have whores, has to have accessible liquor, prohibition or not, has to have a place where a guy can go and shoot craps, either for penny ante or high stakes, has to have a place where a guy can go and play cards. There's no reason putting somebody in jail for it, because it is what all good, righteous Christians do.

Law-Enforcement Agencies

Shared interests stretch farther than mere economic ties. Shared interests occur on a very broad level and should be understood as stemming basically from contradictions which inhere in the political and economic structure of American cities. To understand this, it will help to view the role of laws in the shaping of crime networks. Laws prohibiting gambling, prostitution, pornography, drug use, and high-interest rates on personal loans are laws about which there is a conspicuous lack of consensus. Even persons who agree that such behavior is improper and should be controlled by law disagree on the proper legal response. Should persons found guilty of taking drugs, gambling, or visiting a prostitute be imprisoned or counselled? Reflecting this dissension, large groups of people, some with considerable political power, insist on their right to enjoy the pleasures of vice without interference from the law.

Those involved in providing gambling and other vices enjoy pointing out that their services are profitable because of the demand for them by members of the respectable square-john community. Prostitutes work in apartments located on the fringes of the lower-class area of the city, rather than in the heart of the slums, precisely because they must maintain an appearance of respectability so that their clients will not feel contaminated by poverty. Professional pride may stimulate exaggeration on the part of the prostitutes, but their verbal reports are always to the effect that "all" of their clients are "very important people." My observations of the comings and goings in several apartment houses where prostitutes work generally verified the women's claims. Of some fifty persons seen going to prostitutes' rooms in apartment houses, only one was dressed in anything less casual than a business suit.

Watching those who frequented panorama gave me the same impression that the principal users of vice are middle and upper class. During several weeks of observations (leaning against the wall), I observed that more than 70 percent of the consumers of these pornographic vignettes were well-dressed, single-minded visitors to the slums who came for fifteen or twenty minutes of viewing and left as inconspicuously as possible. The remaining 30 percent were poorly dressed, older men who lived in the area.

Information on gambling and bookmaking in the permanently established or floating games is less readily available. Bookmakers report that the bulk of their "real business" comes from doctors, lawyers, and dentists in the city:

A: It's the big boys—your professionals—who do the betting down here. Of course, they don't come down themselves; they either send someone or they call up. Most of them call up, 'cause I know them or they know Mr. ____ [one of the key figures in the gambling operation].

Q: How 'bout the guys who walk off the street and bet?

A: Yeah, well, they're important. They do place bets and they sit around here and wait for the results. But that's mostly small stuff. I'd be out of business if I had to depend on them guys.

The poker and card games held throughout the city are of two types: 1) the small, daily game that caters almost exclusively to local residents of the area or working-class men who drop in for a hand or two while they are driving their delivery route or on their lunch hour, and 2) the action games that take place twenty-four hours a day and are located in more obscure places, such as a suite in a downtown hotel. Like prostitution, these games are on the edges of the lower-class areas. In Seattle the action games were the playground of men who were by manner, finances, and dress clearly well-to-do professionals and businessmen.

Not all business and professional men partake of the vices. Indeed, some of the leading citizens sincerely oppose the presence of vice in their city. Even larger numbers of the middle and working classes are adamant in their opposition to vice of all kinds. On occasion, they make their views forcefully known to the politicians and law-enforcement officers, thus requiring public officials to express their own opposition and appear to be snuffing out vice by enforcing the law.

The law-enforcement system is thus placed squarely in the middle of two essentially conflicting demands. On the one hand, the job obligates police to enforce the law, albeit with discretion; at the same time, considerable disagreement rages over whether or not some acts should be subject to legal sanction. This conflict is heightened by the fact that some influential persons in the community insist that all laws be rigorously enforced, while others demand that some laws not be enforced, at least not against themselves.

Faced with such a dilemma and such an ambivalent situation, the law enforcers do what any well-managed bureaucracy would do under similar circumstances. They follow the line of least resistance. Using the discretion inherent in their positions, they resolve the problem by establishing procedures that minimize organizational strains and that provide the greatest promise of rewards for the organization and the individuals involved. Typically, this means that law enforcers adopt a tolerance policy toward the vices, selectively enforcing the laws when it is to their advantage to do so. Since the persons demanding enforcement are generally middle-class and rarely venture into the less prosperous sections of the city, the enforcers can control visibility and minimize complaints merely by regulating the location of the vices. Limiting the visibility of such activity as sexual deviance, gambling, and prostitution appeases those who demand the enforcement of applicable laws. At the same time, since controlling visibility does not eliminate access for persons sufficiently interested to ferret out the tolerated vice areas, those demanding such services are also satisfied.

Cooperation and Control

The policy of cooperating in order to control the vices is also advantageous because it renders the legal system capable of exercising considerable control over potential sources of real trouble. For example, since gambling and prostitution are profitable, competition among persons desiring to provide these services is likely. Since legal remedies are lacking, the competition tends to become violent. If the legal system cannot control those running the vices, competing groups may well go to war to dominate the rackets. If, however, law-enforcement agents unofficially cooperate with some, there will be enough concentration of power to minimize conflicts. Prostitution can be kept clean if the law enforcers cooperate with the prostitutes; the law can thus lessen the chance, for instance, that a prostitute will steal money from a customer. In this and many other ways the law-enforcement system maximizes its visible effectiveness by creating and supporting a shadow government that manages the rackets.

Initially, people may have to be brought in from other cities to help set up the necessary organizational structure. Or the system may have to recruit and train local talent or simply co-opt, coerce, or purchase the knowledge and skills of entrepreneurs engaged in vice operations. This move often involves considerable strain, since some of those brought in may be uncooperative. Whatever the particulars, the ultimate result is the same: a crime network emerges—composed of politicians, law enforcers, and citizens—capable of supplying and controlling the vices in the city. The most efficient network is invariably one that contains representatives of all the leading centers of power. Businessmen and bankers must be involved because of their political influence, their ability to control the mass media, and their capital. The importance of cooperating businesses was demonstrated in Seattle by the case of a fledgling magazine that published an article intimating that several leading politicians, in particular the county prosecutor, were corrupt. Immediately major advertisers canceled their advertisements in the magazine. One large chain store refused to sell that issue of the magazine in any of its stores. When one of the leading members of the network was accused of accepting bribes, a number of the community's most prominent businessmen sponsored a large advertisement declaring their unfailing support for and confidence in the integrity of this "outstanding public servant."

The network must also have the cooperation of lawyers and businessmen in procuring the loans which enable them individually and collectively to purchase legitimate businesses, as well as to expand the vice enterprises. One member not only served along with others in the network on the board of directors of a loan agency, but he also helped wash money and advise associates on how to keep their earnings a secret. He served as a go-between, passing investment tips from associates to other businessmen in the community. In this way a crime network serves the economic interests of businessmen indirectly as well as directly.

The political influence of the network is more directly obtained. Huge tax-free profits make it possible to generously support political candidates. Often the network members assist both candidates in an election, thus assuring influence regardless of who wins. While usually there is a favorite, ultra-cooperative candidate who receives the greater portion of the contributions, everyone is likely to receive something.

Like all activities of the criminal network, political influence is obtained in a variety of ways. An ambitious and talented young lawyer decides to run for senator. He is running behind his opponent. He knows that his main problem is inadequate campaign financing. One night he receives a telephone call from a lawyer acquaintance asking to talk with him. They go for a drive, and in an isolated parking lot outside the city the young candidate is given an envelope containing thirty-five thousand dollars in one-hundred-dollar bills. The acquaintance tells him, "This is from some of the businessmen downtown who want to support you in your campaign."

There is, of course, a dilemma posed by accepting the money. As one aspiring politician who found himself in just this situation explained it, "I knew I needed that money for the campaign. And I knew too that that son of a bitch I was running against spent all his time in Washington getting drunk. But I couldn't beat him if I didn't get more funding. So I took the money. I told myself it would go for a good cause."

Perhaps it did. The recipient won the campaign and went on to support many "good" causes. He also paid his debt to those "downtown businessmen," who continued to support him in future elections.

During the late 1920s an aspiring politician was running for the office of county prosecutor. He had a problem raising funds. David Beck, who was rapidly putting together one of the most powerful labor unions on the West Coast, supported this aspiring young graduate from the University of Washington Law School. Warren Magnuson won the race for county prosecutor. Shortly thereafter, when Dave Beck organized a strike against the two local daily newspapers (both of which were owned by the Hearst chain), Warren Magnuson wore a button supporting the strike. The strike was eventually settled on terms favorable to Dave Beck and his Teamsters: not only because of Warren Magnuson but also because Franklin Roosevelt won the Presidency in 1932 and the Hearst newspapers had to come to grips with the reality of a shifting power base in Washington. Roosevelt's son-in-law was made publisher of the Seattle *Times* (the leading Hearst paper in Seattle), and Dave Beck, Warren Magnuson, and the Democrats were well on their way to forging a lifelong alliance that would end only when Dwight Eisenhower won the Presidency in 1952.[6]

David Beck also forged alliances with owners of cabarets,

cafes, and cardrooms. He invested in pinball operations and bingo parlors. He supported and worked for political candidates who were "realistic" and wanted to see Seattle grow economically. The Pacific Northwest was the scene of some of the most vicious anti-union activity in the country. Local businesses employed professional killers to shoot and maim strikers.[7] The Teamsters, for their part, developed "goon squads" of truck drivers and professional fighters to maintain the picket lines.[8] These same people and these same tactics were later employed in the interest of maintaining control over people who worked for or found out about the organization of illegal businesses in the city and state. A restaurateur who refused to pay his tithe (such as Charlie MacDaniel) found Teamsters coming into his restaurant and starting fights with customers and employees. Teamster trucks would not deliver goods to cardroom owners who did not cooperate. Teamsters would not drive trucks to serve the pinball machines of competitors whom Dave Beck did not approve.

The mayor's office was not crucial to the continued success of the network, but it always helped to have a cooperative mayor. When Dorm Braman ran for mayor in 1964, the county prosecutor introduced Braman to a number of Seattle businessmen. They included Robert Murray, Calvin Decker, and "Rudy" Santos. Calvin Decker and Rudy Santos owned some of the most profitable and long-standing "clubs" in Seattle where gambling took place on a regular basis. They contributed heavily to Braman's campaign, and the prospective mayor (who was successful in his campaign) returned the favor after election by announcing that gambling would continue to be "tolerated" in the city.

Within the police department the same theme is repeated but with its own variation. A new police officer is taken out on the First Avenue patrol. After a couple of nights his partner goes into a place that has gambling or into a cabaret that operates on the edge of legality and comes out with a bottle of whiskey and ten dollars. The new patrolman is informed that "from time to time these guys give us something—here you take the whiskey; I've got plenty at home." If the young recruit accepts it, then it builds from there up to regular payoffs, depending of course on the beat and how important his job. If he refuses the "gratuity," then the senior patrolman will tell the sergeant that "Joe ain't gonna play; we're gonna have trouble with him." The next day Joe receives a notice that he has been transferred to a patrol car that works out of Wallingford, the North end, or Georgetown, middle-class neighborhoods where the vices are not so prevalent. It can even be done as a promotion so that the officer believes that his refusal has been noticed by the higher-ups and that he has therefore been promoted away from the First Avenue midnight shift to a comfortable, dry beat.

Bureaucracy Affords Discretion

Contrary to the prevailing myth that universal rules govern bureaucracies, the fact is that in day-to-day operations rules can and must be selectively applied. As a consequence, some degree of corruption is not merely a possibility but rather a virtual certainty that is built into the very structure of bureaucratic organizations.

The starting point for understanding this structural invitation to corruption is the fact that the application of all rules and procedures underpinning an organization inevitably admits to a high degree of discretion. Rules can only specify what should be done when the actions being considered fall clearly into unambiguously specifiable categories, about which there can be no reasonable grounds of disagreement or conflicting interpretation. But such categories are a virtual impossibility, given the inherently ambiguous nature of language. Instead, most events fall within the penumbra of the bureaucratic rules where the discretion of officeholders must hold sway.

Since discretionary decision-making is recognized as inevitable, in effect, all bureaucratic decisions become subject to the discretionary will of the officeholder. Moreover, if one has a reason to look, vagueness and ambiguity can be found in any rule, no matter how carefully stipulated. If ambiguity and vagueness are not sufficient to justify particular criteria being applied, contradictory rules or implications of rules can be readily located that have the same effect to justify the decisions which, for whatever reason the officeholder wishes, can be used to enforce his position. Finally, since organizations characteristically develop their own set of common practices, which take on the status of rules (whether written or unwritten), the entire process of applying rules becomes totally dependent on the discretion of the officeholder. The bureaucracy thus has its own set of precedents, which can be invoked in cases where the articulated rules do not provide precisely the decision desired by the officeholder.

Ultimately, the officeholder has license to apply rules derived from a practically bottomless set of choices. Individual self-interest then depends on one's ability to ingratiate himself to officeholders at all levels in order to ensure that the rules most useful to him are applied. The bureaucracy, therefore, is not a rational institution with universal standards but is, instead, irrational and particularistic. It is an organization in which a set of self-serving goals emerge that often conflict with the organization's ostensible purposes. This is precisely the consequence of the organizational response to the dilemma created by law prohibiting the vices. Hence, the bureaucratic nature of law enforcement and political organization makes possible the corruption of the legal-political bureaucracy.

For the police bureaucracy the goal of maintaining a smooth-functioning organization invariably takes precedence over all other institutional goals. Where conflicts arise between the long-range goals of the law and the short-range goal of sustaining the organization, the former loses, even at the expense of undermining the socially agreed-upon purpose for which the organization presumably exists.

Yet, the law-enforcement agency's tendency to follow the line of least resistance, of maintaining organizational goals in the face of conflicting demands, necessarily embodies a choice as to which demands will be followed. Bureaucracies are not equally susceptible to all interests in the society. They do not fear the castigation, interference, and disruptive potential of the alcoholics on skid row or the cafe owners in the slums. In fact, some residents of the black ghetto and other lower-class areas of the city have been campaigning for years to rid their communities of the gambling casinos, whorehouses, pornography stalls, and bookmaking operations. But their pleas fall on deaf ears. The letters they write and the committees they form receive no publicity and create no stir in the smoothly functioning organizations that occupy the political and legal offices of the city. On the other hand, when the president of a large corporation in the city objected to the "slanderous lies" being spread about one of the leading members of the crime network, the magazine carrying the "lies" was removed from newsstand sale, and the editors lost many of their most profitable advertisers. In time, the magazine folded. Similarly, when any question of the honesty or integrity of policemen, prosecutors, or judges involved in the crime network was raised publicly, it was either squelched before being aired, or it aroused the denial of influential members of the banking community (especially those bankers whose institutions loaned money to prominent members of the network), as well as leading politicians, law-enforcement officers, and the like.

In short, bureaucracies are susceptible to differential influence according to the economic and political power of the groups attempting to exert influence. Since every facet of politics and the mass media is subject to reprisals by network members and friends, exposure of the ongoing relationship between a network and the most powerful economic groups in the city is unlikely. In the end it is cooperation with, not suppression of, the rackets that is in the best interest of the police, the politicians, and the business community.

The fact that the bureaucrats must listen to the economic elites of the city and not the have-nots is, then, one important element that stimulates the growth and maintenance of a crime network. But the links between the elites and criminal associations are more than merely spiritual. The economic elite of the city does not simply play golf with the political and legal elite. There are, in fact, significant economic ties between the two groups.

The most obvious nexus is manifested by the campaign contributions from the economic elite to the political and legal elite. We need not dwell on this observation here; it has been well documented in numerous other studies. What is not always recognized, however, is that crime networks are an important source of money for the economic elite. In 1964 leading bankers and industrialists of the city were part of a multimillion-dollar stock swindle engineered and manipulated by associates of the crime network with the assistance of confidence men from another state. This entire case was shrouded in such secrecy that out-of-state newspapers called me (and others) to find out why news about the scandal was not forthcoming from local wire services. When the scandal was finally exposed, the fact that industrialists and network members heavily financed the operation (and reaped the profits) was conveniently ignored in the newspapers and the courts; the evildoers were limited to the outsiders, who were in reality the front men for the entire confidence operation.

Legal Ambiguities

Owners and operators of the restaurants, the cigar counters, and the taverns where gambling takes place are joined by owners of hotels, taverns, and apartment houses where prostitution takes place. They all pay money into the crime network to stay open and for much the same reason. The laws of the state, county, and city are specifically (and in many cases intentionally) written so as to make it impossible for anyone to operate profitably a tavern, cabaret, hotel or nightclub without violating the law. Two statutes, one governing cabarets, the other governing the jukeboxes, are illustrative.

I earlier described the ordinances that required having a restaurant the size of a football field in order to have a *legal* nightclub large enough to hold enough customers to make a profit. These ordinances are passed with good Christian piety. The required seating distance from the platform would keep people from being too close to sexually stimulating objects; it would require cabarets to have something of a family atmosphere (what is more American family-like than a restaurant?), and it would keep too much sex from going on at once. In effect, however, the ordinance does not create a family atmosphere or reduce the number of girls dancing or keep customers from being too close to the dancing girls; it produces instead a neat mechanism by which the police, politicians, and other law-enforcement agencies can shake down the owners and operators of nightclubs.

The city council also passed a curious law designed to control the distribution of jukeboxes in the city. At the hearing accompanying the passage of this ordinance, it was alleged that organized crime controlled jukeboxes in many cities in the United States. Some of the city council members, therefore, proposed that the city prohibit anyone from owning the jukebox in his/her establishment, thus forcing him/her to rent the machine from a central distributor. How this was supposed to control the influence of organized crime is something of a mystery, especially since the license to operate the jukeboxes was given to a man who had been convicted of a felony and whose reputation held him to be the head of the local Mafia. (He *was not, in fact*, the head of the local crime network but he was an important member of it.)

Numerous other state and local laws serve similar purposes. They make it possible for organized crime to move freely but not without sharing the profits and paying homage to those members of "straight" society who provide the entry permit into these areas of entertainment, extortion, and dealing, where the profits are high and the activities illegal.

The crime network is thus an inevitable outgrowth of the political economy of American cities. The ruling elite from every sphere benefits economically and socially from the presence of a smoothly running association. Law-enforcement and government bureaucracies function best when the network is part of the governmental structure. And the general public is satisfied when control of the vices gives an appearance of respectability without curbing availability.

As we saw earlier, the operators of cardrooms, cafes with pinball machines, taverns, nightclubs, bookmaking establishments, and sundry other enterprises which were in violation of one or more laws had to pay graft to keep open. It will be recalled that these people reported making two payments a month, one to the police and one to the syndicate (or in some cases they thought they were paying one payment to the beat cops and another to the higher-ups). The money went in the same general direction. The policeman who picked up the payment would take a percentage and pass the remainder on up the line. This included the sergeants, lieutenants, and captains of those divisions of the police department directly concerned, especially vice and patrol divisions. The money that was funneled up was then divided into several packages: some for ranking police officers—at one time the assistant chief of police received an average of fifteen hundred dollars a month—but most for people in government offices including members of the city council, the state legislature, and other state offices.

Now all that sounds hierarchical and neat, which apparently contradicts my earlier statement that the payoff system was not so organized. The payoffs from the cardroom operators and taverns were organized in this manner, but these payoffs were only a small part of the revenues.

Network associates paid off in a variety of ways. A drug financier, for example, paid off quite differently from a tavern owner. No one really knew how much he made from his various illegal activities, and no one tried to find out. He contributed heavily to the political campaigns for county prosecutor, city council, state legislature, and governor. His candidates did not always win, but they won often enough to protect him from exposure.

There is always room for many people to operate as independent entrepreneurs. The only requirement is that one pay off the right people in the right way. It could be a payment to the right politician's campaign, or it might even be just giving support when needed. The son of one of the city's founding fathers and the son of another of the city's leading businessmen provided support during crises. Through the county prosecutor and members of the city council, the two were able to enhance their already substantial family fortunes by buying and selling real estate. They invested in loan companies (at least one of which loaned money exclusively to racketeers or people wanting to start businesses such as taverns and cardrooms), from which the crime network took a cut and other business ventures which, "as luck would have it," always netted a high profit on a small investment. The investors were able to turn a hefty profit by investing in an amusement company, which declared bankruptcy and was subsequently found by the court to have committed criminal fraud. Several properties purchased by the investors were, soon after purchase, sought by the city or state, and the price was greatly increased.

There were also opportunities to invest in new business; for example, a new hotel inevitably turned a very high profit to the investors and further indebted them to those members of the network who had recommended the investment. Whether or not those respectable businessmen knew why the investment was so profitable is a moot point. The procedure was so obvious, however, that one must either question their business acumen or assume that they were knowledgeably engaging in fraud.

Over the years the city's and state's most influential banks, newspapers, corporate executives, and private citizens became indebted and embedded in the web of criminal activities organized and coordinated by the network. Exposure of the system was thus effectively squelched: the perpetuation of key people in office was assured and the power to appoint political candidates and key government officials (such as judges, licensing-bureau chiefs, and law-enforcement personnel) was increasingly invested in the hands of network members.

The County Prosecutor

American law is such that the prosecuting attorney sits in a central position of influence over criminal activities. The prosecuting attorney is also a politically elected official, who must therefore depend on the support of many people in order to obtain and hold his position or use the position as a stepping stone to higher political aspirations.

For an offense to move from arrest to consideration by a court it must pass through the prosecutor's office. At this stage of the legal process the case can move in three possible ways: indictment, information, or complaint.

In general, all three possibilities hinge on the prosecutor's willingness to proceed. An indictment is a finding by a grand jury that there is probable cause to believe that the accused committed the crime charged. Since there is no defense before a grand jury, the grand jury considers only the evidence presented by the prosecutor. It is a rare grand jury that defies the prosecutor. An information is a charge of criminal offense filed by the prosecutor on the basis of his own determination of probable cause. A complaint by a citizen charging a person of criminal offense in most states cannot be heard in court but must be made to the prosecutor. The prosecutor stands astride the criminal process, controlling the gates that lead to the trial court.

The articulated norms for police conduct require the police to enforce every violation of the law. Judges, too, are not formally in the position to dismiss a charge, or, if the accused is proven guilty, to find the accused not guilty, although they are given vast powers of discretion in the choice of sentence. Of the three principal actors in a criminal prosecution, the prosecutor alone is to decide formally whether or not to enforce the law and the degree of crime with which to charge the offender.

In England the power of prosecuting criminal cases was originally, and remains in theory today, largely lodged in the hands of private persons, who are not compelled by law to initiate such prosecution initiated and carried on by the sovereign power.

In the United States the office of the public prosecutor was grafted onto the traditional system of private criminal litigation. The public prosecutor thus assimilated the functions of the private prosecutor, and just as the private prosecutor had discretion whether or not to prosecute, so the public prosecutor was endowed with the same discretion. The prosecutor's discretion is almost unlimited.

> As a general rule, whether the state's attorney does or does not institute a particular prosecution is a matter which rests in his discretion. Unless the discretion is grossly abused or such duty is compelled by statute or there is a clear showing that such duty exists, mandamus will not lie.[9]

That is, a court will not issue a writ compelling the prosecutor to prosecute.

His discretion is almost as broad if he wants to decline to prosecute a charge already laid. In some states there are no limits placed on the prosecutor's discretion to stop a prosecution. In most states, however, a small element of judicial control is inserted into the process by permitting the prosecutor to initiate prosecution but requiring judicial approval for a withdrawal of the charges. In fact, however, as in the case of the decision to prosecute, the prosecutor's decision not to prosecute is an enormous power in the hands of one public official.

Prosecuting attorneys do not achieve that office by being neutral and uninvolved in politics. On the contrary, a prosecuting attorney must be nominated by his party, financed by people with money, supported by newspapers, and helped out in times of crisis by influential citizens. The prosecutor is in a position where he or she virtually controls one of the largest industries in the state. At his or her discretion in Seattle was the life or death of a hundred-million-dollar business. It is in the prosecutor's interest to encourage, but at the same time control within certain limits, that kind of industry. Not surprisingly, most prosecutors manage the industry at least to some extent.

The interests of the network become the interests of the individuals and groups who occupy key positions for the network's survival and health. There are, however, forces at work which counteract the shared interests. Although the overwhelming tendency is toward cooperation, there are countervailing forces which tend toward dissension. It is simply impossible for any organization to be so effectively integrated with the individual interests of all its members that conflicts do not arise.

The operation and maintenance of a crime network is no different from the maintenance of social order everywhere. Year in, year out, the leading business people, newspaper people, politicians, law enforcers, cardroom operators, and truck drivers did their job, took their pay or their payoff, and went on vacation. Some got ulcers, some felt guilty, some enjoyed every moment of it. They all shared in the complicity of silence that kept the "good citizens" satisfied that law and order prevailed in their corner of the world. Indeed it did for the bulk of the population, who lived in the middle- and upper-class suburbs that encircle the business district where they worked and the slums where the surplus labor force existed.

Over the years there were innumerable incidents that necessitated the use of various mechanisms of social control by members of the network, which included some instances where the ultimate force—murder—was used to solve a problem.

In the late sixties the network was threatened with exposure and dissolution. One of the key figures in the probe of network activities was Ben Cichy, the pinball czar and head of the Far West Novelty Company who was photographed as he entered Prosecutor Charles O. Carroll's home. Ben Cichy, who was an excellent swimmer according to his family and friends, drowned in May 1969 in front of his palatial lakeside home.

Earlier, in March of 1964, Marvin Stenholm, a former police officer and later a chief investigator for Prosecutor Carroll, drowned while on a fishing trip. It was the opinion of several people close to the top of network enterprises that Stenholm was killed because he was threatening to expose the network.

An attorney, said by many insiders to be one of the "nastiest men alive" and one who was closely allied with illegal businesses, was with his girl friend when she fell out of the window of an apartment building. She died.

In each of these and several other instances, the King County medical examiner, who was the brother-in-law of the county prosecutor, found that the deaths were accidental. The people of First Avenue took these deaths as a warning not to talk to reporters, sociologists, or anyone else "nosing around."

Over the years the network was responsible for the deaths of many people. Drowning was a favorite method of eliminating troublemakers, because it was difficult to ascertain whether or not the person fell from a boat by accident, was held underwater by someone else, or committed suicide.*

Some deaths were arranged in more traditional ways. One man was shot during an argument in a bar. The offender was tried before a judge who consistently showed great compassion for any crimes committed by members of the network. He compensated for his leniency with network members by being unusually harsh in cases against blacks who appeared before him. The case was dismissed for lack of evidence.

Murder is not, however, the preferred method of handling uncooperative people. Far better, in the strategy of the crime network, are the time-honored techniques of blackmail and co-optation. The easiest and safest tactic is to purchase the individual for a reasonable amount, as was attempted with MacDaniel. If this fails, then some form of blackmail or relatively minor coercion may be in order.

A candidate for sheriff was strongly supported by the network in his bid for office. Campaign contributions were generously provided since he was running against a local lawyer who was familiar with the goings-on of the network and had vowed to attack its operations. The network's candidate won the election—network candidates almost never lost local elections—but underwent a change of heart shortly thereafter. He announced, in no uncertain terms,

---

*According to one informant, "Murder is the easiest crime of all to get away with. There are one hundred and one ways to commit murder that are guaranteed to let you get away with it."

that he would not permit the operation of gambling houses in the county, although he did not intend to do anything about the operations within the city limits, since that was not his jurisdiction. Nevertheless, the county, he insisted, would be kept clean.

The network was as annoyed as it was surprised. The county operations were only a small portion of the total enterprise, but they were nonetheless important, and no one wanted to give up the territory. Further, the prospects of closing down the lay-off center operating in the county was no small matter. The center was crucial to the entire enterprise, because it was here that the results of horse races and other sports events came directly to the book-makers. The center also enabled the network to protect itself against potential bankruptcy. When the betting was particularly heavy in one direction, bets were laid off by wiring Las Vegas, where the national betting pattern always takes care of local variations. Clearly, something had to be done.

No man is entirely pure, and the new sheriff was less pure than many. He had two major weaknesses: gambling and young girls. One weekend, shortly after he took office, a good friend of his asked if he would like to go to Las Vegas for the weekend. He jumped at the opportunity. While the weekend went well in some respects, the sheriff was un-lucky at cards. When he flew home Sunday night, he left fourteen thousand dollars' worth of IOU's in Las Vegas.

Monday morning one of the network "players" visited the sheriff in his office. The conversation, according to some-one who heard it, went like this:

Player: "Say, ____, I understand you was down in Vegas over the weekend."
Sheriff: "Yeah."
Player: "Hear you lost a little bit at the tables."

Sheriff: "Uh-huh."

Player: "Well, the boys wanted me to tell you not to worry about those pieces of paper you left. We got them back for you."

Sheriff: "I don't. . . ."

Player: "Also, ____, we thought you might like to have a memento of your trip, so we brought you these pictures. . . ."

The "mementos" were pictures of the sheriff in a hotel room with several young girls. Thereafter things in the county returned to normal.

It should be noted that the sheriff was *not* kept in line by the threat of exposure alone. He was, in fact, subsequently placed on the payroll in the amount of one thousand dollars a month. When his term as sheriff was over, an appointment was arranged for him wherein he could continue to serve the network's interests.

Threats from outside the organization are rarer than threats from within. Nevertheless, they occur and must be dealt with in the best possible way. Since no strategy exists, each incident is handled in its own way. During Robert Kennedy's days as attorney general of the United States, the federal attorney for the state began a campaign to rid the state of the members of the crime network. People who held political office were generally immune, but some of the higher-ups in the operational section of the network were indicted. Ultimately, five members of the network and David Beck of the Teamsters were sentenced to prison. The entire affair was scandalous; politicians whose lives depended on the network fought the nasty business with all their power. They were able to protect major leaders and to avert exposure of network-affiliated politicians. Some blood ran, however, and it was a sad day for the five sentenced to prison terms. Yet the organization remained intact, and, indeed, the five men who went to prison continued to receive a share of the profits from illegal enterprises. Corruption continued unabated, and the net effect on crime in the state was nil.

While I was digging and delving into the business of crime in Seattle, the waters that surrounded the entrepreneurs who profited most were relatively calm. Still, the fact that a "professor" was inquiring into things that were "none of his damn business" was potentially upsetting to some. Upsetting enough to want to cool me out. The easiest way to cool someone out is to find something that can be used against him.

One night I was sitting in one of the higher-class bars owned by a prominent member of the crime network when I was approached by a beautiful woman who offered to buy me a drink. I accepted. As we chatted, she became ever more friendly, until at last she offered to take me home with her. I declined. Within a few minutes another equally attractive woman approached, and the scene was repeated. A good friend told me several days later in a casual manner that I was being set up that night for a possible "photographic session," which, some people believed, would have rendered me vulnerable to blackmail.

That same year I was called by the Internal Revenue Service, and my income-tax return was gone over very carefully. I later learned that the IRS had received a "tip" from someone in government that I was hiding substantial portions of my income. In fact, there had been an error on my return which resulted in my receiving a small refund after the review.

My telephone was bugged, according to friends on the police department, and from time to time I was given a "tail" to find out to whom I was talking and about what. Nothing came of these things, although they did lead me to take some precaution when I talked to people and to make sure that someone knew at all times where I was and to whom I was talking.

The mass media are, of course, always a potential threat to a crime network. Through favorable tax assessment, friendship, tips on good investments, and outright bribes, the local media were for the most part kept very much in line. However, late in 1967 a series of fortuitous events coalesced, which had the net effect of severely threatening the network's existence.

A new magazine devoted exclusively to the state began publishing. The editors were young, open-minded, and hungry for news that would bring their magazine attention. Simultaneously the city's second newspaper got a new managing editor who wanted to make the paper the city's best-selling one.

As it happened, these media people were looking for news just as there were some serious rifts in the network. The alliance between the county prosecutor, the police chief, and the ex-governor of the state had always been an uneasy one. In the late 1960s the alliance was showing one of its periodic strains, as different groups vied for more and more of the declining profits—declining because the economy generally was in the throes of a recession. The internal squabbles made for some rather seriously disaffected players. It was then a good time to recruit informers willing to talk to reporters.

Add to this the fact that quite by accident a scandal which began in Southern California revealed an interstate racket involving one of the network members, the county assessor, Tony Steen. A tax consultant had devised a scheme by which his clients in several states could get lower taxes. His clients paid him, and he in turn would bribe the appropriate people in his client's area. The appropriate people varied from city to city depending on how the political power was distributed. It could have been the county prosecutor, the tax assessor, the mayor, or even someone not in a political office.

As a result of exposure in California implicating Seattle, an audit revealed unusually low tax assessments for the past decade for many of the largest industries in the state—clients of the aforementioned tax accountant. The county tax assessor, who was taking payoffs, was discovered and indicted by a grand jury (only the second grand jury ever called by the county prosecutor during twenty-two years in office). This grand jury, it should be noted, was called only after the accountant's activities in Seattle had been revealed by an extensive investigation in another city.

The county tax assessor confessed, resigned, and was convicted. The prosecutor and the tax assessor spent most of the night before court locked up in the prosecutor's office. The newspapers described the arrest and grilling in a way that made it sound as though the relentless prosecutor had coaxed a confession out of the corrupt assessor during this marathon. In fact, according to a close friend of the tax assessor, he had never received the lion's share of the bribes but had only been following the instructions of higher-ups to lower the taxes on selected establishments. In their all-night discussion, the prosecutor promised that the assessor would not get a jail sentence if he confessed. The tax assessor confessed but was sent to prison despite the prosecutor's protestations to the court.

Thus it was that internal squabbles, inadvertent exposure of a network operation, and the birth of some ambitious news media coincided to weaken the association. It remained, however, for changes to occur in state and national politics before the network came unraveled.

CHAPTER SIX

The Network
Comes Apart

IN THE FIRST few months of 1967 a leading newspaper in
Seattle ran an article which claimed that some policemen were accepting payoffs from tavern owners. The article also claimed that these same officers were drinking and
playing cards while they were supposed to be on duty. Similar allegations had appeared from time to time. It was one
of the "facts of life" with which the network had to live.
There was little need for deep concern. Attempts to expose
more than this most visible, least important aspect of network operations had always failed. Enterprising journalists
who had discovered systematic organization of the rackets
and tried to have their materials published in either of the
city's newspapers inevitably had their materials thrown in
the editor's wastepaper basket and their assignment
changed. There was no reason to suspect that the combination of friendships, business interests, and favorable tax
assessments that had worked for years to control the newspapers would not work again.

It is not entirely clear why this time the newspaper published the article and gave it front-page notice. There were rumors that a tavern owner had complained to the police and the FBI that something was going to happen. The paper may have believed the rumors and responded to make sure it was not scooped by another paper.

There was a minor tremor among network members. There is always the possibility that a small flame may start a brush fire that will spread to the entire forest. The police department responded predictably. They announced that the recalcitrant officers had been reprimanded and given "new assignments." Within the police department the sort of treatment the officers received was seen, however, not as a reprimand but as a clear sign that the network was still in power and protecting its own. The officers were *not* transferred out of the division responsible for enforcing the gambling and vice laws. They were merely moved to another assignment within that division, which means they could continue their previous practices in another area. The message was clear that this "change" represented a difference that made no difference.

The story was not followed up. The reporters who wrote the article continued to gather more information, but nothing more appeared. There was, however, an important move made by the mayor that would in retrospect prove to have consequences for the network.

According to people close to the mayor, he felt under pressure to "do something" because the announcement of reprimands and changed assignments had not placated "the public." Whether someone was putting pressure on the mayor or if it was only his general feeling is unclear. In any event, he appointed a blue-ribbon committee to look into police corruption. The committee selected was handpicked by a major figure in the network and consisted of those businessmen in the community who had been most closely involved with network operations and profits over the years. Two of the men were also from leading families in the city, and thus the committee had all the luster it needed. An attorney was appointed who had worked closely in an attempt to avert the prosecution of Dave Beck, the union official who had been indicted as a result of federal efforts (under Robert Kennedy's impetus) several years earlier. The committee was, then, carefully screened to be sure it would do nothing to threaten the illegal association.

Not surprisingly, the committee seemed determined *not* to discover any payoffs. Their principal source of information was to come from a post-office box to which people could mail anonymous statements telling of police or government corruption. On the street everyone knew who was on the committee and who would be told if they gave information. Imagine also how meaningless anonymity is in such cases. Obviously anyone saying "I paid off so and so" would know that "so and so" would easily be able to identify him. To no one's surprise (except perhaps a few naive observers), the committee reported that they had received "very little" mail. This fact was used as evidence that there was little or no corruption among the police. The committee also interviewed twenty-five tavern owners, all of whom denied any system of payoffs, and a number of police officers, who denied doing anything wrong. The committee closed with a whitewash and a recommendation that the city ask the International Association of Chiefs of Police (IACP) to conduct a study of the police department.

The mayor thanked the committee and reiterated their findings to the press and public. The mayor asked the IACP to look into the police department. Late in 1967 a team of IACP investigators came to Seattle. They were in the city only a short time, but it was long enough for them to discover the extensive payoff system operating in the police department. As a result of their investigation they acted according to the first law of police work: they protected their brothers in blue. The IACP team issued a public report in February 1968 which said they had found only minimal payoffs isolated among a few "bad cops," the impact of which was trivial. This was the only report available to the press or the public. There was, however, another report for the eyes of a selected group of police officers only. The private version maintained that there was in fact an extensive payoff system involving several divisions of the police department (including the entire vice division) and centering around the coordination and imagination of the assistant chief of police, M. E. "Buzz" Cook. This report warned that unless the police did something to change these circumstances, a scandal was almost certain. It recommended that the centralization of power in the hands of the assistant chief of police be broken, and that four separate but equal divisions be assigned different officers each with the power to control his own division and report directly to the chief of police. The IACP also recommended that assistant chief of police Cook be asked to resign or be demoted. Instead, somewhat later Buzz Cook was appointed acting chief of police. But that gets us ahead of the story.

The IACP report that was made public also recommended that the police department be reorganized. It noted that, as presently organized, the police department power was heavily concentrated in the hands of the assistant chief, to whom all lower-level officers had to report.

Whatever furor might have been left from the relatively innocuous, and certainly understated, article in the paper about police payoffs was sufficiently defused by the IACP report. The pressure was thus taken off the police. Reporters continued to "discover" payoffs and corruption. Editors continued to refuse to publish their findings.

Until . . .

A new editor came to Seattle and took over the editorship of the city's second newspaper: second in sales, second in advertising, second in reputation. One of the older reporters went to the new editor with information about corruption implicating the county prosecutor, Charles Carroll. The editor decided to publish it. Without consulting the owner of the paper, he ran an article that showed the prosecutor meeting in his home with Ben Cichy. The article claimed that the pinball magnate went to the prosecutor's home on the first of every month. The implication was that the prosecutor was being paid off to permit pinball machines to operate. The reporter claimed to have much more evidence implicating the prosecutor in a variety of criminal acts, but newspaper lawyers advised that the accusations might be libelous. Only a relatively safe and unaccusing article was published, along with a photograph showing Cichy on his way into the prosecutor's lavish home in an exclusive residential area of the city.

When this article appeared with the picture, was there a great hue and cry from "the public" or even from "the ruling elite" of the city? Was there a call from politicians or law-enforcement people for an explanation from the prosecutor? Was there anything said that called for an explanation as to why the county's leading law-enforcement officer met monthly with a known gambler?

No. On the contrary, leading citizens spoke vociferously in defense of the prosecutor: the same true blue citizens who were business associates, the same citizens who had sat on the mayor's blue-ribbon council to look into allegations of police corruption. Instead of asking for an explanation, they attacked the newspaper for engaging in "yellow journalism." The prosecutor threatened suit and explained only that he and Cichy got together once a month because they shared an interest in classical music.

The newspaper's lawyers became more and more nervous. The new editor got an object lesson in the power structure of the community. The reporter continued the investigation but was unable to find anywhere to publish his findings. Eventually he was given a comfortable job with the state and resigned from the paper and from "yellow journalism."

A group of Eastern-educated, ambitious, and enterprising young men had just moved to Seattle and had been appointed editors of a local magazine being established by one of the leading broadcasting corporations in the city. *Seattle* was attempting to make a mark on the publishing world by showing that a local magazine outside New York City could be profitable and innovative. The smell of scandal attracted the editors like death attracts poets. They pursued the rumors and leads collected earlier by the reports for the newspapers. They also contacted me and asked for an outline of what they called "organized crime" in Seattle. Without revealing the names of informants or jeopardizing people to whom I had an obligation, I outlined the system for them and also agreed to publish an article speaking generally about the tolerance policy and organized crime. The next issue of *Seattle* contained an article by the editor, my article on the tolerance policy, and a front-page editorial calling for the prosecutor's resignation.

Result: some major advertisers cancelled their advertisements, newsstands refused to sell the magazine, the owners of the magazine put pressure on the editor, revenues declined, the prosecutor threatened suit, the business community attacked the magazine, and in the end the magazine went out of business. This was not solely because of its attempt to expose the crime network but that was a major reason for its demise.

Interestingly, the prosecutor was especially concerned about the article I wrote for the magazine. He found out about its pending publication and threatened suit if the editors published it. How he discovered the existence of the article is still a mystery but does indicate the extent to which he controlled many facets of the city. Only the managing editor, an associate editor, and the secretary to the managing editor were aware that I sent an article to the magazine. The article went by air mail, registered, from Santa Barbara, California. The magazine received a telegram from the prosecutor which threatened them with a libel suit if they published the article before they even received it.

The prosecutor survived this attack, as he had many others over the years, with the complicity of many and the active aid of a few leading citizens. For the moment the prosecutor and the crime network had weathered the storm.

In retrospect these early, halting efforts to bring the network to an end were the first breeze of what would become a major hurricane. The first, ineffective efforts by the media demonstrate the inability of the media to serve as a guardian of public morality among politicians and law-enforcement people. Indeed, the only real threat to an association of illegal businessmen comes from competitive forces amassing sufficient power to overthrow them, not from public exposure.

The Network and Political Alliances

The political party composition of Seattle's crime network was a coalition of strange bedfellows. For years the state government had been controlled by Democrats. On

WESTERN UNION
TELEGRAM

WESTERN UNION
TELEGRAM

WESTERN UNION
TELEGRAM

UNION
RAM

M◆

KING AM TV SEA

WU SEA
  WU A251 PD

            SEATTLE WASH AUG 15 1968 1147A PDT
PETER BUNZEL, DLR DO NOT PHONE
  PUBLISHER SEATTLE MAGAZINE

  WE HAVE ADDITIONAL INFORMATION CONCERNING CONTENTS OF SEPTEMBER
  ISSUE. IT NOW APPEARS THAT YOU ARE PUBLISHING AN ARTICLE BY A
  SOCIALOGIST CONCERNING THE ROLE OF PROSECUTING ATTORNEYS IN
  RELATION TO POLICE DEPARTMENTS AND OTHER PUBLIC OFFICES AND THE
  CONTENT OF THE ARTICLE IS DEROGATORY TO PROSECUTING ATTORNEYS.
  IF THE INFORMATION IS ACCURATE YOU ARE MANIFESTING YOUR MALICIOUS
  INTENT BY PUBLISHING IT IN THE SAME ISSUE WITH THE ARTICLE ON
  ME ANDTHIS OFFICE
    CHARLES O CARROLL
                1227P PDT

  KING AM TV SEA

  WU SEA

the state level network members were Democrats, and
funds from illegal business activities were used to support
Democratic candidates, including U.S. senators and congressmen. Seattle, however, was largely Republican for
over thirty years. The mayoralty was nonpartisan in principle but Republican in fact. The King County prosecutor
was a right-wing Republican of long standing. He was also
the major power in city and county Republican Party

organization with, of course, the support of leading businessmen.

There was strong local representation of the Democratic Party in the network. Union officials instrumental in network affairs were Democrats as were the sheriff and several other leading figures.

When it came time to utilize profits for political campaigns, the spoils divided according to control. With businessmen and the leading city politicians involved in illegal activities supporting Republicans, the Republicans got the lion's share. In the county the Democrats were better off (with respect to the contributions from illegal profits), as they were on the state level.

There was, then, an uneasy alliance between right-wing Republicans and Democrats, who shared management policies and competed for political control of the state and local governments. It was a widely based spectrum, which is in part the reason why it survived so long with such stability of investment and profit. There was, however, one political group clearly left out, the liberal-to-moderate wing of the Republican Party. The late 1950s, early 1960s was not a good time for this brand of Republicanism. Barry Goldwater, whom the leading local Republicans supported for the nomination, ran for the Presidency in 1964. It was a time for regrouping among moderate and liberal Republicans.

Within the state of Washington the governorship, both U.S. senators, and the statehouse were, and had been, controlled by Democrats for many years. The Democratic governor, who had cooperated with and supported members of the crime network throughout his tenure in office, was defeated in 1964 by a Republican who clearly divorced himself from the national policies of Goldwater. He also clearly divorced himself from that wing of the state and local Republican Party controlled by the county prosecutor and his business associates. The new governor's power was limited, however, because he inherited a Democratically controlled house, two Democratic U.S. senators, and even a Democratic attorney general. Not surprisingly, he made only minor moves to undermine the power of the local Republican Party during his first four years.

The election of 1968 shaped up as an exciting one. The attorney general of the state, John O'Connell (a Democrat), ran for governor against the incumbent Republican, Dan Evans. He needed campaign issues, however, if he were to win the election. He found one in the corrupt politics of Seattle. As attorney general, he needed the governor's request to investigate corruption on the local level. The governor refused to request an investigation. The attorney general made this an issue. He accused the governor of hiding something. He made it sound as though the governor were protecting "organized crime." In a "White Paper To the People of Washington" (see Appendix F for an excerpt from this paper) Attorney General O'Connell wrote:

On Wednesday, August 21, the Seattle *Post-Intelligencer* disclosed that an official of the Far West Novelty Company* had been a regular visitor at the home of King County Prosecutor, Charles O. Carroll, once a month at about the same time each month. Far West Novelty Company is the association of county pinball operators which has held the only master license issued for pinballs in King County since 1942. . . .

The same day, August 21, I conferred with members of my staff who were generally familiar with allegations concerning a possible breakdown of law enforcement in King

*The attorney general's White Paper is in error by referring to this as the Far West Novelty Company. The correct name is The Amusement Association of Washington.

County. . . . I concluded that there was a distinct possibility that a number of the state's criminal laws were not being properly enforced in King County (especially those relating to gambling and prostitution) and that there were also indications of a system of payoffs to public officials.

State law . . . gives the attorney general power and duty, upon written request of the governor, to investigate violations of the criminal laws of this state to determine if those criminal laws are being improperly enforced in any county.

However, as Attorney General O'Connell pointed out in this White Paper, Governor Evans failed to give him a "written request" to investigate the allegations. Astute political observers sensed that O'Connell's campaign was gaining ground, that the attorney general was embarrassing the governor and appealing more and more to the voters, although throughout the campaign the incumbent governor stayed several points ahead of the challenger in public opinion polls.

The attorney general appointed two special investigators to report directly to him their findings of corruption in law enforcement and politics in Seattle. They reported a great deal more than the attorney general had expected. Among other things they informed him that one of his closest and most trusted political allies in Seattle, the King County sheriff, was enmeshed in the crime network.

As the investigation was peaking, a curious thing happened. Two reporters from the city's leading newspaper who had themselves unveiled extensive information about crime networks in Seattle discovered a line of credit the attorney general had been given with which to gamble by a Las Vegas hotel. The check was for ten thousand dollars, a substantial amount of money for someone on an attorney general's salary to be gambling with in Las Vegas. No wrongdoing was ever uncovered, and it never came out* exactly how the reporters for the Seattle *Times* discovered that Attorney General O'Connell had obtained a ten-thousand-dollar line of credit at a Las Vegas hotel.

Was it mere coincidence that the two reporters who revealed this information had for several years been investigating and gathering substantial information about Seattle's crime network? They never published most of the information they gathered. Their first and only major scoop in connection with corruption and vice in Seattle was the information which implicated the attorney general.

The stigma of the line of credit was enough to ensure a victory for O'Connell's opponent. The people of Washington chose a man who refused to request that the attorney general investigate the alleged corruption and payoffs in Seattle over a man who had obtained a ten-thousand-dollar line of credit in a Nevada hotel and whose campaign manager for King County was one of the chief targets of the payoff scandal. The people of Washington were offered no middle ground between those two extremes.

Meanwhile, Richard Nixon was elected President in a campaign against Hubert Humphrey. The American people were offered no middle ground either.

The Republican governor (a moderate Republican) and the county prosecutor, although of the same party, were arch enemies. Neither supported the other in his political campaign. In the 1968 election their enmity became increasingly public. Furthermore, at the 1968 convention the prosecuting attorney had openly supported Ronald Reagan against Nixon. The governor had supported Rockefeller but was much more congenial to the Nixon nomination. With Nixon's election and the governor's reelection, the

---

*One informant reported to me that the reporters received the "tip" on O'Connell's line of credit from the chairman of the state GOP committee.

time was right for an attack on the network, which played into the hands of political interests in opposition to those presently in power.

The U.S. Attorney Cometh

One of the prerogatives of office for a President is the right to recommend to the Congress hundreds of prestigious, high-paying government jobs. Among the appointments at the discretion of the President are the U.S. attorneys, who sprinkle the land. As with any law-enforcement officer, the incumbent in these positions may use his discretion to enforce the law in a variety of ways depending on the political and economic forces impinging upon him (or her in those rare instances where a woman is appointed).

When Richard Nixon was elected following a reign of Democrats, the privilege of appointing U.S. attorneys was his. Crime networks everywhere held their breath. And well they should have, for Nixon was well aware (a) that crime networks are an important source of political money, (b) that these networks were more often than not sources of Democratic campaign contributions, and (c) that a U.S. attorney who was properly (from Nixon's perspective) diligent could break the stranglehold the Democrats had over big-city crime networks. Especially if, as was to come to be, new legislation were introduced making it possible for the U.S. government to actively prosecute local corruption, something which until 1970 was impossible by federal law.

An outside observer might well have anticipated that the Nixon appointee would be one who would be free from local Republican Party influence since the local party was dominated by anti-Nixon forces; it was therefore essential that the network organize an effort to have a "friendly" U.S. attorney appointed. They chose as their nominee a man who had served as assistant prosecuting attorney and who was known by them to be someone who "understood local problems" such as the tolerance policy.

The governor had other ideas. He too knew the importance of the U.S. attorney and he wanted to break the network's stranglehold on Seattle politics. So did the people in the White House, one of whom, John Ehrlichman, had been closely associated with the political and economic features of the network before moving to Washington.

There ensued a battle of considerable proportions, although it was a battle that went on quietly so far as the public was concerned. The governor recommended a man who was prosecuting attorney of a rural county in the state. He was young, ambitious, and in the right part of the Republican Party, that is, the governor's camp. He also had spoken out at a state prosecuting attorneys' convention in opposition to the tolerance policy.

The most active members of Seattle's crime network worked diligently for their nominee. Two leading network businessmen flew to Washington, D.C., to enlist the aid of the Republican congressman from the state, a congressman who had spent large amounts of money to gain his victory. He strongly supported the crime network's nominee for U.S. attorney. They also contacted a White House adviser with whom they had some influence. The message was the same: convince Nixon to nominate its candidate for U.S. attorney.

The governor was also actively pushing for his candidate. When it became clear to the county prosecutor that his candidate was unacceptable, he offered to withdraw his nominee if the governor would do likewise. The governor refused. Nixon appointed the antitolerance-policy, liberal Republican from the rural county as U.S. attorney, and the walls of the network began to crack noticeably.

Meanwhile, the police department was reorganized. As recommended, the new organization created four bureaus within the police department each with its own assistant chief who reported directly to the chief of police, Frank Ramon. To give the change substance and to convince the skeptics that there really was reform in the department, two of the assistant chiefs chosen were among the most respected police officers on the force: at least one of them, Tony Gustin, had in his twenty-year career on the force remained completely aloof from the payoff system. As a result he had spent most of his career in the juvenile bureau and other branches of the department where payoffs were nonexistent and where he could not interfere with the payoffs of his colleagues. Two of the other assistants, George Fuller and Buzz Cook, were not as clean as Gustin but they were nonetheless as uninvolved as anyone. George Fuller had completed his master's degree in sociology at the University of Washington and therefore brought some added credentials to the reforms. The centralization of authority in the hands of the assistant chief of police thus was eliminated.

As if that were not enough, the state attorney general, who was a Republican, for the first time also began a war against the network. He had replaced the Democratic attorney general who had run for governor and been defeated. One of his first rulings as attorney general was to declare the licensing of pinball machines illegal. Perhaps because of their visibility, pinball machines have always been a favorite target of people attempting to reform illegal business enterprises, although pinballs are of minor importance compared to the annual profits from bookmaking, high-stakes poker, drug importation, and so on. Nevertheless, the new state attorney general was advised to attack pinballs, and he did.

Within the police department there was a predictable response to these political machinations taking place outside the department. Without articulating or even understanding the implications of the storm being created by the loss of control of critical offices, police officers began lining up on different sides. The old established network bagmen were too entrenched to change. A few officers who had either been only tangentially involved or been uninvolved could shift and maneuver. It was "in the air" that the outcome of all the changes would be a new police chief. Choosing the right side in this fracas would be crucial in determining whether or not one had a chance of becoming chief. After the reorganization of the department two of the assistant chiefs began what came to be called a "palace revolt." Most important was an idealistic officer who in his capacity as head of a bureau began briefing selected members of the city council (people he thought to be uninfluenced by criminal activities) and the press. Knowledge may not be power, but at some point in the political infighting the public exposure of inside information can be a powerful weapon. The media were being carefully and intelligently informed and primed for the right moment. The price the media people had to pay for receiving this inside information was cooperation. They would not release information until the cooperative police officers were ready, lest they explode the plans too early and destroy the chances of "reform." Ironically, it was in part the same argument, and the same technique of control (giving inside information to selected reporters who will reveal only what the police want revealed as the price for this inside information), which had enabled the crime network to survive with minimal publicity for as long as it did.

Within the network itself the cracks grew wider. Newspaper, radio, and magazine publicity increased. The U.S.

attorney, who openly opposed the tolerance policy, was the political enemy of the county prosecutor. The state attorney general had refused to permit the continued licensing of pinball machines. Investigators were scouring the bushes for informants, for someone on the inside to turn state's witness in return for immunity from prosecution. The police department organization was being shaken.

Ben Cichy drowned beside his house next to his fifty-five-foot, twenty-nine-ton seagoing yacht. On the day he died Cichy had two appointments. The first was with two of the network's most trusted members, a former assistant prosecutor and an undersheriff in the county sheriff's office. The second appointment was with a special investigator whose evidence had been crucial in developing the case against the crime network. Cichy's death was seen by network members from top to bottom as a desperate move on the part of desperate men to keep the cracks in the wall from destroying the foundation. But it was too late. The foundation had already been moved. The revolution had already begun, and there was no stopping it.

In July 1969 the city council voted to end the tolerance policy. This was an interesting piece of "legislation" in view of the fact that the policy was originally established not by vote but by fiat. Regardless, the vote did have the effect of publicly declaring that the old system was dead.

Police Vibrations

It will be recalled that, as a result of Mayor Braman's invitation, the International Association of the Chiefs of Police did an investigation of the Seattle Police Department. Their public statement suggested only minor difficulties with a few isolated police officers taking small payoffs. Their full report, however, which was given to only a very few people in government and in the police, suggested much greater potential problems.

To break the payoff system in the police department required that police officers who were not involved be willing to take some risk. In a police force where payoffs had been funneled from bottom to top for over fifty years, this was not an easy task. When the police department was reorganized along the lines suggested by the IACP, Tony Gustin became head of one of the four divisions.

Gustin began immediately to transfer anyone he knew to be collecting payoffs. He also assigned into his division men whom he believed he could get to close down gambling establishments. They had orders to begin slowly and in the safest areas; predictably they began harassing and arresting gamblers and whorehouse operators in the black ghetto.

Things grew more and more tense. Efforts were made to get Gustin transferred out of the division. But he wisely allied himself with some newsmen and an investigator from the attorney general's office. It would be dangerous to try to oust him when he was only doing his job and had support from some powerful interests. With the state attorney general investigating as well as the U.S. attorney, it was clearly a time to try to let things cool off rather than heat them up by firing a "good cop" or letting more dirty linen get aired in public.

Gustin grew bolder. It became clear that hard evidence against some of the leading network politicians and policemen was necessary. Charlie Berger, who owned the Lifeline Bingo Club, kept extensive records including a mutilated check made out to the county prosecutor for five hundred dollars, which the prosecutor had sent back to Berger uncashed.

Investigators for the attorney general had developed a substantial amount of information connecting Berger with gambling and with payoffs to police and politicians. Compared to many of the other illegal activities known to Gustin and the investigators, the bingo operation was relatively inconsequential. Yet what was needed was some evidence of gambling and payoffs that would stand up in court.

In August 1969 Gustin met with a newspaper reporter and a special investigator for the attorney general. The three of them went to a quiet bar and discussed the possibilities open to them for exposing the payoff system and particularly for forcing some of the key players in the police department to resign. Over several of "the strongest Scotch-and-sodas I've ever had in my life" (as one of them recounted the meeting) it was decided that the Lifeline Bingo Club would be the target of a raid.

There was of course considerable risk in such a move. If it backfired, if the records that were alleged to be there were not, or if the entire operation could later be painted by the higher-ups in the police department as merely harassment of innocent citizens by overzealous moral entrepreneurs, then the entire effort might go for naught. The three people felt that with their own strengths—the investigator's thorough knowledge of the club and its operation, the newsman's ability to influence media coverage, and Gustin's ability to pull off the raid—they stood a good chance.

At the time this decision was made the bingo clubs in the city had been temporarily closed down. Berger, among others, was putting pressure on the police to allow the clubs to reopen. Gustin was confident that the assistant chief, Buzz Cook, would give the word to reopen the clubs soon:

> So it was decided to do it. We would justify the raids on the grounds that we know the records are there. Now we sit back and wait for Buzz to open them up, and then we get an

agent inside several times, prior to the raid, to determine that gambling is being conducted, somebody to go out and get an affidavit to get a warrant. And we take them.

The completion of the operation required a certain amount of intrigue. Few of the police officers could be trusted. Gustin enlisted the aid of George Fuller. Together they planned a deceptive maneuver. He brought into the "inner circle" one person who was tangentially involved in the payoff system. To him and others Gustin announced that there would be a raid of the Alpha Bingo Club. Fake plans were drawn and left in desks overnight, desks known to be rifled every night and the information contained in them passed on to the assistant chief of police. Only a few trusted people knew where the raid was actually to occur. After several weeks of such planning and shenanigans, Gustin gathered thirty-five policemen together and prepared for the raid.

The invading force dressed in slickers and First Avenue garb. Thirty-five clean-cut policemen gathered at a predetermined spot and were told, only then, where they would go. With Gustin and the special investigator in the pack and the reporter following, they walked like an ill-trained army through the rainy streets of the skid row area of the city.

They went quickly up the back stairs of the bingo club. The owner of the club couldn't believe it, nor could the elderly men and women with their strings of ten-cent bingo cards, when the lieutenant in charge strode across the floor of this den of iniquity, took the microphone from the hand of the caller, and announced, "You are all under arrest."

Gustin chose a time of day when there would be the fewest people playing. He was after the records and the proprietor, not the good citizens. Still, at the time of the raid there were over eighty elderly women in the place.

The police issued all of them traffic citations for being in a place where gambling was occurring. It must have been far more excitement than anyone had bargained for. Suddenly the bingo players with shopping bags were criminals. What would they tell their sons and daughters?

The owner of the club and ten employees were arrested. The employees all spent the night in jail. The establishment newspaper used this as a central issue to discredit the raid. The chief of police tried to cover for himself and for the crime network (in that order). He criticized the police officers and especially Gustin. He emphasized the irregularity and inhumanity of locking in jail ten women who "had children and families," who only ran the lunch counter and called the bingo games. It was a poignant issue and a clever diversionary tactic that might have worked under normal conditions.

Normal conditions were a time when the network still had control of the support it had always relied on in crises: businessmen to issue public statements of support, U.S. and state attorney generals to provide countervailing information and evidence. But these sources of control were either split or frightened. The police chief was left alone in his efforts as people began trying to hide their own trails and let someone else take the blame.

The pressure on the chief was horrendous. The prosecutor, who had a private line to the chief's office (a number known only to the chief's wife and the prosecutor), demanded that the chief get the department under control. City council members were screaming likewise. The prosecutor was, in turn, getting calls from all over town asking, "What the hell is going on?"

At one point the chief of police stood up at his desk in front of a reporter, a reporter who had interviewed him hundreds of times over the past five or so years, and the chief began emptying his pockets of everything—keys, wallet, notepaper. He said, "Look, Ron, I never got a dime. I don't care what anybody says, I never got a goddamn dime."

In fact, the chief of police was not stretching the truth too far. He had received a lot of free whiskey, Christmas presents, and a job he liked. But in comparison to those who organized and coordinated the payoffs within the police department, the chief never did profit very much from his cooperation. He had kept his job, which was more than he would be able to say a month later.

The chief left town. Wisely or unwisely, he went to an IACP meeting in Miami. Ironic—Miami is one of the most thoroughly corrupt cities in America. Ironic—the IACP meeting in Miami was filled with lobbyists from organized crime networks from all over America. Ironic—the IACP had issued a report to the public saying Seattle had a clean police force. Ironic—the IACP had warned that if the assistant chief was not neutralized there would be a scandal. Ironic—the IACP had recommended a change in the structure of the police department which made possible the Gustin raid on the bingo club. When the forces of change that emanate from higher powers are set in motion, even those who most want to protect the established relations end up playing into the hands of those who are moving the strings.

The chief was not the only one under pressure. Gustin's life was threatened. He had risked his career. He had violated one of the sacred norms of police work: at all costs protect your brothers in blue. Both of the people above him on the police force, the chief and the former assistant chief, would fire him outright if they could. His other less-direct bosses, the city council and the county prosecutor's office, were also out to have him fired or at least neutralized, which meant demotion at best. Once he had dealt the cards, his only option was to play out the hand.

Gustin had the support of the U.S. attorney and of the state attorney general, as well as the cooperation of several media people and some special investigators. It was a fairly weak, though not irrelevant, power base from which to try to manage the palace revolt.

There was, however, an alternative open to Gustin. He could join the network. He had the chance. A police officer linked with the network but still close to Gustin told him quietly that he had been instructed to offer Gustin forty thousand dollars if he would defuse the revolt. He refused. He also refused to reveal the source of the offer.

During the chief's visit to the IACP convention, Gustin and two other division commanders decided to confront the chief with allegations of corruption. The newspapers and other media were reporting part of the contents of the records found in the bingo club. They carefully screened the information to protect many people. There were cancelled checks in the safe that showed payments to state legislators, city councilmen, and many other people. This information was never fully made public. Bits and pieces of it were unclear enough for them to start looking out for their own interests first and other people's second.

When the chief of police returned from Miami, Gustin called him and asked him to come to his office. He did. With the aid of other police officers, Gustin gave the chief a military-style briefing on corruption in the police department. The chief was, of course, fully aware of all these things. Indeed, everyone knew that everyone knew. . . . Finally the chief asked what they wanted of him. One high-ranking officer (who had himself participated in payoffs from time to time), according to one of the people present, said, "What we're saying is that you are either a thief, a liar, or a fool. And I think I know which one of them you are."

Then an affidavit was presented, which was signed testimony to the effect that the chief had received a large payoff from an illegal operation. When the evidence was presented and the chief's role in it spelled out, he said, in effect, "What do you want of me?"

Gustin replied, "I want a demotion to captain or I want you out." As a major in the department, Gustin was not civil service. This meant he could be dismissed or demoted at the discretion of the chief without cause being shown. But as a captain, a position Gustin held previously, he was civil service and therefore both his job and his pension were protected. Gustin quite accurately sized up his position and realized that either the chief had to go, or he had to get a secure position in the department.

Interestingly in this meeting all that the participants save one had in mind was to try to get the chief to cooperate with a thorough investigation of the department's complicity in the criminal network, with an eye to "cleaning it up." The one person who had a different idea was Gustin. He wanted the chief's resignation. He knew better than others that it was the chief or him. The others could have survived a reform program with the chief as head. But Gustin had already gone too far with his independent efforts to expose the system. He had to have the chief's resignation to protect himself.

Following the meeting with the chief, the group went over to the mayor's office; a representative from the city council was present at the meeting, and the group repeated the entire scenario outlining the police-connected criminal activities.

At the end of the meeting the mayor asked the policemen what had to be done. Gustin again supplied the answer: the chief had to go, or they all wanted to be demoted to captain.

The chief retired. The mayor appointed an acting chief of police. Whom did he appoint with the advice and encouragement (one might say, demand) of both the King County prosecutor and the president of the city council? Assistant Chief of Police "Buzz" Cook, the man accused of being a key figure in the crime network, of course.

The division heads who had engineered the palace revolt let it be known to the acting chief they could not work with him. They forced him to resign too.

As in every other community, the police of Seattle had a "guild." It was controlled by members of the network. The guild recommended that Frank Moore, who was the right-hand man of the former assistant and then acting chief of police, be appointed. The mayor made the appointment immediately.

Outside the police department the newly appointed U.S. attorney set to work to gather information and expose the network. He first contacted the local office of the FBI. Presumably the FBI is subservient to the U.S. attorney, but in fact it is highly independent. When the U.S. attorney contacted the agent in charge of the office who was responsible for Seattle, he was told that the FBI had too many other pressing things to do—watching student demonstrations, catching Communists, and the like. The U.S. attorney tried to pull rank but to no avail.

The U.S. attorney was not totally stifled, however, as he had been given the files collected by the state attorney general, who had wanted to use local corruption as a stairway to the governor's mansion.

With the large body of information now available to law-enforcement officials on the extent of the crime network, even the newly appointed U.S. attorney was quickly convinced that a case could be developed against leading politicians and law enforcers.

The U.S. attorney called Washington, D.C., for support.

In particular he wanted to be sure that his bosses in Washington would not oppose his attack. They gave their approval. More particularly, he needed the help of the local FBI, and he hoped to get it by going to the White House. Attorney General John Mitchell, through his assistant, Richard Kleindienst (both of whom would later be indicted on criminal charges), assured the U.S. attorney of their support. Kleindienst personally contacted J. Edgar Hoover of the FBI, and instructions went out to the Seattle office to cooperate. As one observer put it, "After that [the U.S. attorney] was up to his elbows in FBI agents."

There remained, however, a major technical problem. There was at the time no suitable federal law under which a government or law-enforcement official could be indicted for permitting gambling, accepting bribes, corruption, or any of the offenses systematically committed by members of the network. Some gamblers, such as those operating bingo parlors and pinball machines and bookmaking operations, could be indicted for transporting or conspiring to transport gambling devices across state lines. But the purpose of the investigation was not to send some businessmen engaged in illegal businesses to prison; the purpose was to break the network. The strategy decided on was to call a grand jury and subpoena leading members. While the witness was on the stand before the grand jury, an attempt would be made to get the witness to perjure himself. The principal questions would be: "Did you know of the existence of a payoff system within the police department? Did you yourself ever accept a payoff from anyone?"

If the witness answered "No" to either of the questions and if the U.S. attorney could then get testimony from informants contradicting the witness's statement, then the witness could be indicted for perjury. On the other hand, if the witness admitted knowing of or accepting payoffs, then this admission could be used as ammunition against the county prosecutor and others at the top of the network.

The U.S. attorney convened a federal grand jury. At the January session witnesses were called, and network members questioned. In the end only one indictment came out of the January session. An ex-sheriff, who had also served on the state parole board, was indicted for perjury. The February session of the grand jury culminated in indictments against three people for conspiring to transport gambling devices across state lines.

These indictments were a start. They fanned the flames and kept the issue alive. They warned network members that there was much danger afoot. Two people who were under questioning were killed. The police department palace revolt took heart, and even some of the most trustworthy network members secretly smiled at the realization that some of the worst of the city's finest might be in for a bad time.

The early indictments, however, only scratched the surface. To make sure that the network was broken, the U.S. attorney was well aware that he had to indict someone close to the top. A crucial election was pending for county prosecutor. If the incumbent prosecutor were reelected, the prospect for breaking the network would be severely threatened. If, however, the prosecutor could be discredited and defeated, then a new prosecutor might be elected who would "clean up the mess" by indicting people for violating the state and county laws against gambling, bribery, and corruption.

At the April session of the grand jury the U.S. attorney called as a witness Buzz Cook, who had been a key figure in the crime network within the police department for twenty years. His testimony contradicted that of some key witnesses, and the U.S. attorney persuaded the grand jury to indict Cook for perjury.

They had indicted one of the police department's leading officers, a man who had served as acting chief on several occasions. These indictments put pressure on the county prosecutor to call a county grand jury to look into charges of bribery and corruption. To do so, however, would be very dangerous for the prosecutor in view of the possibility that such a jury might get out of his control. Not to call a grand jury or make any move whatsoever to investigate the allegations being made by the U.S. attorney would expose the prosecutor to severe criticism from the press, as well as from within his own political party. Politicians were quick to sense that the incumbent prosecutor's jugular was exposed, and several people, both Democrats and Republicans, immediately announced their candidacy for prosecutor.

There were, as we have seen, two main political factions enmeshed in the network: the prosecutor's right-wing Republican faction and the Democratic Party's statewide faction. When Assistant Police Chief Cook was indicted, a county supervisor immediately declared his candidacy for prosecutor. So too did a moderate Republican who was closely tied to the moderate Republican governor.

In the course of testimony before the grand jury not only was former Acting Chief of Police Cook implicated, but so too was the current acting chief, Frank Moore. Thus, in short succession following the chief's resignation, both of the next two mayor's appointees were also implicated in the payoff system in the police department. Acting Chief Moore resigned.

The mayor was unable to reach into the police department without taking a great risk. He had already appointed two known members of the network. He, therefore, was under considerable pressure not to make the same mistake again. There were no candidates inside the police force that were both safe from possible indictment by the grand jury and supported by a powerful segment of the police. The mayor, therefore, selected as acting chief a man who was chief of police in another state. The new chief brought with him, as his assistant, a man who was the former chief of police in the same city.

One of the most blatant acts engaged in by the new chief of police was to establish a police investigation unit. The unit was composed mainly of people connected with the crime network except for Gustin. This move looked very good publicly. Within the police department, however, two things very quickly became clear: Gustin had no authority on the investigative unit, and, furthermore, the new chief was out to punish those men within the police department who had forced the resignation of the old chief. Not Gustin, but another of the leading officers behind the former chief's resignation was also implicated in payoffs, albeit far more mildly than any of the heavy network members who were exposed. He was threatened with being reduced in rank to captain or being fired from the police department, thus losing his pension. He retired instead. His early retirement meant a reduction in pension, but that was far better than no pension at all.

The new acting chief of police harassed Gustin incessantly. He tried to force him to resign. Gustin refused. During one argument Gustin told the chief that he was "sick and tired of guys like you." Gustin also told him he was taking the next day off and was going to stay home and get drunk. About 12:30 P.M. the next day, the assistant to the chief called Gustin and demanded that he report for duty. The speculation was that Gustin might be drunk and could be fired as being unfit for duty. He reported to duty sober. Such were the kinds of harassment Gustin was subjected to, the price he paid for exposing the corruptness of the police department and breaking the network. The acting chief served only as long as he was on leave from his regular duties. When he returned to his regular post, his assistant was made acting chief. Finally, a police officer from another Nixon-Republican city was brought in as chief of police to replace the acting chief. After a few more moves and countermoves, the task force and the acting chief recommended that a permanent chief of police be appointed from out of state. They recommended a former Los Angeles County sheriff's department captain and presently a chief of police of a city notorious for tolerating gambling.

The appointment was made by the mayor. The new chief moved to Seattle and immediately demoted Gustin to captain and placed him in charge of the juvenile bureau. The demotion meant a salary reduction of three thousand dollars a year. Within the department some of the major figures who had run the network were promoted, even in the face of being implicated by the federal grand jury, including one of the most prominent bagmen in the department. Another member was made acting assistant chief of the technical division, and later permanent assistant chief in charge of that division.

Of the other three officers who were instrumental in exposing the corruption in the police department, one was forced to retire early on threat of being sanctioned for taking payoffs, and the other two were demoted.

The Republican Party split. The old established network businessmen continued to support the incumbent prosecutor. So too did many other local business groups. The

young Republican and the liberal and moderate wings of the party, however, supported a candidate handpicked by the governor. The primary race for the Republican nomination was close, but the scandals, the indictments brought by the U.S. attorney, and the implication that the incumbent prosecutor tolerated much more than the tolerance policy implied were sufficient to give the Republican nomination to the governor's candidate.

The Democratic Party's nominee was closely linked to Democratic politics. The race was so close that the outcome was determined by absentee voters. The absentee ballots were two-to-one Republican, and the new Republican Party took over the prosecutor's office. The newly elected prosecutor immediately began investigations into corruption. A county grand jury was called and provided with enough evidence so that eventually *fifty-four* public officials (politicians and law-enforcement officers) were indicted on charges of bribery, corruption, and misuse of office.

The indicted public officials included the former county prosecutor, the former chief of police, two former assistant chiefs of police, the president of city council, the county sheriff, the undersheriff, the head of the county jail, a former sheriff, the head of licensing bureau of the county, and so on. Basically, indictments were brought against selected local political and law-enforcement officials. State-level members of the crime network were untouched, as were most of the businessmen.

The forces of change were successful. The network came apart. "Right" prevailed. At least some sort of right.

One year after the indictments were brought, most of those indicted had either been exonerated or the charges had been dropped. There was really no reason to pursue the matter too far. The network as it had existed was broken and that, after all, had been the purpose of the investigation.

It was, however, necessary to find a fall guy, someone who could be made to take the brunt of the attack so that there would at least be some small illusion that the entire process had been a sincere effort to find and bring to justice criminal types. But whom? The prosecutor? The mayor? The chief of police? The sheriff? The vice-president of the bank? The president of the city council?

In the end none of these people were found guilty or sentenced to jail, but others were. Acting Chief Buzz Cook was sentenced on federal charges as well as state charges, serving a total of six months. Lyle J. LaPointe, one of his assistants, was sent to the county jail for one year. A former sheriff and member of the parole board, Tim McCullogh, received a three-year suspended sentence. The person who drew the stiffest sentence was not a public official but a bagman, not a police officer but a racketeer: Frank Colacurcio, a tavern owner, was given three years on a federal charge, of which he served two years and one month in a federal penitentiary.

Others either were found not guilty or, for most, their cases were dropped.

From the Vancouver *Sun*, May 24, 1972:

SEATTLE POLICEMEN GUILTY

Associated Press

SEATTLE—Verdicts of guilty against the remaining two defendants in what started out as Seattle's largest political cor-

ruption trial have finally been returned by Superior Court
Judge James Mifflin.

Milford E. Cook and Lyle J. LaPointe, former high-
ranking Seattle police officials, were found guilty after a
one-day defence presentation by Cook, who testified on his
own behalf. LaPointe's attorney rested his case without calling witnesses.

Cook and LaPointe were the last 19 defendants named in
a conspiracy indictment returned by the 1971 King County
grand jury which charged the 19 former and present law
enforcement officials conspired to promote and allow
gambling, bribery, extortion, blackmail and liquor law violations through a system of police payoffs.

The eight acquitted by Mifflin last Thursday after the
prosecution rested its case included Charles O. Carroll,
who for 22 years as county prosecutor was considered one of
the most powerful figures in Republican state politics.

Charges against former Seattle city council president
Charles M. Carroll were dropped without explanation last
year. The state supreme court in March ordered charges
dropped against six others including former police chief
Frank Ramon.

Cook, 58, retired as an assistant police chief June 1, 1970
after 29 years on the force. LaPointe, 57, a former inspector
and 22-year veteran, retired on a disability pension May 4,
1971. The maximum sentence for the crime of "conspiracy
against a governmental entities" [sic] is up to five years in
prison, a fine of up to $10,000, or both.

A year after the indictments I found abundant poker
games, bookmaking operations, prostitution, and drug
trafficking still in the city. Pinball machines and bingo parlors were gone. Gone too were the openly advertised
"amusement centers." The buildings where these businesses had thrived a year before were now rundown and
boarded up.

One year later my informants and my observations indicated the beginnings of a new crime network in Seattle. A network that would pay homage and share profits with a new political alignment of Democrats and Republicans, which would be more subtle than the older one, less open, without pinballs, but in most important respects different from the older one only in the faces that ran the enterprises and shared the profits.

CHAPTER SEVEN

The Higher Circles

DURING ONE OF Seattle's seemingly endless winters, I began to feel permanently enveloped in the greyness of sunshineless days. Basking in the gloom cast by the drizzle, I sat with a prominent local attorney in one of the better restaurants in the city. The attorney had on occasion invested in illegal ventures. We had become friends during the course of my research, and he had helped me penetrate the upper echelons of the criminal network that managed Seattle's illegal businesses. On this occasion he had called and asked me to lunch. After an appropriately unfocused conversation of fifteen minutes he paused and said, "Did you know that Meyer Lansky was in town the other day? You know his son lives in Olympia?" This attorney and I had talked about Meyer Lansky before. We both knew him to be one of the major financiers of illegal businesses in the United States. He continued, "Meyer contacted _____ [a lawyer known to be a principal go-between for network members]. He told him to pass the word to Rosellini that Meyer would pay everything necessary for Rosellini to run for governor."

That was as gloomy as the weather. It nonetheless brightened the conversation. We talked at length about why Lansky would be willing to invest such a large sum of money in the state's governorship. We did not unravel the mystery that afternoon, but this information started me in the direction I needed to understand not only Lansky's unusual offer but the connection between what was happening in Seattle and what was happening elsewhere in the United States at that time.

Outside Connections

When the crime network was in full swing, on the fifteenth of every month a member of the state House of Representatives flew from Seattle to a city a thousand miles away carrying a satchel full of one-hundred-dollar bills. This was "washed money," which had been filtered from gambling profits through a bank. The amount in the satchel varied depending on how much of the bookmaking profits had to be "laid off" during the preceding month, how much the investors from other cities had coming as their share of profits from various illegal transactions in the city, and how much (if any) local profiteers wished to invest in businesses run by network operators in other cities.

Despite the mythical character of the idea of a Mafia, there is nonetheless a national crime network, the structure and organization of which parallels rather closely the structure and organization of the network in Seattle. That is to say, it is a loose affiliation of businessmen, politicians, union leaders, and law-enforcement officials who cooperate to coordinate the production and distribution of illegal goods and services, for which there is a substantial consumer demand.

The satchel the state congressman carried out of Seattle

every month flew with him to an expensive bar, to a lawyer who represented illegal interests in that city. The lawyer took the satchel with him to his office, where he added its contents to an even larger amount gathered from his own city's illegal businesses. The entire amount was then flown to Las Vegas, where a representative took the money. A few days later the currency was converted to larger bills, added to the "skim" from Las Vegas casinos, and flown to Florida. Meyer Lansky took his share of the profits and sent the remainder off to investors and associates in other cities— New Orleans, Cleveland, Detroit, and New York—whose investments entitled them to a certain share of the profits from Seattle, San Francisco, Las Vegas, and Miami.

Crime networks flourished in the cities of America during prohibition. Many of the leading personalities in these associations had begun their upwardly mobile ascent out of poverty earlier, when they were employed by businesses as strikebreakers. Some were later employed by or actively engaged as members of labor unions to combat the violence of businesses that tried to break union inroads.

But prohibition was the impetus for the emergence of organized efforts to provide the illegal commodities that people wanted, namely alcoholic beverages, and the services they were willing to pay for: gambling, prostitution, high-interest loans, and so forth.

Following World War II the growth in wealth and power of crime networks was unmatched by the growth rate of any other industry. The nation's economy, which was thriving on the discovery of credit buying, on the wealth to be had from the expropriation of resources of less-developed nations, and on the markets won by dividing the world up with the Soviet Union, created an affluence that seemed boundless. Commodities and services that were illegal were in heavy demand. Profits were incredible. Restrictions were minimal.

The associations shared similar problems of existence. They had incredibly high profits from gambling, drugs, and usury which they wanted to invest. But where? How? The economy and criminal operations were expanding everywhere, and the investment of excess capital was critical. Furthermore, with their expanded operations, they were also in need of federal influence. The growth of the bureaucracy in Washington posed an ever-increasing threat to criminal operations. Payoffs and cooperation of local and state governments were sufficient to ensure relatively trouble-free operations locally, but federal agencies, controlling drugs and federal crimes as well as federal legislation that could either facilitate or impede operations, became increasingly important. Crime networks benefited from the same economic and political climate that benefited other businesses from 1945 on.

The situation was replete with opportunities for someone who could provide investment opportunities and federal political clout. As is always the case in situations such as this, someone came along for the job. That person was a man long associated with criminal operations in New York and a close associate of most of the leading crime figures of the thirties, Meyer Lansky.

Meyer Lansky had a shrewd businessman's eye for discovering new territories and creating impressively high profits for his associates, namely people who ran or profited from network operations in cities like Cleveland, New York, Cincinnati, and Kansas City.

Lansky's empire began with a fairly modest investment in Broward County, Florida. The Colonial Inn was south Florida's first major gambling and entertainment establishment outside of Miami Beach. Investors in the club included the major figure in Detroit's crime network, Mert Wertheimer, who owned one-third of the Colonial Inn, and Joe Adonis, leading racketeer in one of New York's networks, who owned 15 percent. Lansky kept 16 percent for himself and distributed the remainder among his close friends and relatives. The profits were staggering, even by syndicate standards where profits less than 20 percent are considered losses. From Florida, Lansky moved into Cuba, where profits were even more impressive and where he also purchased the goodwill, friendship, and protection of Fulgencio Batista, the Cuban president before the socialist revolution. To top off these investments, Lansky invested heavily in the heroin traffic from Turkey and France and opened a hotel gambling casino in Las Vegas. By so doing, Lansky assured himself of the undying loyalty and admiration of even the most anti-Semitic members of crime networks across the nation. Mark it, however, that he was no "godfather." He was simply a well-respected, trustworthy investor with excellent political connections—connections which were able to get even Lucky Luciano out of prison on a pardon.

Lansky also had an almost unerring eye for the political payoff system. He chose his candidates well, but he also covered himself (and those who depended on him for help) by financing candidates who competed with each other. Thus, he paid handsomely into the campaigns of both Thomas E. Dewey and Franklin Roosevelt. He contributed to the political campaigns of Lyndon Johnson, as well as Hubert Humphrey, George Smathers, Russell Long (and Huey Long before him), John Connolly, Richard Daley, Albert Rosellini, and Edmund Brown, to mention only a few.[10] But he paid more here than there, a fact that was ultimately to be his undoing. Those who play the political payoff game take the chance of financing the loser. When that happens, their fortunes fall as surely as they rose when they financed the winner.

Like his brothers and sisters in private industry, a syndicate leader is measured by the profits he produces. The stockholders are the profiteers from crime operations in New York, Trenton, New Orleans, Las Vegas, Seattle, Portland, and cities across the country. Also, like his brothers and sisters in private industry, a successful syndicate operator must manage political payoffs to ensure the protection of crime network interests. Meyer Lansky probably has done both jobs better than anyone in the history of organized crime.

The years from 1932 until 1964 were Democratic years almost everywhere. Naturally Lansky placed his money, at least a disproportionate amount of it, in the hands of Democrats. In Seattle as elsewhere he worked diligently for Democrats. It paid off. Judges were appointed, legislation passed, and protection provided. Lansky's investments in the Democratic Party were often coordinated with, or given through, trade unions, especially the Teamsters.[11] Whether given directly or indirectly, the money funneled to politicians in the form of "campaign contributions" or bribes was designed to purchase influence. As newscaster David Brinkley observed:

> George Meany of the AFL–CIO is fawned over in Washington but not entirely for his intellectual brilliance. And not because he can deliver labor's votes. He can't. What he can deliver and does deliver is political money.
>
> The present U.S. Ambassador to Great Britain was not appointed for his contributions to creative foreign policy and diplomacy but for his contribution of political money. This is not new. Back in the fifties, the President appointed one of his big contributors ambassador to a country, then it was found he didn't even know where the country was.
>
> So, jobs like that, and Washington influence, are in effect for sale. All it takes is money, political contributions in election years. If you give enough, Washington's favors can

be yours—influence, flattery, social success, invitations to
swell affairs, and even ambassadorships to countries with
nice climates and cheap servants. Perhaps more important,
influence on domestic policy, such as taxes, affecting your
own business and income.

Running for office has become incredibly expensive, and
candidates have to get money somewhere. The Democrats
get a lot of it from the unions, and the Republicans get a lot
of it from rich individuals and corporations.

No doubt, there are some rich unions and people of
charitable soul, who will give money expecting nothing in
return, but they are scarce. A big political contribution
usually is seen as an investment. It's a scandal everyone
admits. But it's worse now, because running for office costs
more. Public cynicism about politics and politicians already
runs high. If this is not cleaned up, the political system will
come apart—with influence, dominance, and even control
put up for sale to the highest bidder. [12]

It has been commonly accepted by those who play the
political game seriously that a major source of Democratic
Party revenue for the past fifty years has been a labor-
union–crime network coalition.

The most important source of political money for the
Democrats and Republicans alike is, of course, the contributions that flow from "legitimate" business, that is, from
those businesses whose principal product is a legal one,
although the means by which the business is conducted
may be highly illegal. The means of conducting the business and the business itself may, in fact, be far more harm-
ful to more people than the business of organized crime.
Nonetheless, it makes sense to differentiate businesses
whose main product or service is illegal, since this difference in legality does create important differences in the
way the businesses are managed and how they function.

Despite the fact that both Democratic and Republican parties receive their major share of financing from legal businesses, the sad fact (from the Democratic Party's point of view) is that the Republicans receive the greater share of that political money. However, the labor-union–crime-network funds that oil the Democratic Party's machinery help to equalize the disproportionate share of political money that legitimate business and industry give to the Republican Party.

From the 1930s and into the 1960s, there emerged an unspoken détente between Republican and Democratic leaders with respect to some of the major sources of campaign contributions. The Democratic and Republican parties came to control different sources of the available political money. Obviously, if either party could undermine a major source of the other party's political money, the balance of power so crucial to any workable détente would be severely threatened as the money shifted into the coffers of one party.

Shortly after his election to the Presidency in 1968, Richard Nixon began a campaign which, had it been successful, would have shifted much of the labor-union–crime-network political money from the Democratic to the Republican Party. Whether this was a knowledgeable plan on the part of Nixon and his political advisers is something we do not know. Judging from the now available insights into how this group of men planned numerous political forays to increase their position of power, one suspects that the attempt to corner funds for their political interests may have been quite rationally made. In any case, whether by design or simply as a by-product of other decisions, the consequence for the balance of power between the Republican and Democratic parties would have been the same.

Nixon had long-standing and very close ties to a number

of people whose business profits derived at least in part from illegal businesses. Regardless of how heavily involved in crime enterprises these associates and partners of Nixon were, it is tempting to speculate that they were involved enough in such places as Dade County, Florida; the Bahamas; Costa Rica; and Las Vegas, and in such enterprises as drug trafficking, stock frauds, bank swindles, and gambling casinos to have the wherewithal to run illegal businesses profitably.

The Nixon administration's campaign against "organized crime" was in fact a campaign against those crime networks that were most closely connected with Nixon's political foes, Republicans and Democrats. This campaign had the effect of eliminating the entrenched owners and managers of crime cartels, thus affording Nixon's associates and partners an opportunity to increase their share of criminal enterprises. To bring this about, the Nixon administration systematically exposed networks in Democratic Party strongholds, while ignoring networks who supported Nixon's wing of the Republican Party.[13] At the same time, the campaign against organized crime attempted to purge Meyer Lansky from his position as a major link between different organized crime interests and the Democratic Party.

Lansky's empire was vast. The Republicans' first attack was on his Las Vegas holdings. For this attack Howard Hughes was available to invest in the casinos and hotels, which Lansky was being forced to sell by state political pressure that threatened to end the skimming of profits which made the casinos so profitable, by subpoenas and indictments brought by Republican-appointed U.S. attorneys where Democrats had reigned heretofore, by Internal Revenue agents under Republican control, and by FBI agents under Republican control. So he sold out of Las

Vegas, and Howard Hughes came in. Immediately the profits that were for political payoffs began moving into the Nixon campaign fund and out of the Democrats'.

In south Florida Lansky was indicted by a Republican-controlled grand jury for perjury. In Las Vegas he was indicted for tax evasion.

Control of a Miami-based bank shifted from Lansky to Nixon associate Bebe Rebozo. Union funds that had gone to Lansky for investment and into Lansky's banks were transferred. Law firms that had had lucrative union contracts lost them to Republican firms; the Teamsters hired Nixon's own law firm. For all of this, the Republicans paid off: Nixon granted Jimmy Hoffa executive clemency, and Hoffa was released from prison. Frank Fitzsimmons, who was the replacement for Hoffa as head of the Teamsters, was publicly acknowledged by Nixon as being "welcome in my office any time; the door is always open to Frank Fitzsimmons."

It was not only the door to his office that was open; so too was the door to his airplane. In January 1973 the Los Angeles office of the Federal Bureau of Investigation learned that a syndicate leader from the Midwest was coming to Los Angeles to work with Teamsters officials to arrange a billion-dollar health insurance contract for Teamsters' members. Frank Fitzsimmons came to attend the final meeting. The FBI bugged the offices for seventy-two hours preceding the major meeting, but when they requested permission to continue the bug (which by federal law they had to do), the attorney general's office turned down the request. The meeting between Fitzsimmons, a Midwest associate, and insurance company officials took place, and the contract was signed. Fitzsimmons left immediately to meet Richard Nixon in Palm Springs, and they flew back to Washington, D.C., together. The International *Herald-Tribune* reported these events in the April 30, 1973, edition as follows:

Two ranking officials to the Department of Justice eight weeks ago turned down a request by the Federal Bureau of Investigation to continue electronic surveillance that had begun to penetrate Teamsters's union connections with the Mafia, according to reliable governmental sources. Attorney General Richard G. Kleindienst and Assistant Attorney General Henry E. Petersen were said to have made the decision after 40 days of FBI wiretapping had begun to help strip the cover from the Mafia plan to reap millions of dollars in payoffs from the welfare funds of the International Brotherhood of Teamsters. The officials acted on the grounds that investigation had failed to show "probable cause" to continue eavesdropping, the sources said.

They reportedly acted after having received a memorandum, prepared at the direction of L. Patrick Gray III, who was then the bureau's acting director. The memorandum, which made no recommendations, indicated the sensitivity of the investigation, which was reportedly producing disclosures potentially damaging and certainly embarrassing to the Teamsters' president, Frank E. Fitzsimmons, the Nixon administration's staunchest ally within the labor movement.

Endorsement

The administration's cultivation of the two-million-member union culminated last year in a Teamster endorsement of the President's reelection, and Mr. Nixon has made it clear that the door to his office is always open to Mr. Fitzsimmons.

The Kleindienst–Petersen decision came less than a month before Charles W. Colson, special counsel to the President, left the White House to join a Washington law firm to which Mr. Fitzsimmons had transferred the union's legal business.

Before leaving the White House, Mr. Colson had been instrumental in formulating administration political strategy regarding organized labor.

The electronic surveillance began on January 26, under an order of the Federal District Court in Los Angeles authorizing the FBI to tap 11 telephone numbers in the offices of People's Industrial Consultant, 9777 Wilshire Blvd., Los Angeles, Justice Department sources said.

The consulting firm is a Mafia front set up to channel Teamster welfare money to underworld figures, the sources said.

On February 14, the court authorized an extension of the tap until March 6. The taps were requested and installed under the omnibus Crime Control and Safe Streets Act of 1968.

FBI Affidavit

What was learned from the taps was described in an FBI affidavit submitted to Justice Department lawyers. The affidavit asked for continuance of the existing surveillance for 20 days and installation of new taps on a public telephone and the office telephone of an alleged mobster implicated in the plot to siphon money from the Teamsters.

The affidavit said that investigation up to then, including the use of electronic listening devices, had indicated "a pattern of racketeering activity—that is, a series of payments of commissions or kickbacks" flowing from corporations controlled by a doctor in league with the mob through People's Industrial Consultants "to the officers and agents of the employee-welfare benefit plan," in violation of federal statutes.

Mr. Petersen and Mr. Kleindienst, however, would not allow an application for renewal of the court order.

A request Friday to the Justice Department for comment from the two government officials went unanswered.

The FBI affidavit cited information reportedly given to

the bureau by an informant in contact with an associate of Allen Dorfman, consultant to the Teamsters' billion-dollar Central States, Southeast and Southwest Areas Pension Fund, who began a federal prison term a month ago for conspiring to receive a kickback in connection with a loan application made to the pension fund.

"Source No. 3"

The informant, identified in the affidavit as "source No. 3," said that on February 8, at the Mission Hills Country Club in Palm Springs, California, Dorfman's associate introduced Mr. Fitzsimmons to Peter Milano, Sam Sciortino and Joe Lamandri, identified by the FBI as southern California members of the Mafia. The Teamster leader was in Palm Springs participating in the Bob Hope Desert Classic golf tournament.

Justice Department sources reported that, according to the informant, the three men presented to Mr. Fitzsimmons a proposal for a prepaid health plan, under which members of the union covered by its welfare program would be provided with medical care by Dr. Bruce Frome, a Los Angeles physician. Monthly medical fees for each union member would be paid by the central states fund from the millions of dollars contributed to it by employers under Teamster contracts.

In a 15-minute conference with the three, the informant added, Mr. Fitzsimmons gave his tentative approval and sent the group to a Palm Springs residence for definitive discussions with Dorfman.

The FBI were said to have learned that the next day Mr. Fitzsimmons met with Lou Rosanova, identified by Justice Department sources as an envoy for a Chicago crime syndicate, which sought a percentage of the Los Angeles mob's take on the health plan.

Justice Department investigators say that they have evidence that the Chicago branch of the Mafia is determined to retain the access it had to the pension fund through

Dorfman during James R. Hoffa's Teamster presidency. Hoffa was imprisoned after being convicted of tampering with a federal jury and pension fund fraud.

As a result, according to the federal agents, the Chicago Mafia members have kept a sharp eye on Dorfman and Mr. Fitzsimmons since Mr. Fitzsimmons gained clear control of the union.

In 1971, President Nixon commuted Hoffa's eight-year prison sentence, with a provision that precludes his holding union office until 1980.

Nixon's Plane

Rosanova and Mr. Fitzsimmons had talks again on February 12 at La Costa, a plush resort and health spa in San Diego County, according to the Orange County and San Diego County authorities. The same authorities reported that a few hours after that meeting Mr. Fitzsimmons boarded President Nixon's plane and flew to Washington with the President. Both Rosanova-Fitzsimmons meetings were reportedly observed by informants of the Orange County District Attorney's Office. On February 27, at La Costa, the same informants say that they heard Rosanova boast of a future payoff split between him and Mr. Fitzsimmons.

In its affidavit seeking an extension and a broadening of electronic surveillance, the FBI cited as a basis for its request Title 18, Section 1954, of the U.S. code, which prohibits commissions and kickbacks to union and welfare plan officials in return for the placement of union business.

Corroboration

During the 40 days the devices were in operation, the sources said, recorded conversations greatly supplemented and tended to corroborate information gathered in other phases of the investigation being carried on by the bureau and authorities in Los Angeles, Riverside, San Diego, and Orange Counties.

On February 9, the day after Milano, Sciortino and Lamandri allegedly met with Mr. Fitzsimmons and Dorfman in Palm Springs, the taps at People's Industrial Consultants were said to have picked up a conversation between Dr. Frome and Raymond de Derosa, identified by the California authorities as a muscle man for Milano, who operates out of the consulting company's offices.

The FBI affidavit said that de Derosa had told the doctor that "the deal with the Teamsters is all set." De Derosa indicated to Dr. Frome, according to the affidavit, that People's Industrial was in the line for a 7 percent commission, and they talked about a possible $1 billion-a-year business.

In other tapped conversations, de Derosa reportedly said the PIC would get a 10 percent cut of the medical payments. He reportedly complained that the concern had to "give away three points (3 percent) to get the deal."

This is apparently a reference to that part of the deal surrendered by the Los Angeles Mafia figures to pacify the Chicago representatives.

Meyer Lansky was left out of the Teamsters-Republican Party coalition. Several years later it was reported that Nixon could get $1 million from the Teamsters Union. He told John Dean that this fund could be used for hush money. The Washington *Star* reported on Sept. 29, 1977:

> . . . the $1 million may have been what Nixon referred to in the March 21, 1973, White House meeting with Dean concerning the Watergate burglars, demands for huge sums [of] money in return for keeping quiet.
>
> According to a transcript of a tape of that conversation, Nixon said to Dean: "What I mean is you could get a million dollars . . . And you could get it in cash. I know where it could be gotten. . . . We could get the money. There is no problem in that."

But Lansky's empire was much more than a link with the Teamsters. His investments in Las Vegas were supplemented by major holdings of casinos and hotels in the Bahamas, which he helped open up after Cuba was brutally thrust outside the gambling circuit for American tourists. Businessmen who supported the Republican Party attempted to wrest control from Lansky in the Bahamas by manipulating political leadership. Bebe Rebozo made extensive investments in hotels and casinos and tried to buy up and compete with Lansky's enterprises. Someone attempted to murder a leading politician who was favoring Rebozo in the struggle.

The final attack on Lansky was probably the most successful and the most serious. The Republicans attempted to close off his sources of heroin. They did this by pressuring the Turkish government to enforce the law prohibiting the growing of opium, the plant from which all heroin is refined. At that time (late 1960s) Turkey accounted for probably 90 percent of the opium processed into heroin and shipped to the United States. By 1972 Turkey was accounting for less than 40 percent, and Lansky had lost control over a major source of his financial empire.[14] The Republican administration also pressured the Latin American governments whose countries were layover points in the heroin route to America, and Lansky's principal Latin American coordinator of heroin traffic, Auguste Ricord, was forced out of Argentina, where he had been managing the traffic for years. He was eventually arrested in Paraguay.[15]

Meanwhile, the heroin traffic from southeast Asia, especially from the Golden Triangle of northern Thailand, Burma, and Laos, expanded production and a new source of heroin for the incredibly lucrative American market opened up. It is unknown whether this new heroin source was linked to Republican politicians, but the fact that the

CIA and the South Vietnamese governments under generals Ky and Thieu actively aided the development of this heroin source suggests that such a link is not beyond the realm of possibility.[16]

Lansky must have known he was fighting for his life. Always a heavy contributor to the Presidential election, in 1968 he outdid himself by a good margin. Through his agent, Sam Levinson, Lansky contributed at least $240,000 to Hubert Humphrey's campaign against Nixon. Lansky also contributed heavily in support of the Democratic governor of Washington. In fact, so heavily did he contribute that according to political observers there the Democratic candidate was able to ignore altogether the usually time-consuming task of raising campaign contributions.

The format of the attack against Democrat-controlled crime networks was much the same everywhere. Newly appointed Republican U.S. attorneys called grand juries to investigate corruption and racketeering. In Chicago one of Illinois's leading Democratic politicians, Otto Kerner, who had formerly been the governor of Illinois and was at the time of his exposure a U.S. judge, was indicted, tried, found guilty, and sentenced to prison for accepting a payoff while he was governor. As we have seen, in Seattle the bulk of the political, law-enforcement network members and even a few of the racketeers were indicted.

In the state the Democrats lost the governorship despite Lansky's heavy financing. Moreover, the state attorney general's office was also won by a Republican, and to make matters totally unliveable for the existing network, a Nixon-affiliated Republican won the county prosecutor's office. These shifts in state and local political fortunes would mean considerably less money for Democrats in the state, because the new network would be formed around a moderate Republican-oriented group. It would thus mean considerably more money for the Republicans.

Thus it was that the network in Seattle came to its demise. Newspaper reporters who reported the comings and goings of the network, and law-enforcement officers who exposed the guilty culprits took well-deserved pride in their role. The county prosecutor and the U.S. attorney, who worked long hours to build cases against network members, were pleased with their role. It was a marvelous experience in which the righteous thought they were spearheading a campaign against evil. What they did not realize was that they, in fact, were only pawns in a much larger game that was going on at the highest levels of government.

This began to dawn on some when, after the indictments were brought and some key players in the network had been removed from their positions of power and sufficiently compromised so that new appointments could be made, the word came from Washington, D.C., to stop further investigations. The governor suddenly cooled on the idea of seeing the indictments through to prison sentences. The FBI and other investigative units denied the rumor that gambling, drug trafficking, and prostitution were coming in again under new management. The Republican judge, whom the defendants had all agreed on as presiding judge, dismissed the indictments on all but three of the key defendants.

Or maybe those most involved in the network's demise simply turned their heads and began looking to their careers and their political futures. Maybe the reaction of a reporter who early on tried to expose the network was typical: "It's all over. There is no more gambling." This same reporter, six years before, had gone to *see* whether or not there was gambling. Now he was willing to accept the myth that prevailed that the network had been broken, that Seattle was "clean."

The network's demise did not usher in a new era of freedom from the rackets or from the influence of crime. The evidence at hand suggests that the whole process of exposing the crime network resulted from political and economic struggles taking place outside of Seattle, King County, and the state.

CHAPTER EIGHT

The Enemy Is Us

I N THE MIDDLE AGES, when Anglo-American criminal law was being formed, there was no pretense of applying the law uniformly across class lines. When prostitution, gambling, public intoxication, drug use, and the like were made criminal, it was not intended nor was it the practice to apply these laws indiscriminately to all social classes. The upper classes were free to gamble, engage prostitutes, or take drugs without fear of interference from the state.

In time the emerging commercial, mercantile, and industry-owning classes sought to use the state as a means of equalizing their position vis à vis the heretofore dominant landed aristocracy. The law was one of the means through which this struggle was resolved. By insisting on the right to a trial by jury, by establishing an adversary system of justice, by creating a set of social relations built around contractual obligations, the emerging class of businessmen and manufacturers was able to bring the landed aristocracy to heel; at least the two ruling classes were made more or less equal in the law. The lower classes were of course excluded from this equality. The necessity of paying an attorney for protection in the courts assured that neither the aristocracy nor the nouveau riche would have to share state power with the working classes.

Thus was a solution forged: but so too were the seeds of conflict planted by that solution. Relying on the moral principle of equality before the law and depicting the state as a value-neutral organ for settling disputes gave rise to endless criticism from those who observed that "some are more equal than others."

This process is lived over and over in the history of law: a solution is forged which attempts to resolve conflicts that arise out of basic contradictions in the structure of social relations created by the political and economic forms of the era. The solution, however, creates social relations which themselves generate further conflicts reflecting underlying contradictions which generate further attempts to resolve the contradictions.

The first laws prohibiting gambling, bribery, official corruption, vice, prostitution, drug use, and usury were each in their turn an attempt to resolve problems stemming from contradictions. Some were intended to help control the "teeming masses of urban dwellers who walk the streets seeking money by any means fair or foul." Others, such as anti-opium laws, came as a consequence of international competition as it developed into a worldwide, all-encompassing economic system.

Laws against usury are illustrative. They helped stabilize the banking industry by reducing competition. Laws were enacted that established legal limits to the amount of interest that could be charged. They solved a problem of competition among moneylenders, helped stabilize financing for both industry and banking, made life more predictable and monopolies better able to form in the banking industry. At the same time, usury laws opened up the possibility for people to operate illegally. If the banks could not charge excessively high rates of interest, then they would not loan to people who were highly risky. Alas, risky people have as much need for money as those with good credit. Not being able to get credit in a bank does not reduce one's desire to borrow, but it may increase one's willingness to pay higher than legally allowable interest. Enter the usurer. For the usurer can charge excessively high interest and therefore make a profit even from customers who are a greater risk than banks will accept as borrowers. Result: a structurally induced illegal business is created as soon as the solution to competition and "chaos" in the banking industry is solved by establishing legal limits to interest. All, of course, done with the best of intentions.

Notice, however, that those who engage in usury face a number of administrative problems not faced by banks. Most important is the fact that usurers, because they are engaged in illegal acts, cannot turn to the state and ask that the law be invoked to force debtors to pay back what they have borrowed. Usurers thus, in order to protect their investments and guarantee their profits, must establish their own law-enforcement arm. They must employ a staff of people who are capable of "persuading" those who have borrowed but failed to pay back their debts that it is better to pay the debts than to have them hanging over their heads. Usurers utilize many of the same techniques that the law employs in the service of banks: they confiscate property, threaten to expose the person to public shame, and if none of these are effective they resort to corporal or at times even capital punishment. The latter is of course utilized only as a means of demonstrating to other would-be renegers that it is unwise not to pay your debts. The same principle, need it be said, underlies the justification for capital punishment when it is imposed by the state on people who presumably have committed acts that are "beyond the tolerance limits of the community." The acts vary;

the problem that gives rise to them is identical, namely, that some people are not living up to the standards others with more power think they should. To keep the heresy from spreading, a life is taken.

It is ironic that those who are least likely to be able to afford the high interest of usurers are those most likely to have to turn to them for loans: the poor as well as the rich are protected from being charged more than the legal limit on interest by banks and licensed financiers.

It is an ironic manifestation of political economic contradictions that the laws that keep many illegal activities from being rampant in the "better neighborhoods" have the effect of concentrating them in precisely those parts of the city where the people are most likely to be already disillusioned by "The System," that is, in the slums. Thus a further contradiction: laws which were not initially intended to be enforced against the rich result in pushing illegal businesses into areas where the poor and working classes live and are thereby exposed to the hypocrisy of the law in everyday life.

Other Networks, Other Times

Robert Winter-Berger was for five years a lobbyist in Washington. On one of his frequent visits to the office of John McCormack, Speaker of the House of Representatives, the back door to the Speaker's office suddenly burst open and Lyndon Johnson, President of the United States, exploded into the room. Winter-Berger in *Washington Pay-Off* reports:

> Johnson disregarded me, but I can never forget the sight of him, crossing the room in great strides. In a loud, hysterical voice he said: "John, that son of a bitch is going to ruin me. If that cocksucker talks, I'm gonna land in jail." By the

time he had finished these words he had reached the chair at McCormack's desk, sat down, and buried his face in his hands. Then I knew why he had come here, and I realized how desperate the situation must be.

To the best of my recollection at that shocking moment, McCormack said: "Mr. President, things may not be that bad." He got up and went to Johnson and placed a hand on his shoulder.

"Jesus Christ!" Johnson exclaimed. "Things couldn't be worse, and you know it. We've talked about this shit often enough. Why wasn't it killed, John?" When Johnson looked up at McCormack, I could see he was crying. He buried his face again.

"We tried, Lyndon," McCormack said. "Everybody did."

Johnson said: "I practically raised that motherfucker, and now he's gonna make me the first President of the United States to spend the last days of his life behind bars." He was hysterical.

"You won't," McCormack said helplessly.

"How much money does the greedy bastard have to make?" Johnson said. "For a lousy five thousand bucks, he ruins his life, he ruins my life, and Christ knows who else's. Five thousand bucks, and the son of a bitch has millions."

"We all make mistakes," McCormack said, glancing at me. "How could he have known, Mr. President?"

"He should have *given* him the goddam machines," Johnson said. "He should have known better. Now we're all up shit creek. We're all gonna rot in jail."

"We'll think of something," McCormack said. He rubbed Johnson's shoulder. "Please. Calm down. Control yourself."

In a burst, Johnson said: "It's *me* they're after. It's me they want. Who the fuck is that shit heel? But they'll get him up there in front of an open committee and all the crap will come pouring out and it'll be my neck. Jesus Christ, John, my whole life is at stake!"

"Listen, Lyndon," McCormack said, "remember the sign Harry had on his desk—THE BUCK STOPS HERE? Maybe we can make this buck stop at Bobby."

"You *have* to," Johnson cried out. "He's got to take this rap himself. He's the one that made the goddam stupid mistake. Get to him. Find out how much *more* he wants, for crissake. I've got to be kept out of this."

"You will, Lyndon," said McCormack. "You will."

The President moaned. "Oh, I tell you, John, it takes just one prick to ruin a man in this town. Just one person has to rock the boat, and a man's life goes down the drain. And I'm getting fucked by two bastards—Bobby and that Williams son of a bitch. And all he wants is headlines."

"It'll pass, Lyndon," McCormack said. "This will pass."

Johnson got angry. "Not if we just sit around on our asses and think we can watch it pass. You've got to get to Bobby, John. Tell him I expect him to take the rap for this one on his own. Tell him I'll make it worth his while. Remind him that I always have."

"All right, Lyndon."[17]

Johnson had gone through this tirade with scant notice that Winter-Berger was in the room. When he finally took note of him, he asked McCormack if he was "all right." Assured that Winter-Berger was all right and a friend of Nat Voloshen, a major Washington lobbyist, Johnson asked Winter-Berger to take a message to Voloshen: "Tell Nat that I want him to get in touch with Bobby Baker as soon as possible—tomorrow, if he can. Tell Nat to tell Bobby that I will give him a million dollars if he takes this rap. Bobby must not talk. I'll see to it that he gets a million-dollar settlement. Then have Nat get back to John here, or to Eddie Adams later tomorrow, so I can know what Bobby says."

Bobby Baker, the "motherfucker" Johnson had "practically raised," began his Washington career at age fourteen as a page for the Senate. By 1955 he had been hired by Johnson, then Senate majority leader, as his secretary. His salary was nine thousand dollars a year, and his net worth, he stated, was eleven thousand dollars. By 1963, only eight years later, his personal fortune had grown to over two million dollars. Presumably another million was added when he "took the rap" and did not implicate the President. Baker's rise to fortune came by selling favors and influence and information and by investing in businesses owned and managed by racketeers: among them the vending machine business, which was in the end his downfall. Among the racketeers Bobby Baker was closest to was his and Lyndon Johnson's neighbor, Sam Levinson, one of Meyer Lansky's closest associates and a partner with Lansky in Las Vegas holdings. Levinson contributed $250,000 to Hubert Humphrey's 1968 Presidential campaign against Nixon.

The crimes for which Lyndon Johnson thought he might be the first President to end his term of office in prison— the crimes he was willing to pay Bobby Baker one million dollars to conceal—were never disclosed. Abe Fortas, one of Johnson's appointees to the U.S. Supreme Court, was less fortunate, and, when his links with a notorious financial wheeler-dealer in Florida were revealed, Fortas had to resign from the Supreme Court. It is even possible that had Baker revealed even part of what he knew about Johnson's involvement in criminal acts, they would have paled what is publicly known now about Richard Nixon's involvements.

Richard Nixon continued the Johnson tradition of selling favors and protecting investments for those who supported him politically. The textile industry contributed over $400,000 to Nixon's reelection campaign and the oil industry over five million just one day before the law went into effect requiring public disclosure of campaign contributions. For their contribution the textile industry won a tariff on the importation of textiles from Japan which assured them of a high stable price for their products for years to come. According to columnist Jack Anderson, in 1972 the president of McDonald's hamburger chain contributed $250,000 to Nixon's election and won in return an exemption of high school employees from the minimum wage law—an exemption personally written in by President Nixon and one which exempted most of McDonald's employees in the race to cover America with hamburgers. (In 1968 he contributed only $1000.)

The milk industry contributed a million dollars to Nixon's campaign and was rewarded with a boost in milk prices during a period when prices on everything were frozen to curb inflation. ITT promised to contribute $400,000 to underwrite the expenses of the Republican National Convention. The Department of Justice subsequently dropped an antitrust suit against ITT.

As Richard Kleindienst said: "I am not a prophylactic sack with respect to the White House."[18] Meanwhile, as assistant attorney general, Kleindienst, it will be remembered, was one of the principal people in the Justice Department giving the green light for the U.S. attorney in the state of Washington to investigate and expose the organization of illegal businesses there. He was not, however, quite so concerned about such phenomena elsewhere. During his confirmation for U.S. attorney general, when John Mitchell resigned to take over the management of Nixon's reelection campaign, it was revealed that Kleindienst had cleared a U.S. attorney, Harry Steward, who had been charged with obstructing investigations into corruption in San Diego: Nixon territory.[19]

Nixon, Johnson, Kleindienst, Mitchell: these men are not aberrations in an otherwise well-working machine. They are merely acting out roles that emerge time and time again. Lincoln Steffens was not writing about 1900, and I am not writing about 1970. The story is told over and over.

George Washington started us off by unashamedly using the office of the Presidency to enhance his personal fortune. During the administration of Ulysses Grant the Union Pacific Railway directors were caught pocketing money from government bonds, and Grant's vice-president was implicated in the plot. During Grant's second term of office, frauds totaling some seventy-five million dollars were unveiled, and Grant's secretary of war (who was forced to resign) as well as his personal secretary were involved.

In the 1840s Martin Van Buren was reported to be so corrupt that there were songs written eulogizing his willingness to sell anything he controlled.

Warren Harding was perhaps less fortunate than his predecessor or those to follow, since his administration's scandal ("Teapot Dome") has become a pseudonym for political corruption (perhaps soon to be replaced by "Watergate"). The Teapot Dome Scandal was only one of many rumored during Harding's administration, and he was spared much of the torture of the scandal by his well-timed death. The scandal involved the leasing of government land at Teapot Dome, Wyoming, to the oil magnate H. D. Sinclair. In the end, the secretary of the interior, Albert B. Fall, was proven to have personally benefited substantially from this and other land leases. Fall was eventually tried, convicted, and sentenced to jail (one year) for having accepted a bribe.

President Roosevelt's administration was relatively free from scandal, although this is probably more a result of the crises (Depression and World War II) during that administration acting as a smokescreen than the purity of the politicians.

Harry Truman's administration saw a White House military general, Harry H. Vaughn, accepting a deep freeze in return for using his influence. Donald Dawson, a close

Truman aide, was implicated in a scandal involving the misuse of public funds and influence by the Reconstruction Finance Corporation. The Internal Revenue Service was involved in yet another Truman-era scandal which culminated in a conspiracy trial against Truman's former appointments secretary.

Sherman Adams, one of Eisenhower's closest associates, was found to have accepted numerous gifts (among them a vicuna coat) from Bernard Goldfine, who was at the time trying to influence the Federal Trade Commission. Sherman Adams ultimately resigned as Eisenhower's special assistant.

On the state and local levels corruption of police and politicians is revealed with a regularity that is as certain as physical laws. On August 3, 1974, the Knapp Commission, which had been investigating rumors of corruption in the New York City Police Department, reported:

> We found corruption to be widespread. It took various forms depending upon the activity involved, appearing at its most sophisticated among plainclothesmen assigned to enforce gambling laws. . . . Plainclothesmen, participating in what is known in police parlance as a "pad," collected regular biweekly or monthly payments amounting to as much as $3,500 from each of the gambling establishments in the area under his jurisdiction, and divided the take in equal shares. The monthly share per man (called the "nut") ranged from $300 and $400 in midtown Manhattan to $1,500 in Harlem. When supervisors were involved they received a share and a half. . . .

The Commission found evidence that payoffs were widespread (though not always so well organized) in the other divisions of the New York Police Department as well. Frank Tannenbaum wrote in *Crime and the Community*:

It is clear from the evidence at hand—that a considerable measure of the crime in the community is made possible and perhaps inevitable by the peculiar connection that exists between the political organizations of our large cities and the criminal activities of various gangs that are permitted and even encouraged to operate.[20]

Just as criminal liaisons between law, economics, and politics are a mainstay of buying and selling public favors, so are they also a mainstay of regular business practices. The Far East and African sales manager for a leading European business-machine manufacturer explained to me how he sells his company's products by bribing government officials. In some countries the bribes are exorbitant; in some they are "a reasonable five or ten percent," but everywhere, whether selling to government, large corporations, or retail outlets, the principle is the same: the people who give you large orders expect and receive a bribe.

An example of a particularly exorbitant (but not unusual) transaction consummated by the above-mentioned sales manager was the sale of one million dollars worth of business machines to the Congolese government. To secure the sale it was first necessary for him to meet and wine and dine the fifteen top government officials who would have to approve the order. Once the order was placed, the company kicked back $250,000 to the fifteen people, including the minister of finance, the purchasing agent, and so forth. To mark the final irony, the machines were unusable as delivered since the order did not include requisition of an auxiliary machine necessary for the base machine to be operative. No one complained; the company was delighted not just by the size of the order ($750,000 after kickback) but also because the corrupt nature of the purchase enabled the company to double its usual price and thus vastly increase its profits. And of course the sales manager re-

ceived credit for making a very impressive sale. Only the
farmers and workers whose taxes supplied the funds were
harmed by the transaction.

Kickbacks, bribes, collusion, and corruption are as much
a part of corporate business as they are a part of crime
networks everywhere. So too are public lies and disclaimers
of businessmen and politicians caught in the act. In 1967
and 1968 the top executives and accountants of Lockheed
Aircraft, with the complicity of high-ranking officers of the
Air Force, falsified public reports of the cost of overruns on
the C-5A airplane. Complicity of the Pentagon was purchased by the favors Lockheed does for the high-ranking
officers, including, perhaps most significantly, the prospect
of high-paying jobs in the aircraft industry upon retirement
from the service.

Investigative agencies such as the FBI and the IRS are
co-opted in similar if not identical ways. Retired FBI agents
become "special investigators" or are employed by banks,
corporations, or state governments at high-paying jobs.

Meat inspectors for the U.S. Department of Agriculture
are systematically bribed by the meat industry through
extra pay for overtime, free meat, and a variety of smaller
"courtesies."[21] Those who do not accept the bribes or who
push too hard to enforce meat-processing requirements are
isolated, fired, or in some cases even criminally charged for
malfeasance of office.

We could of course go on indefinitely with such examples
but the point would be the same: there is an inherent tendency of business, law enforcement, and politics to engage
systematically in criminal behavior. This is so not because
there are too many laws but rather because criminal behavior is good business, it makes sense, it is by far the best,
most efficient, *most profitable* way to organize the activities
and operations of political offices, businesses, law-

enforcement agencies, and trade unions in a capitalist democracy.

It should not surprise us, then, that crime networks in the larger cities of the nation are ubiquitous. City after city has been exposed and particular network members purged, usually the least powerful ones: the owners of the taverns, gambling halls, whorehouses, and businesses that produce illegal goods and services. Occasionally the cleanup includes some political and law-enforcement people, normally lower-level, relatively powerless ones in the political economy of the city, state, or nation. Occasionally higher-level people are implicated, even at times the President of the United States.

At the turn of the century the cities were New York, Philadelphia, Minneapolis, St. Louis, Kansas City, and Chicago. In the last ten years scandals have broken in New York, Seattle, Portland, Newark, Philadelphia, Chicago, Detroit, and Miami, to name but a few. Like the persistent "white-collar crime," nothing changes as a result. Networks come and go but the process by which they are produced goes on and the consequences remain the same. Whether it is Meyer Lansky or Santo Trafficante, Lyndon Johnson or Richard Nixon, the network remains in control of large segments of America's political economy.

By now it should be clear that the logic of capitalism is a logic within which the emergence of crime networks is inevitable. Capitalism is based on the private ownership of property. Property is acquired by selling products, providing services, or selling one's labor. By law most of the products and services which can be exchanged for money at a profit are legal—that is, the state has decreed that it is permissible for people to buy, sell, and exchange these goods and services. At one time in American history most of the products and services which support the crime industry were legal: gambling, high-interest loans, even prostitution and heroin. Thomas Jefferson himself established a brothel near the University of Virginia for Virginia's young intelligentsia to have a readily available outlet for their sexual urges.

In time some commodities and services came to be defined as illegal. But the demand for these things did not disappear with their transference from legality to illegality, nor did the profits to be had. Indeed, in some cases the profits increased as a consequence of their newly established illegality. Marketing procedures had to be adapted to the fact that these things were now illegal—new methods of collecting debts for example—but the process remained the same. Businessmen and politicians and entrepreneurs invested in, coordinated, and managed these (now) illegal industries in the same way they had managed them when they were legal.

Capitalism provides the basic conditions, but it is the organization of politics in the U.S. that joins the capitalist mode of production to make the ground fertile for crime networks. The key feature of American political organization that combines with markets and profits in illegal goods and services to create networks is the peculiar necessity for American politicians to spend vast sums of money in order to get elected to office.

Only recently has it been necessary for politicians to declare the size and sources of their campaign contributions. The results of their declarations are staggering. Richard Nixon admits to spending over sixty million dollars on his 1972 Presidential campaign. Disclosures of unreported campaign contributions suggest that even this figure may be a gross underestimate of the actual amount spent.

Nelson Rockefeller is reported to have spent over sixty million dollars in his campaign for the Presidential nomination and the governorship of New York.

An American politician must obtain an incredible amount of money if he or she is to be successful. Sources of funds are or course limited. Individual donors giving ten and twenty dollars cannot begin to provide the necessary funds. Especially desperate are those politicians who would run on a platform that does not appeal to the interests and ideology of the wealthiest people in their area. Thus a great irony results: it may even be that the politicians most likely to be vulnerable to the influence of crime networks are those who espouse the more egalitarian, working-class, or populist economic and political principles.

So far as election to public office in the U.S. is concerned, money is everything. In 1974, out of thirty successful candidates for the Senate, twenty-eight of them spent more money than their opponents.

Crime networks with access to billions of dollars in untaxed, unreported, and unaccountable funds are a valuable source of money to oil capitalism's political machinery. In the natural course of events some politicians will come to cooperate more fully than others, some will come to compete for a larger share of network profits, and some will come to reap the profits for their personal as well as their political use. Still others will grow dependent on the money to finance campaigns and occasionally to meet "personal emergencies." Through it all the crime network becomes an institutionalized, fixed, and permanent link in the chain of a nation's political economy. That is what has happened in America. That is why crime networks persist year after year with only the faces and methods of operation changing.

Nor have other capitalist countries escaped the plague. In 1969-70 I researched the relationship between illegal and legal businesses in Nigeria and found essentially the same sorts of interrelations between politics, business, and systematic violation of the law that one finds in America.

What is perhaps more surprising, given our biases, is to discover that crime networks are also pervasive throughout Europe and Scandinavia. In 1975-76, a team of sociologists–lawyers from Sweden and I researched illegal businesses there. Despite the constant claims by the Swedish National Police to the contrary, we discovered an immense and highly organized consortium of businessmen with international connections and local penetration of politics that was firmly entrenched in the illegal enterprises of drug trafficking, gambling, usury, and even the ancient shakedown of "legitimate" business for "protection."

This is not to deny that there are differences. For some purposes the differences may be more important than the similarities: the extent to which the police are corrupt from the top to the bottom may vary from place to place. The variations, however important they may be, should not obscure the fact that the systematic organization of illegal activities for profit is as characteristic of capitalism as bureaucracy is characteristic of the modern state.

Is this to say that capitalism alone creates the networks? Hardly. I did not research systematically in Eastern Europe, but I was not on land ten minutes in Poland before I was offered the opportunity to exchange U.S. dollars on the black market for ten times the official rate. Stories of high-level payoffs and corruption abound. A large percentage of people in Poland report that they have to pay bribes to obtain official favors. Whether these isolated facts add up to a crime network and the systematic penetration of the political economy by the organization of illegal activities for profit is only guesswork, but it is suggestive of that possibility.

Does this weaken the argument that it is the structural characteristics of capitalist democracies (especially the contradictions that inhere in these political economies) that create and sustain crime networks? Not at all. Cigarette smoking causes lung cancer but other things cause lung cancer as well. The kind of "socialism" that is extant in the Soviet Union and Eastern Europe shares with Western capitalism many essential features: a rigid class system, the use of money for exchange, and the alienation of workers from the product of their labor, to mention only a few. It may be that these essential characteristics are fundamental. Unfortunately we lack the systematic comparisons with other countries to be very confident about such speculations.

What can be done? The answer depends on the question implied. To stop gambling, drug taking, prostitution, and usury would require a change in the political economy possible only through revolution. At the moment, that possibility seems rather remote. We must then lower our sights substantially and recognize that, as Murray Morgan said with respect to prostitution in Seattle in the early days of that city's checkered history, "where demand was so sustained and so obvious somebody was certain to try to hustle up an adequate supply." As long as providing things that are heavily in demand is illegal, then, given the political economy of capitalist democracies, crime networks of one sort or another are inevitable. Thus, to eliminate or at least reduce the magnitude and change the character of crime networks requires first and foremost the decriminalization of these things.

There are already some clear lessons to be learned from other countries. Years ago Great Britain placed the problem of opiate addiction (heroin, morphine, etc.) squarely in the hands of the medical profession. While the results of this move have not been to abolish completely traffic in opiates in Great Britain, the extent to which the enterprise is profitable, the degree to which the market has been controlled, and the general effectiveness of the program have kept crime networks from forming around the illicit traffic in opiates in Britain in anything like the same way they have formed around opiates in the United States, France, Sweden, and The Netherlands—to mention but a few countries.

The proposal that heroin use should be decriminalized and medical doctors permitted to prescribe heroin for addicts has been made time after time. After an extensive inquiry into the subject, the American Medical Association and the American Bar Association proposed that this policy be "seriously considered" over twenty years ago. Opposition by the federal agencies responsible for enforcing the laws (whose agents benefit directly and indirectly from the existence of crime networks) has meant certain defeat for such proposals.

We may, however, be in a somewhat better position with respect to the possibility of legalizing gambling. As the economic recession–inflation we are presently witnessing puts pressure on state and federal governments to increase tax revenues, gambling is more and more attractive as a source of untapped revenue. In other words, there are some powerful interests (the state itself) capable of legalizing gambling in order to increase their own revenues. When this happens we would be naive to suppose that the networks that have previously profited from the gambling would suddenly be replaced by legitimate businessmen. The networks, it must be remembered, are already populated by legitimate businessmen. The management would not change but legalized gambling would provide taxes, a reduction of associated illegal actions dictated by the illegal nature of crime networks, and a somewhat greater ability to oversee network activities. In short, we could expect to have the government and its bureaucracies relate to the organizations which supply gambling in much the same way they relate to other businesses. Is it better to have ITT buy my congressman and lobby for its own peculiar self-interests, or is it better to have Meyer Lansky and Company doing it? Perhaps it makes no difference in the long run. I suspect that at least having a small amount of tax benefit that goes into welfare or education or roads is better than the present situation.

It seems quite certain that if drugs and gambling were decriminalized, crime networks as we have known them since the turn of the century would disappear. The fortunes made in these illegal enterprises could then become respectable in the same way that the fortunes of the robber barons—the Mellons, Rockefellers, Vanderbilts, and Kennedys—have become respectable. It would then be possible for us to see, in another generation or two, those who inherit the wealth of Meyer Lansky, David Beck, and Jimmy Hoffa running against a Dupont, a Rockefeller, a Mellon, a Heinz, or a Kennedy for President of the United States. That may not be progress, but it is consistent with historical precedent.

Whatever changes might be forthcoming, one fundamental truth must be grasped: It is not the goodness or badness of the people that matters. The people who ran (or run) the crime network in Seattle were (and are) not amoral men and women. On the contrary, they are for the most part moral, committed, hard-working, God-fearing politicians and businessmen. It seems paradoxical perhaps that someone could kill, threaten, and coerce people to protect himself and still adhere to a set of moral principles to which "all of us" adhere. But from his point of view he may be protecting far more important things than merely his own skin. He may be protecting an ideology for which he stands. He may be protecting the community from being taken over by people whose ideas are, from his viewpoint, bound to lead the community and the nation down the road to ruin. "The Fourth of July oration is the front for graft," Lincoln Steffens wrote. It is often the sincere belief of the grafters that they are also performing a public service and living up to the principles of the Fourth of July oration.

The people in the crime network in Seattle and those who cooperated with it were simply acting within both the logic and the values of America's political economy. They were operating to maximize profits, to protect their investments from competition, to expand markets, and to provide services and goods demanded by "the people." These are all the logical implications of a capitalist economy. These—or closely related—ideas also become values. Profit is a value: something intrinsically worth striving for. Being shrewd, pragmatic people, they know that whatever value one chooses to stress inevitably involves a compromise with some other values. Profit may necessitate compromising strict adherence to the law, but then so does mere survival in the realities of political life. You use whatever resources you can to maximize profits and increase capital. Whenever possible, you also operate to help your friends and business associates. These are values which all persons in crime networks share with many if not most other contemporary Americans. The members of crime networks fought for the protection of these values; some even died for them. Not surprisingly, they were willing to violate many laws—"mere technicalities"—to live up to the logic and values of their world.

SOURCE NOTES

INTRODUCTION

1. New York: Harcourt Brace, 1931, p. 8.
2. National Commission on Law Observance, Washington, D.C.,
U.S. Government Printing Office, 1931.
3. *Theft of the Nation* (New York: Harper and Row, 1969), p. 1.
4. Ibid., p. 21.

CHAPTER THREE

I met Bob Williams several months before he was killed. He
was willing to talk rather freely about his own work but hesitated
to provide much information that would implicate anyone else.

By accident I first heard about how he died from an M.D. who
was working as an intern at the county general hospital. He told
me about a "young black man" who had been brought in on
successive nights as I have described it. I did not know that it was
Bob Williams at the time, but I decided I should look into it.
Interviews with some of the police officers to whom I had talked
about other matters confirmed the story told to me by the doctor.

Primarily the data on the size and degree of criminal involvement of illegal businesses come from informants who either were
themselves principals in the enterprises (and thus in a position to
know) or were close enough to the principals to have such knowledge. Some of the data provided here on the magnitude of illegal
enterprises were later confirmed in testimony before federal and
county grand juries between 1969 and 1972.

In general I did not accept as "fact" data provided by only one
informant. Furthermore, even if more than one informant told
the same story, the story was not taken as fact until I was able to
hear it from someone intimately involved in a particular transaction or event. Often, as in the poker games, I observed for
myself the truth of what I was told.

189

CHAPTER FOUR

Much of what is reported in this chapter is "common knowledge" among people who played, organized, and observed the rackets. This included small-time burglars, petty thieves, waitresses in cardrooms, and cardroom managers. I first heard most of the stories and connections outlined in this chapter from these people. I was, however, suspicious of the accuracy of their picture. Later I was able to get confirmation from some of the principals involved—two of them in particular being a leading member of the network who worked in the sheriff's department (who is now deceased) and a city police officer who, although not himself involved, had at one time been an active "player" in the network and knew exactly who was involved and how the system worked. In addition there were my numerous phone calls, midnight meetings, and casual conversations with fellow-gamblers and "bridge players" which confirmed the basic outline of the network as well as specific facts.

There were in addition my own observations of meetings and occasionally an overheard conversation. One of my most highly placed informants was also willing to let me see notes he had kept of some of the meetings and decisions made by various groups.

The question naturally arises as to why people, especially people at the top, would be willing to talk to a sociologist. Unfortunately I have no easy answer to that question. Individuals' motives for doing what they do remain a dark mystery to social science despite centuries of speculation and inquiry. Some informants wanted revenge for a wrong they felt had been inflicted on them. Others were interested in getting rid of competitors and enemies and saw in me a possible source of outside intervention. Still others were genuinely indignant and incensed at the corruption they had witnessed and in some cases participated in. Some were retired and wanted perhaps to "set the record straight" since they were no longer involved. Some just liked to talk.

There was also a point of pride that helped loosen some otherwise sealed mouths. I developed a strategy of interviewing which began by telling a prospective informant what I had heard. Often what I told the person was some piece of information I already knew was false. But the fact that I, a sociologist interested in a scientifically accurate picture, might believe an erroneous piece of nonsense led many people to want to set me straight. It was not difficult to push for facts and dates and further sources of information under those circumstances, because the interviewee was put in the position of having to give me more than just opinion as to why I should *not* believe what someone else had told me was true.

Finally, since I was myself an active participant in many of the illegal enterprises, it was impossible to put me off with a glib denial. I offered, in fact, to take the sheriff and a high-ranking police officer to see the gambling, prostitution, and drug transactions, which, of course, they already knew about. Nor could they simply fall back on the age-old defense that these things were "so difficult to prosecute," because they knew that I knew they were fully capable of closing down all the gambling, prostitution, and drug dealing in the city (with the exception of things like marijuana) if they chose to do so.

In a sense, then, my position as an insider not only gave me access to casual conversations with cardroom managers, tavern owners, and low-level racketeers; it also gave me information that made it difficult for law-enforcement officials and politicians to dismiss me with the standard excuses and rationalizations that seem to placate the press and the public so readily.

In 1964, when I was in the midst of trying to establish the truth or falsity of the stories, rumors, and innuendos I had heard, I met a reporter for the Seattle *Times*, Don Duncan. I had put together a picture of the crime network very close to the one outlined thus far in the book. But despite the fact that I was convinced of the accuracy of my picture, I was nonetheless uneasy about it. Don Duncan agreed to talk to me about the results of his earlier investigations into corruption and vice in the city. We spent several days together, one session lasting almost eight hours. I said very little except to ask questions. At the end of the discussion I was astounded to discover how closely his findings fitted with mine. This was particularly impressive in view of the fact that with a few exceptions his sources of information were not mine. Don also told me how he had been unable to get any of the articles disclosing these practices published in the paper and how he had been told to stop wasting his time on "yellow journalism." This experience was an important one in convincing me that I was gathering accurate data in a worthwhile way, even if I did not have questionnaires or government statistics to back up my research findings.

CHAPTER FIVE

For the information in this chapter I focused on that subterranean level of political and economic life in a city that is usually ignored. I interviewed former FBI agents and businessmen, many of whom were willing to discuss their involvement with the crime network quite candidly. Lawyers were a different story. Because lawyers are eager to present a united front whenever they scent outside attack, it was very difficult to get substantial evidence on the involvement of individual attorneys. Most of my information came from observing businessmen and law-enforcement officials who had dealings with some lawyers and law firms who were in turn involved with the network. Although it was possible to make inferences based on a lawyer's clientele, I have avoided speculating beyond what I could verify by private conversations. Although some attorneys were directly involved in the network's affairs, the legal fraternity seemed for the most part totally unaware of the nature of law practised in the firms that served as go-betweens for politicians and racketeers. It was of little value to talk to persons in law firms not directly associated with the crime network.

Some of the information reported in this chapter can be found in the court trial record of David Beck and in the McClelland Committee hearings. Further information is found in the federal and King County grand jury hearings, which will be discussed in the next chapter.

5. Seattle *Times*, Feb. 22, 1964.
6. Murray Morgan, *Skid Road* (New York: Ballantine Books, 1951), pp. 241-47.
7. Ibid.
8. Walter Sheridan, *The Fall & Rise of Jimmy Hoffa* (New York: Saturday Review Press, 1973).
9. William J. Chambliss and Robert B. Seidman, *Law, Order and Power* (Reading: Addison Wesley Publishers, 1971), p. 396.

CHAPTER SIX

Several police officers provided the insights and information on which this chapter was based. In addition, David W. Keown researched the demise of Seattle's crime network for his master's thesis, "Seattle: A Case Study of the Exposure of Organized Crime and Corruption," Department of Sociology, University of California, Santa Barbara, 1973.

Ron Henson of KIRO radio and Reg Bruce, who was formerly a special investigator for the state attorney general and is presently head of the Citizens Council Against Crime, very generously shared their time and knowledge with me. Both men were intimately involved in gathering the information and evidence on the crime network. Reg Bruce was also an adviser to the policemen who staged the "palace revolt." He was present during many of the crucial meetings within the police department, and he was privy to a number of private meetings with informants. Ron Henson followed the exposure and the indictments assiduously and brought his considerable talents to bear in clarifying to me the history and events that took place.

Reg Bruce's experiences are worth mentioning because they reflect the political nature of criminal investigation. While Reg was working as a special investigator for the attorney general (O'Connell), he developed an informant who would testify to the effect that Charlie Berger paid Frank Colacurcio $3,000 a month: "During an election year it's a great time to investigate. Because people come out of the woodwork. But it's a bad time to prosecute because it's an election year." Reg reports that he and some of the policemen were trying to get a judge to call a county grand jury, with the hope of indicting some of the people in the payoff system, but no judge would do it because it was an election year. During this time someone from the city Licensing Department came to Reg and threatened to have his private detective's license rescinded.

O'Connell was defeated. Reg and two other special investigators recommended to the new attorney general, a Republican, that the investigation into corruption in King County be continued. The new attorney general declined to do this, and the three resigned in January 1969.

Later, when the U.S. Attorney became interested in what was going on, Reg was rehired by the attorney general's office. Reg became friendly with Tony Gustin and helped plan the Lifeline Bingo Club raid, which started the dominoes falling.

Eventually Reg had a falling out with the attorney general: "I quit because I consider myself a professional investigator and I wasn't willing to screw around with that circus."

About the present situation Reg recently commented: " . . . from the word I get, the new payoff system will not involve the tremendous numbers of officers that the old one involved. That was obviously a very dangerous system. I am led to believe that the payoffs will be more political in the future. . . ."

Following his resignation from the attorney general's office, Reg became executive director of the Citizens Council Against Crime. He comments that in his new job he "has no illusions of stopping crime and corruption" but "I believe we can stop a full-bore payoff system like we had before . . . they are coming back but it's more sophisticated. Before, there was a lot of extortion as well as bribery. Now the payoff system is more bribery—people who want to pay as a form of insurance."

CHAPTER SEVEN

The symbiotic relationship between politics and the illegal business ventures of some of the state's citizenry was constantly suggested by people at all levels of the crime network to whom I talked. The people with the most thorough knowledge of these relationships were the practicing attorneys. I found several who were willing to impart some interesting and important information. In contrast to people "closer to the action" (gamblers, prostitutes, bookies, and beat policemen for example), however, lawyer-informants were characteristically elusive. They were more likely to suggest that I watch "the home of" a certain person "in the prosecutor's office," or observe "who eats together at Vito's every Thursday" than to give any very precise information. Nevertheless, the few lawyers in the state who were both knowledgeable and willing to discuss things with me were extremely helpful. It was largely from leads provided by them that the information in this chapter was developed. I checked the suggestions and "facts" provided against my observations. For example, when told of a meeting between people, I tried to be present or to confirm that the meeting took place from other informants or from newspaper reports.

Newspaper reports were also essential in constructing the overall picture of symbiosis and complicity between criminal money and national politics. It is characteristic of the profession of journalism, however, that the separate accounts of meetings, law-enforcement omissions and political contributions are never brought together into a single picture. Deadlines and the requirement that there be another story tomorrow preclude such collating of facts and events. To some extent this is the task of the social scientist concerned with contemporary history.

It was from a lawyer–politician that I first learned that campaign contributions from illegal businesses were an important source of income for successful politicians. It also became clear as I put the various bits and pieces together that businessmen and racketeers vying for political allies supported different candidates and that their fortunes as gamblers, racketeers, and entrepreneurs were closely linked to whether or not their favored politician won.

Murray Morgan published a fascinating little book, *Skid Road* (New York: Ballantine Books, 1951; see Appendix A, for excerpt), which is a history of Seattle from the lumbering town of shanties and labor unions to the colorful politics of the 1950s, when Dave Beck ran the Teamsters (and many politicians) and Vic Meyer ran for lieutenant governor with a band and a promise to stop corruption by making everyone pay him directly. Although Morgan paid scant attention to the booming illegal businesses of Seattle, his history provided some important insights into relations between politics and illegal money.

The late 1960s also witnessed a heady growth of journalistic accounts of national crime networks and their local affiliates. I would not endorse any one of these accounts as an unbiased or even accurate picture of a national crime network, but each contained fragments and pieces of information which helped clarify the picture in Seattle and especially the national links so essential to an understanding of what was and is going on there. A few of the books that provided pieces of the puzzle were Evert Clark and Nicholas Horrock, *Contrabandista* (New York: Praeger, 1973); Fred J. Cook, *Mafia* (New York: Fawcett World, 1973); Hank Messick, *Lansky* (New York; Ballantine, 1969) and *Syndicate in the Sun* (New York: Macmillan, 1968); Donald Cressey, *Theft of the Nation* (New York: Harper & Row, 1969); Alvin Moscow, *Merchants of Heroin* (New York: Dial Press, 1968); Robert Wilder, *An Affair of Honor* (New York: Bantam, 1969); Martin A. Bosch and Richard Hammer, *The Last Testament of Lucky Luciano* (New York: Dell, 1974); and Walter Sheridan, *The Fall and Rise of Jimmy Hoffa* (New York: Saturday Review Press, 1973).

In addition there are thousands of pages of testimony before Senate and House committees on organized crime. Making sense of these documents is a task requiring no less sociological imagination than it does patience. Yet they, and the journalistic accounts, supplemented by interviews with lawyers, businessmen, politicians, and people close to the action are the only data base we have to draw on.

10. Martin A. Gosch and Richard Hammer, *The Last Testament of Lucky Luciano* (New York: Dell, 1974); Hank Messick, *Lansky* (New York: Ballantine Books, 1969).

11. Sheridan.

12. NBC Evening News, Nov. 16, 1971.

13. See, for example, Anthony Sampson, *The Sovereign State of ITT* (New York: Stein and Day, 1973), pp. 217-88.

14. William J. Chambliss, "Markets, Profits, Labor and Smack," *Contemporary Crises*, vol. 1, no. 1 (January, 1977), pp. 53-76.

15. Evert Clark and Nicholas Horrock, *Contrabandista!* (New York: Praeger, 1973), pp. 89-93.

16. Alfred W. McCoy, *The Politics of Heroin in Southeast Asia* (New York: Harper and Row, 1973), pp. 52-75.

Chapter Eight

17. New York: Dell, 1972.

18. Sampson, p. 221.

19. Ibid., p. 214.

20. New York: Columbia University Press, 1938, p. 128.

21. Peter Schuk, "The Curious Case of the Indicted Meat Inspectors," *Harper's Magazine*, 1972.

Appendixes

A NOTE ON THE
SOURCE MATERIALS

In these appendixes I have included bits and pieces from a variety of sources. Obviously not even a tiny fraction of the interviews can be presented here. Most of the interviews were confidential and I promised never to quote or reveal them. The people who talked to me must above all else be protected. Some of the interviews, however, were with people willing to have their observations made public. I have selected excerpts from these interviews (Appendix B), but in no sense are the opinions and materials presented here either representative or sufficient. They are merely glimpses designed to help the reader obtain a better feel for the materials.

I have also included some written documents: Appendix E is an accountant's report to Albert Rosellini when Rosellini was accused of accepting bribes from Frank Colacurcio and Charlie Berger. It is amusing to see the ex-governor's own accountant saying in a letter that the accountant found no record of payoffs received by Rosellini from either Berger or Colacurcio.

Some of the police memos that were distributed in the early 1960s pertaining to the tolerance policy are also included, for what they are worth (Appendix C). It is interesting that these memos clearly contradict one another and were circulating at a time when the network was operating at its peak.

An excerpt from Murray Morgan's book *Skid Road* (Appendix A) pointing out the connection between David Beck and Warren Magnuson and the Seattle newspapers makes for interesting reading. I would call attention to the fact that the Hearst Newspaper Corporation, which owned both the Seattle *Times* and the *Post-Intelligencer* appointed Franklin Roosevelt's son-in-law to be publisher of the *Times* after Roosevelt was elected President in 1932. David Beck's attorney in 1928 who defended him against charges of misusing union funds was later appointed by Truman as Secretary of Commerce. The links in the chain go on indefinitely.

Mainly for future historians who might want to see if the action is now where it was then, I have included a list of the places holding public cardroom licenses in 1968 and a list of places that had licenses for panorama (Appendix D).

Appendix F contains a letter from Attorney General John O'Connell to the governor of the state, Daniel Evans, requesting that Evans request O'Connell to investigate the allegations of bad conduct on the part of Seattle law-enforcement people. Wonderful commentary on the politics of law enforcement. Also included in that appendix is the White Paper referred to in Chapter 6 in which O'Connell tried to explain his ten-thousand-dollar line of credit at the unnamed Las Vegas hotel.

Appendix G is "The Investigative Task Force Report of the Seattle Police Department," which was put together after the fall of the old network.

Appendix H consists of facsimiles of the legal briefs of the grand jury indictments of some of the Seattle network members.

APPENDIX A

"Dave Beck and Labor Politics" from Murray Morgan, *Skid Road* (New York: Ballantine Books, 1951), pp. 241-47

In 1933 the National Recovery Act was signed by President Roosevelt. Section 7a stated that "employees shall have the right to organize and bargain collectively through representatives of their own choosing, and shall be free from interference, coercion, or restraint of employers of labor or their agents." Across the land the great drive to unionize the workers began.

Dave Beck was ready and waiting, willing and able. He had by this time rounded up everything on wheels in Seattle. He was perfecting his technique of unionizing a plant by "organizing the boss"—convincing him that he could make more profit by paying higher wages and thereby creating stability. Where other union leaders were calling the bosses names, Beck soft-soaped them. "Some of the finest people I know are employers," he kept repeating. He was too shrewd to rely mainly on propaganda. Behind the sweet words was the economic force of the Teamsters, who could refuse to haul supplies to any outfit that fought Beck. Professional bullyboys made it unhealthy to drive anything for pay if you didn't wear a Teamster button. Trucks were sideswiped and overturned, men who voted wrong at the Central Labor Council were beaten up. People heard the apocryphal Teamster slogan, "Vote no and go to the hospital."

Seattle had three papers in 1936 and none of them liked Dave Beck. The dominant papers, the *Times* and *Post-Intelligencer*, which Hearst brought in 1921 had a running feud to see which hated him the most. In May of that year the Newspaper Guild began a drive to organize the *Post-Intelligencer*. Two of the most active members in the Guild chapter were Everhardt Armstrong, the drama editor, and Frank Lynch, the chief photographer; they

201

were good men who had been with the paper for more than fifteen years. Shortly after they let the management know they were in the Guild, Lynch was fired for "inefficiency" and Armstrong for "insubordination."

The Guild tried to negotiate for their reinstatement, but the management refused to talk about it. The Guild filed an appeal with the National Labor Relations Board and also put the matter before the Central Labor Council. Beck dominated the council, and it voted to put the *Post-Intelligencer* on the unfair list. That meant strike. Beck ordered the Teamsters to join the picket line and the union men turned out in force. To everyone's surprise, so did hundreds of unorganized citizens who didn't care for the paper or for William Randolph Hearst. There were housewives in trim frocks, faculty members from the University of Washington, lawyers, clerks, and at least four ministers of the Gospel on a picket line that jammed the streets for a block in each direction from the plant. The typographical unions refused to pass the picket line. A few non-Guild reporters slipped through and covered their beats by telephone; they pecked out copy in the echoing city room, but without the backshop men no paper could be printed, and even if one were printed it would have been difficult to distribute. . . .

Hearst took to the air. He brought in a battery of public-relations men, bought hours of radio time, and filled the radio channels with sound and fury. Beck was pictured as a racketeer and—of all things—a Red. Beck sued the *P-I* and the stations for $500,000, and later settled out of court for $15,000. The Hearst orators shifted their attack; they argued that freedom of the press was endangered and that a labor dictatorship was being established. The Guild had no money to buy radio time but it had plenty of supporters, so it organized some of its well-wishers into a telephone brigade. Whenever a station carried a pro-Hearst broadcast, the telephone brigade swamped the switchboard with indignant demands that the Guild's side of the story be told. Station managers began to give the Guild free time to reply to charges made on purchased time.

The Hearst people formed a Law and Order League, which

started to take an inventory of firearms owned by its members; there was talk of an armed phalanx which would crash through the picket line around the plant. That talk died down after a mass meeting of Guild supporters, at which not only ministers but the mayor and the prosecuting attorney spoke on behalf of the strikers. Warren G. Magnuson, the handsome young prosecuting attorney of King County, carried a Teamster card in his wallet and had the Commonwealth Federation endorsement for the late Marion Zioncheck's seat in Congress. Magnuson cited laws guaranteeing the right to strike and the right to picket. Those laws must be obeyed, he said. The mayor, John F. Dore, once friend of the businessman, told the cheering crowd of five thousand that if the Law and Order League appeared with guns, the city police would take the weapons away from them in the interests of law and order. "I don't care if the *Post-Intelligencer* ever publishes," he said, "and I think it would be a good thing for the town if it didn't." . . .

When Dore ran for mayor again in 1936, this time with the backing of the Teamsters, he won handsomely. "Brother Dave Beck was the greatest factor in my election," he told the State Federation of Labor after the vote was counted, "and I say again that I am going to pay back my debt to Dave Beck and the Teamsters in the next two years, regardless of what happens."

Beck's political flank was guarded; neither police nor private guards were going to disrupt a Teamster picket line. The *P-I* strike settled into a siege. It became apparent that ultimate victory might hinge on the state and national election results. The Republican gubernatorial candidate was campaigning on the issue of the *P-I* strike. "If I were in Olympia," ex-Governor Hartley said, "I'd smash that strike." Nationally the Hearst chain was pouring out editorials in favor of Alf Landon; the Democrats made no secret of their delight that one of Hearst's spigots was plugged. Both sides waited for the political decision in November. The Republicans lost and Hearst surrendered. He wrote an editorial praising Roosevelt as the possible successor of Andrew Jackson, and a little later he announced that the *Post-Intelligencer* would resume publication with Roosevelt's son-in-law John Boettiger, late of the *Chicago Tribune*, as its new publisher. Hearst said that Boettiger would have a completely free hand.

The handsome young publisher arrived in town with Anna Roosevelt as helpmeet and assistant publisher and editor of the homemaker page. The President's son-in-law was not unmindful of the role Dave Beck had played in his rise from the editorial ranks to that of publisher. Boettiger told the assembled dignitaries at a welcoming banquet that he considered Seattle a "model industrial community." Never again did the *Post-Intelligencer* attack Beck, and when Westbrook Pegler or one of the other syndicated columnists made unfriendly remarks about the Teamster leader, *P-I* editors protected the public by deleting the heresy.

Nor did the *Times* find anything wrong with Beck after 1936. Its editorials, which once had equated Beckism with bolshevism and the Teamsters with terror, suddenly became models of restraint. It was not that General Blethen loved Beck the more; it was that there had appeared on the labor scene a man he loved much less. He was Harry Bridges, president of the Pacific Coast Longshoremen's Union, CIO. . . .

APPENDIX B

Selections from Interviews

A: . . . the cardroom and the bookmaking are slightly separated at the lower levels. The lower-level people don't even feel very confident. It was pretty much by accident that I found this out myself. It was a couple of years before I knew how the operation was. In fact, it was the pinball operators and that faction of them wanted ____ and his bunch, group, to lay off of me and in view of this they offered me, in place of my cardroom license, a panorama license. Now you know what a panorama is, don't you?

Q: Yes, I think so.

A: A panorama is the viewing of naked women through a—yes. Well, there is payoff in that too, you see, and what they were angling at was to get me out of gambling entirely and put something else in there that may be more palatable to me and no problem to them, but in the same tone you have to make a payoff here, so then it would have me two ways. It would get me out of gambling, making me willing to pay off, and I couldn't make any moves that way anyway. So it was kind of fudgey, but this is what was offered to me just before I left.

Q: I would like to get a picture now of what it looks like as an organization.

A: The structure of it.

205

Q: Right. Where does ____ fit into the organization? Is he at the top?

A: Well, ____ was right up at the top for a number of years. When he was having trouble in Portland he was no longer at the top, but he was an important figure. He had to retire for a while as a prominent figure. The only reason the government caught him in these indictments is they made a pinch of the Turf and he didn't have his name on the licenses, but what they were doing is making a gradual transfer over—he was going to become a partner. But his share in the partner hadn't completely materialized. . . .

Q: What about ____?

A: I think he was one of the prime movers in getting bookmaking set up. One of the more clever ones, but he's lower on the ladder, is running a place out of the city called the ____ Smoke Shop, and he is a details man. But this goes beyond the immediate people down there; it goes up into the city hall itself, and if you want my personal opinion, I feel that ____ is definitely the big brains behind most of it. He stayed in the background of the city council for years. . . . Now you probably heard about ____ in the city council. He is just a front man for the boys, but he has no knowledge, I don't think, of the inner workings of this very, very close-knit organization. The government tried very hard to break it but they couldn't get anybody to come forward that knew beyond what I did. I mean they didn't know the thing that they wanted but where could they go from there bit? This is the things they couldn't get, they probably had lots of leads on, but they couldn't get anybody to testify that knew this, you see, so I don't know, it's a pretty close-knit organization, there are people that even I know that probably don't have no knowledge that they are in it.

Q: Is it your opinion that this organization is not tied to organizations outside the state?

A: I would say so that with the exception of the small portion of lay-offs and the wire service. Those two areas I think pretty well have to go out of state, but I would say this is a close-knit group playing to the _____ group. You see, I can now see that _____ started way back when the first licenses were issued in the early thirties, you know. The stories around here is that if you were in the Seattle area in which he was running a law practice, you couldn't go up to the state and ask for a tavern license without getting turned down and sent back. But you had to go through _____ to do it. So he was starting his organization clear back then, and he built it through Seattle. . . . And Seattle was wide open. At that time my place, Battersby and Smith, had just plain wide-open gambling. Nothing was hidden at all.

Q: When was this?

A: In the early thirties.

Q: This was in the early thirties?

A: Yes.

Q: You had no connection with them then?

A: No connection at all, but I get this knowledge from previous people in the rackets.

Q: Yes, but Battersby and Smith, you kept that name, is that right?

A: Yes, but it isn't under that name now.

Q: Oh, it isn't?

A: After I left I think they changed the name. The Golden Apple. I think it changed hands again. They didn't have a gambling establishment after that. They used it more for a dine and dance.

Q: Did they have bookmaking after that, do you know?

A: No.

Q: They never have gone back into that?

A: No, I don't think so. In fact, I feel very confident in that, no. They had already established a place over there in the Pennyland Arcade, up a block and across the street by one of the former owners and one of the fellows that got convicted in this federal deal. But he is no way up the ladder, but he is in that group.

Q: Now, you commented on _____. Is it your opinion that he is, was, actively engaged in organizing this group, or was he simply taking payoffs, or is he, or, and I'm not so concerned about _____ again as I am the structure of the thing. What is the relationship between say _____, _____, these guys? Is the relationship where they give them money or is the relationship where they actually are helping direct the decisions? I know this is going to be a lot of guesswork and that's all right. It's your opinion that I'm interested in.

A: I went down to the legislature last year and one of the senators said that the only difference between _____ now and _____ of several years ago is that he doesn't allow the same cronies, the same corrupt officials to come in the front door. They come in the back door. This is what he said. Yes, I believe he is a strong factor in it.

JANUARY, 1966

Q: _____, former King County sheriff, is now on the parole board?

A: Yeah, he's just notorious.

Q: Is he corrupting the parole board?

A: I don't think there's any question about it. Those guys who come through the parole board . . . he just puts the screws on those guys who come through there for marijuana or something and he lets the hoods go free. He lets them out for three or four years. If they're doing a bit he gets them off. And ———. . . .

Q: What do you mean, "if they're doing a bit"?

A: I mean if they've got a sentence that they're serving.

Q: Does he take money for getting people off?

A: I'm not sure it's in the form of taking money for each case. I don't think so. He will take money for a case, and I'm sure he does that, but that's aside from the relationship with the syndicate. But anyone who comes in that the syndicate wants him to get off he gets off because that's the syndicate's kind of contract, but it's not a question of taking money . . . for each case. He's on the payroll, as it were.

And ———, who's the head of the parole board, I think, is a straight guy, at least he was when he became head of it. And I haven't been there since then. I think he probably still is. And he's no dope! And I suspect he sees this. . . .

OCTOBER, 1972

A: It was desperately important that Ben had to die.

Q: Why would that have been the case?

A: Your guess is as good as mine. He may have been on the verge of talking; they may have decided he was so old he was getting loose-lipped; he might have been asking to pay less money to the boys downtown; he might have been holding out on them; he might have been keeping two sets of books. Who knows?

Q: Who decided he had to die?

A: I don't know.

NOVEMBER, 1972

. . . cities take on their character from social outcasts. Creeps built this city, and creeps make it go. And creeps usually end up deciding whether they survive or not. Tacoma didn't have enough creeps; that's why, even though they got the first railroad out there, they wound up taking second place. Most of the creeps gravitated to Seattle in the formative years. Seattle was a fun town in 1910. It was a wide open town. It was a wide open town during World War Two to a certain extent. But from the time of prohibition on, Seattle had taken on this strange character that we all know it has. . . . Everybody knew that a decent city that was growing had to have whores, had to have accessible liquor, prohibition or not, had to have a place where a guy could go and shoot craps, either for penny ante or high stakes, had to have a place where a guy could go and play cards. There was no reason putting somebody in jail for it, because it was what all good, righteous Christians did. . . .

In his testimony at the Cook trial, Palmer Hughes, who was the star witness for the government, said that he came on the police force in 1936. And in his testimony he said that within a week or two of when was sworn in, he took his first payoff. I think you'll find the question is asked, "How old was this system when you got into it?" And he specifically says that they locked up a police chief and some other people in 1925, but they had resumed this thing in 1926. And it had been going on on this basis since then; this organized system of handing the money up. So much to the patrolman, so much to the sergeant (there were no lieutenants then—when they added that rank to the chain of command they really screwed things up), it went from sergeant to captain. So many sergeants contributed to one captain; so many captains contributed to one inspector; so many inspectors to the chief's office, and so on. A regimented system. He said it was ten years old when he came on in 1936, and he took his first payoff within a week or two of when he was sworn in.

. . . about 1946, Mayor _____ and the Restaurant Association guy, and somebody whose name you've got, and someone representing the Teamsters Union—and I didn't have the chance this week to find out who the guy from the Teamsters was—and Police Chief _____, and _____ sat down, and they apparently decided that it ought to be more carefully guarded . . . they decided that they had to keep a lid on. Okay, you had cardrooms in the city, and they were giving out licenses. It just didn't look right when guys had stacks of hundred-dollar bills on the table in broad daylight. Some lady might be shopping downtown and look in the window, you know, and see this. And then is when the paperwork that I sent you comes into play. Finally they decided that these cardrooms, everything, a lid oughtta be kept on, that the cardrooms should be for amusement only.

Q: Was there any crisis that precipitated that?

A: Not to my knowledge, other than occasional newspaper articles and editorials saying, "My God, they're having a high-stakes card game down at the such and such place. . . . By God, a guy takes his son downtown to buy fishing tackle and sees these men sitting there playing cards with two thousand dollars on the table, what kind of a community are we? So they set limits. _____ believed, and I think most people who would accept the "tolerance policy" would think, "Ah, I've solved the problem. I've created penny-ante poker!" All he did was create what the Washington state liquor control board had through its regulations. And here I want to draw a rather detailed analogy. The Washington state liquor control board's regulations are impossible to observe. Washington state liquor board's leverage on licensed premises, for graft, for political favors, the leverage that permits an enforcement or an inspection officer to collect a bribe, is that any bar, any tavern in the state of Washington can be closed at any moment. When _____ . . . set these detailed regulations, three raises, all this stuff outlined in the memos, all he did was give the police department an increased control over the survival of each separate license. They immediately grasped upon this, and went around and explained to the boys that they knew and they were gonna help them—still had their high-stakes games late at night when the house got a five-thousand-dollar cut out of a hundred-thousand-dollar game (I mean, they were still gonna make their money). But so long as these regulations were so detailed, it was gonna be hard for them to be observed. Somebody was gonna want to play poker for five dollars an ante, instead of one dollar.

Q: You think he was aware of that?

A: He should have been. It's a long time ago. . . .

Q: When you used those figures of a one-hundred-thousand-dollar game with a five-thousand-dollar cut, are those figures that have actually been . . . ?

A: These are figures that certain people have told me were common for certain games at certain locations: the Turf cardroom, from its inception; the Ram. The Turf is, I think, gone, but it was on Second Avenue. The Ram is on Pike Street between First and Second. The Ram, one of the two, now, the Ram or the Turf, had reported the fourth or fifth highest income, supposedly, a few years ago on its federal income-tax return, from gambling that any licensed, federal, stamped gambling establishment in the U.S. reported.

APPENDIX C

Police Department Memos from 1962 to 1963

form 1.11
411 21. 16

INTRA-DEPARTMENT COMMUNICATION
SEATTLE POLICE DEPARTMENT

FROM   Assistant Chief C. A. Rouse   DATE December 11, 1962

TO   Precinct Commanders, Precincts I, II and III

SUBJECT   Gambling Enforcement Policy

A. All forms of public gambling are subject to complete enforcement. No license issued by the city gives permission to violate the state laws.

   1. Punchboards, pull tabs, counter dice, pools, lotteries and similar paraphernalia are contraband and shall be seized arbitrarily. Operators and players shall be arrested on view in every instance consistent with available evidence.

   2. Coin operated machines of any kind, such as pinballs, claws, ski-ball, mechanical bowling and mechanical baseball are in themselves not contraband. No payoff shall be made by an operator or his agent to any player of any coin operated machine. Whenever payoffs are observed or come to the attention of the police officers by legal techniques, arrests shall be made and all participants and evidence seized.

B. Non-public gambling is not legal and is not permitted under any license of the City of Seattle. Official policy of the Seattle Police Department is to seek voluntary compliance on the part of private persons, churches, clubs, fraternal organizations, service clubs, charitable agencies, veterans organizations or philanthropic societies. Officers of the Seattle Police Department will investigate every complaint, develop the necessary evidence and arrest all participants. The arrest of participants will include the seizure of all gambling paraphernalia.

   1. Bingo games are gambling and the paraphernalia used must be seized incident to arrest. Organizations and/or individuals conducting bingo games will be subject to arrest after January 1, 1963.

   2. Lotteries, pools or drawings of any nature are illegal.

   3. Raffles of any nature are illegal.

   4. Other games: private persons, churches, fraternal, veterans, service PTA, clubs, philanthropic agencies or other groups sometimes organize bazaars. Games of skill, such as wheels, boards, roulettes, dice, 21, door prize lotteries, name or number lotteries, throw or toss games, pitches, coke ring, balloon darts, Hoopla, spot pitch, and variations, are frequently employed. Games of this type played for money or consideration are illegal.

   5. Reno Nites, Western Nites and Las Vegas Nites are illegal if the activities in any way include any gambling game or device. The pre-sale or sale at the time of admission of script or chips does not make these games legal. Such devices will only make the collection of evidence difficult.

213

Form 1.11
C11 21.10

INTRA-DEPARTMENT COMMUNICATION
SEATTLE POLICE DEPARTMENT

FROM   Assistant Chief C. A. Rouse   DATE December 11, 196

TO   Precinct Commanders, Precincts I, II and III

SUBJECT Gambling Enforcement Policy - Page Two

    a. Most "Nites" described require dice, likewise 21, likewise faro, likewise roulette wheels, dice cages or other gambling contraband. Such items commonly recognized as gambling paraphernalia shall be seized as evidence - even though circumstances do not make possible physical arrests.

C. Licensed cardrooms are not authorized by the license granted to conduct, participate in or condone any form of gambling on the licensed premises. No device such as markers, chips, trade checks or any other device or scheme makes gambling by the licensee or players legal. Failure on the part of the licensee to suppress gambling on the licensed premises will result in recommendations designed to revoke the license (in addition to other appropriate charges.)

D. Bookmaking on any event is illegal. Commonly, books are made on horse racing or other sporting events. Bookmaking is difficult for uniformed officers to combat. However, uniformed officers are responsible in the area of their assignment to seek out and report every possibility of bookmaking activity.

                                                                C. A. ROUSE
                                                                Assistant Chief of Police

CAR/rh

Copies:
Inspector W. W. Crow
Captain L. K. Greiner
Captain E. T. Corning

cc: Chief F. C. Ramon

Form 1.11
CSS 21.10

INTRA-DEPARTMENT COMMUNICATION
SEATTLE POLICE DEPARTMENT

FROM   Chief F. C. Ramon   DATE December 26, 1962

TO   Deputy Chief M. E. Cook, Staff Division

SUBJECT   Cardroom Operations

On January 1st and thereafter, card games in cardrooms will be for amusement only. Taking rummy as an example, the allowable procedure will be that the two losers each pay 25¢ to the house. The house can give the one winner trade check or checks in amount of less than 50¢. These checks cannot be redeemed by the house for cash. Games will not be permitted where there is direct betting on every hand or where betting amongst the players is an integral part of the game. A reasonable interpretation of the rummy procedure can be extended to other games, such as pinochle, bridge, whist or a similar game where betting on each hand is not a part. No games will be allowed where there is continuous betting between the participants.

The management may not participate in the game in any fashion except as indicated above. No money is to be on the tables. The management will be obligated to discourage gambling of any type amongst the players. It will be pointed out to management that part of their responsibility is to comply with the state law which prohibits gambling.

F. C. RAMON
Chief of Police

FCR/rh

Form 1.11
css 21.19

INTRA-DEPARTMENT COMMUNICATION
SEATTLE POLICE DEPARTMENT

FROM   M. E. Cook, Deputy Chief, Staff Division   DATE 11/15/62

TO

SUBJECT Gambling Enforcement Procedure and Policy

Today I had lunch with Chief Frank Ramon, Assistant Chief C. A. Rouse and Attorney Paul Moates, at which various aspects of the gambling policy, to be instituted on January 1, 1963, were discussed.

There was general agreement on the following items:

(1) The department would be very careful to make arrests only for violations of the State Gambling Laws which were so flagrant, or, in which the arrest was so reasonable that there could be no loss of public support and the case would be as certain of conviction as we can make it.

(2) We will not confiscate gambling devices or items used in conducting gambling games unless they are clearly those devices which are inherently gambling devices and recognized as such in previous cases, such as: punchboards, pull tabs, or pinball machines on which a payoff in cash has been witnessed. We will not confiscate the merchandise from punchboards nor additional equipment, such as, where there are 10 pinball machines and a payoff was made on only one, we will confiscate just the one which is involved in the current case.

(3) We will not concern ourselves in the beginning with gambling in bowling alleys or golf courses or in private clubs or in churches or in any other place other than those open to the public.

(4) Arrests will not be made on the holiday, January 1, 1963, be= cause of the difficulty encountered in posting the bail. We will confiscate the evidence and inform the suspect that he will probably be arrested at a future time by warrant. This will give the prosecutor's office an opportunity to review the case prior to the final decision of whether or not an arrest is to be made.

(5) We will file none of these cases in McGoverns Court or, at least, none of the cases in which the offense involves City Licensed operations.

Form 1.11
css 21.19

INTRA-DEPARTMENT COMMUNICATION
SEATTLE POLICE DEPARTMENT

FROM   Sgt. J. Brozovich, Vice Investigation Unit   DATE __2/5/63__

TO   M.E. Cook, Deputy Chief, Staff Division

SUBJECT   Investigation on Information Furnished by HARRY RICHARD SHUTTS

On February 1st, 1963, Sgt. J. Brozovich and Officer George
Cuthill checked Ben Paris, The Pike Recreation, The Silver
Spot (Ballard), the B & G Cafe (Lake City). All were closed.
The barber shop next door to The Silver Spot was checked with
negative results; 611 Union Street has been checked four times
since January 14, 1963, on two occasions there was a bridge game
in progress, Joe Gasparavich states there are no bets on the
bridge game (this is doubtful). On the other two visits there
were no games.

Checked Sam's, Union St. Smoke Shop on January 31st, 1963,
doors were locked, dust and debris both inside and out, appears
to have been closed for several weeks. The complaint on The
Fiddlers Inn, 35th N.E. & E. 85th, also the tavern across the
street from the main gate of Sand Point for selling beer on
Sunday turned over to Wash. Liquor Control Board.

A close surveillance will be kpt on The Athens Cafe for any
games or gambling.

It is this investigators belief that all the information furnished by Mr. Shutts occurred prior to January 1st, 1963.

Respectfully submitted

Sgt. J. Brozovich
Vice Investigation Unit

JB:ed
(4)

orm 1.11
css 21.19

INTRA-DEPARTMENT COMMUNICATION
SEATTLE POLICE DEPARTMENT

FROM   Sgt. J. Brozovich, Vice Investigation Unit   DATE___2/23/63_____

TO   M.E. Cook, Deputy Chief, Staff Division

SUBJECT 611 Union Card Room

611 Union Card Room, owned and operated by Joseph Gasparovich (Gaspipe). This card room has received more individual attention than any card room in the city. It is the only Public Card Room that did not close. I have personally visited this card room at least 8 times since January 14, 1963. On my first visit a Bridge Game was in progresss. I talked to Mr. Gasparovich about the game, he stated that each player pays the house 50¢ an hour, that no money exchanges hands after each game, that he is remaining open until the Legislature meets and passes a bill legalizing some form of gambling. I observed two men plaing "Pan" and asked Mr. Gasparavich to cease this game immediately.

On the other visits, on three occasions, no game was in progress, on four visits both bridge and "Gin" were being played. I again informed Mr. Gasparovich that it was inconceivable to me that anyone would play"Gin" for the mere pleasure of playing or that he could afford to furnish cards, chips, lights and other equipment for $2.00 an hour.

On February 15, 1963, after receiving the complaint from Chief Ramon, I immediately went to 611 Union St. Mr. Gasparovich was standing outside, I informed him again,as I had previously, that the Bridge players were not playing Bridge for just pleasure and that I would make every effort to effect an arrest and would secure a warrant for his arrest whether he was on the premises or not as he was soley responsible for the actions of his employees. He waved his arms and shouted for a period of five minutes and then asked me if I wanted him to close his doors and padlock them. I informed him that that was a decision he would have to make but that it sounded like a good idea. Later in the evening, Officers Rothuas and Cuthill paid the premises a visit, also Sgt. Ramon and Officer Bailey, of the Patrol Division, had a conversation with Gasparovich,a short while later the cardroom closed and has remained closed. However we will keep a close check on it.

Respectfully submitted.

Sgt. J. Brozovich
Vice Investigation Unit

cc: Chief F.C. Ramon

Form 1.11
C&B 21.19

INTRA-DEPARTMENT COMMUNICATION
SEATTLE POLICE DEPARTMENT

FROM   Sgt. J. Brozovich, Vice Investigation Unit   DATE Feb. 27, 1963

TO   M.E. Cook, Deputy Chief, Staff Division

SUBJECT   Alaska Boosters Association

I received information that Alaska Boosters Association had moved to 517½ - 3rd Avenue (Old China Lane) with the intention of playing Bingo. I investigated the above premises and talked to Mr. Harold G. Bittner, the President of the Association. Mr. Bittner informed me that the Association moved to 517½ - 3rd Avenue from 1120 - 4th Ave. He has a charter issued on October 21, 1961 - File #156190. Secretary of the Association is A.W. Paisley, 1304 N.E. 62nd. Treasurer is Jewel Paisley (Bittners sister).

Purpose of the Association, to boost Alaska. Any person 21 years of age or older, who is a resident of Washington or Alaska, and has manifested an interest in the progress and development of the State of Alaska may join.

Mr. Bittner states the association is in debt $26,000.00, trade dollar loss, transit and billboard advertising. He states further that he has a membership of about 375 of which 200 are residents of Alaska and 175 local members. Dues are $12.00 per year, payable quarterly.

Mt. Bittner then inquired about operating a Bingo game once a week. My answer was "NO". He then asked if I would object if he talked to Chief Ramon. I informed him that I had no objection.

Respectfully submitted

Sgt. J. Brozovich
Vice Investigation Unit

APPENDIX D

Public Cardroom
and Panorama License Holders, 1968

PUBLIC CARDROOM LICENSES

Ben Paris Sporting Goods &
Recreation Co.
1609 Westlake Ave.,1
7-4-43   8 tables

M.C. Honeysuckle
2032 E. Madison St., 22
7-4-43   4 tables

F.H. Strickler
Cosmo Recreation
2020 E. Madison, 22
_____   4 tables

Gilroy-Nebzger, Inc.
211 Union St., 1
_____   8 tables

A. V. Santos
Filipino Social & Improve-
ment Club
515½ Maynard Ave. S., 4
_____   4 tables

Spiro Ulasic
Occidental Tavern
116 S. Washington, 4
2-1-44   4 tables

Dan Sarusal
200 5th Ave S., 4
3-16-54   4 tables

John L. Pape
Labor Temple Card Room
2800 1st Ave., 1
11-16-52   4 tables

Wah Lee Club, Inc.
669 S. King St., 4
_____   4 tables

Alvin Lewis
Trigar Al Lewis Place
673 Jackson St., 4
_____   4 tables

Fred Henderson
Robbers Roost
1309 E. Yesler, 22
_____   3 tables

Edward B. Washington
Madrona Tavern
2700 E. Union St., 22
1-9-56   ($1,000)

220

Santoro & Santoro
Viji's
1311 3rd Ave., 1
8-5-63   4 tables

Rossi & Perry
Virginia Inn
1937 1st Ave., 1
6-23-53   4 tables

Robert Wong
418 Maynard Alley S., 4
5-1-68   4 tables

Demetrios, Begleris
Tumwater Tavern, 1
3-21-55   4 tables

Transco Investments, Inc.
The Ram Restaurant
120½ Pike, 1
5-27-57   8 tables

Bitts, Inc.
411 2nd Ave., 4
8-15-57   6 tables

Martin Ervin
Hilltop Recreation Center
1200 Jackson, 44
6-12-67   4 tables

George V. Papapangiatou
Athenian Social Club
319 Yesler Way, 4
3-20-59   4 tables

J & M, Inc.
J & M Tavern & Cafe
201 1st Ave. S., 4
7-1-59   9 tables

Estate of Arthur O. Sanders
Nite Cap Tavern
8500 14th Ave. S., 8
1-1-61   4 tables

Endia Dahl
Airport Way Inn
3903 Airport Way, 8
1-1-61   4 tables

Elmer L. Nelson
Seaport Tavern
200 1st Ave. S., 4
4-16-62   4 tables

Frontier Restaurant, Inc.
Frontier Restaurant & Lounge
1-1-62   4 tables

Magres Lee
Blue Bird Inn
701 23rd Ave., 22
7-13-65   4 tables ($1,000)

Byes & Walseth
Pike Recreation
1429 4th Ave., 1
7-1-62   8 tables

Phillips & Phillips
Angelo Tavern
501 S. Jackson St., 4
1-30-63   4 tables

Sports Center, Inc.
Turf Grill
1407 3rd Ave., 1
3-1-63   8 tables

Victory Recreational Club,
Inc.
514 S. King St., 4
9-1-63   4 tables

Willard J. Casey
Archer Inn
1200 1st Ave., 1
1-1-64   1 table

Alex & Alex
Fireplace Tavern
1408 3rd Ave., 22
1-22-64   2 tables

Jean Kimbrough
The Silver Spot
5233 Ballard NW, 7
2-4-64   6 tables

John A. Lazaga
CRS Recreation
506 S. King St., 4
10-13-65   4 tables

Joseph John Gasparovich
Union Card Room
611 Union St., 1
5-1-65   4 tables

Florence Bellotti
Casino Card Room & Cafe
172 S. Washington St., 4
5-1-65   4 tables

Gerald J. Shelden
Go In Tavern
1107 1st Ave., 1
9-25-67   4 tables

James E. Kamitchis
Travelers Tavern
800 Howell St., 1
12-13-65   4 tables

Boulder Enterprise, Inc.
1423 1st Ave., 1
1-1-66   4 tables

Logal F. Bailes
Casbah Tavern
2038 E. Madison, 22
1-28-66   4 tables

Superior Enterprises, Inc.
Ballard Smoke Shop
5443 Ballard Ave. NW, 7
1-1-66   4 tables

Ralph E. Miller
Denty's Tavern
1319 3rd Ave., 1
5-1-66   4 tables

Harry L. Naon
Rainbow Club Cafe
614 Pike St., 1
7-1-66   4 tables

Duchesneau & Duchesneau
Alex Tavern
4915 Rainier Ave. S., 18
9-1-66   4 tables

Central Cafe & Tavern, Inc.
207 1st Ave., W., 4
11-10-66   4 tables

Conguista & Conguista
New Italian Cafe
1515 Rainier Ave. S., 44
1-2-67   4 tables

Donna Matos
605 Club
1531 1st Ave., 1
5-1-67   4 tables

Bellecy & Bellecy
Ramble Inn
5901 Airport Way S., 8
7-18-67   4 tables

Harold A. Brown
Smokey Joe's Tavern
706 Pike St., 22
8-23-67   4 tables

Jimmie Sumber, Jr.
South Side Recreation
2314 S. Jackson St., 44
1-1-68   4 tables

George W. Evans
Malmen's Fine Foods
5231 Ballard NW, 7
3-17-68   4 tables

PENDING

Daron, Inc.
611 Union St., 1
1-2-68   5-13-68 Applying for
refund, withdrawing application from city council

Robert Scott
Central Recreation
2301 S. Jackson St., 44
5-1-68   4 tables
Change of owner

Hull & Hull
Greenlake Recreation Center
411 NE 72nd St., 15
5-1-68   4 tables
Change of location

Panorama Operators Licenses

Western Amusement, Inc.
Lou's Grill
1406 1st Ave., 1
12-8-67 $200, 12-8-67 $500

Ernest M. Graig
Sportland Amusement
P.O. Box 1141
Tacoma, Wn. 98041
____ $835
35 devices at
High's News Lunch
32 at Pennyland

Bittner & Co., Inc.
Sportland Arcade
1123 1st Ave., 1
12-15-67 $290   12-15-67 $500
58 devices

Panorama Service, Inc.
1414 1st Ave., 1
2-1-65 $670
34 devices

Mary Sherman
The Champ Arcade
1413 1st Ave.
Mail to P.O. Box 1184, 11
12-7-67 $500
1-11-68 $315
63 devices

Panorama Location Licenses

Western Amusement, Inc.
Lou's Grill
1406 1st Ave., 1
____ 40 devices

Amusement Center Arcade,
Inc.
1414 1st Ave., 1
1-1-58   34 devices

Bittner & Co., Inc.
High's News Lunch
1411 1st Ave., 1
2-1-61   35 devices

Bittner & Co., Inc.
Sportland Arcade
1123 1st Ave., 1
____ 58 devices

Pennyland Arcade Incorporated
1003 1st Ave., 4
1-1-65   32 devices

Mary Sherman
The Champ Arcade
1413 1st Ave.
mail to P.O. Box 1884, 11
12-1-65   63 devices

APPENDIX E

Letter from Ernest A. Jonson, Public Accountant, to Albert D. Rosellini

November 2, 1972

Albert D. Rosellini
1429 Washington Building
Seattle, Washington 98104

Dear Mr. Rosellini:

Attached hereto is a copy of financial statement at November 30, 1971 which has been prepared from the books without audit by us. I am also enclosing herewith a summary of your income tax returns for the years ending November 30, 1965 through November 30, 1971. Your attention is called to the year ended November 30, 1966 which shows a sale of property for a total of $250,000, with a gain of $240,672.78. This property, amounting to approximately five acres, was acquired by you prior to November 30, 1953 and was sold to the Great Northern Railroads since it was a necessary acquisition by them for the completion of their Industrial Park in Renton.

We have examined your cash received records for the period from 1965 to the present and there

have been no fees received by you from Colacurcio, Berger or the Lifeline Club.

Very truly yours,

ERNEST A. JONSON AND CO.

Signed

Ernest A. Jonson,
Certified Public Accountant

ALBERT D. AND ETHEL ROSELLINI
INCOME SUMMARY FROM FEDERAL INCOME
TAX RETURNS

NET INCOME FOR THE YEARS:

1965	$ 66,382
1966	317,239
1967	109,565
1968	52,571
1969	42,400
1970	63,197
1971	58,372

Total $709,726

Total Taxes Paid $218,363

Note—Net income before exemptions. Capital
gains are shown as total gain.

APPENDIX F

Attorney General John O'Connell's White Paper to the People of Washington

AUTHOR'S NOTE

On August 21, 1968, the Seattle *Post-Intelligencer* ran a photograph showing Ben Cichy, president of the Amusement Association of Washington (referred to in the White Paper as the Far West Novelty Company) and a major owner of pinball machines in the state of Washington, going to the home of Charles O. Carroll, then King County prosecutor. The attorney general of the state of Washington at that time was John O'Connell.

According to a White Paper to the People of Washington issued by O'Connell, this news item stirred him to begin a preliminary investigation into the possibility that state laws were not being "properly enforced" by local law-enforcement officers. However, the attorney general has no authority to investigate such allegations. To do that he must be instructed by the governor to carry out an investigation. O'Connell, a Democrat, was a candidate for the governorship and was at the time running against the incumbent governor, Dan Evans. Thus, if Governor Evans requested the investigation, he would doubtless be providing a platform from which his opponent for governor could marshall considerable political support. On the other hand, the governor's refusal to authorize such an investigation could easily be turned into a campaign issue suggesting that he was protecting some questionable practices.

It was in the context of this controversy and the allegations going back and forth between the governor and the state attorney general that O'Connell issued the White Paper. The excerpt that

227

follows deals with the fact that in the course of the governor's race it was revealed that O'Connell had cashed a large check at a hotel in Las Vegas where he was gambling. This information, when made public, was probably a turning point in the governor's race, which, in the end, was won by Dan Evans. I have excerpted here the attorney general's discussion of the revelation that he had cashed the check, for I believe it shows the incredible intertwining of political and economic interests that are enmeshed in the network of people and activities surrounding illegal businesses.

October 7, 1968. Three members of my investigative staff and I met with the Executive Committee of the King County Superior Court Judges. At this meeting we laid out the procedures and methods which our investigative staff was using, preliminary information which we had gathered, and the general directions which our investigation was pursuing. We named some names of the persons whom we were investigating.

Although no publicity was given to the fact that I would meet or had met with the Superior Court Judges Executive Committee on October 7, 1968, the fact that the meeting was held was known generally to members of the Press, including the Seattle *Times*. I did not disclose any of the details of that meeting and I have full confidence that the Judges with whom I met were equally discreet. However, it was a relatively simple matter for the Press to learn that the meeting has been held. Prior to the meeting, I had stated that I would disclose details to the Judges, so it was logical for the Press to conclude that I had done so.

I take the pains to point this out because of what happened at 8:45 A.M. the following morning, Tuesday, October 8. At that time I received a telephone call from John Wilson and Marshall Wilson, reporters for the Seattle *Times*, stating that they wished to see me. My secretary informed them that I was tied up and would speak to them later. Fifteen minutes later, the Messrs. Wilson arrived at my office in Seattle and demanded to see me. I told them I was not available at that time and set an appointment for 8:30 A.M. on Thursday, October 10, 1968.

October 10, 1968. Messrs. John and Marshall Wilson from the Seattle *Times* arrived at my office at 8:30 A.M., and immediately began interrogating me about alleged checks which they stated I had cashed in Las Vegas, Nevada, in 1965 and 1967. After several requests by me for documentation, they showed me a $10,000 counter check used to secure a line of credit, which I had signed in December, 1965. I decided not to discuss the matter with the *Times*, but rather to spell it out fully to the people on television, which I did on Sunday, October 13, 1968. The *Times'* reporters released their story immediately upon leaving my office on October 10. It was broadcast by the noon news on that date, and appeared in all editions of the Seattle *Times*. From that time on, the opposition has attempted to make the fact that I play cards for money, sometimes for large sums of money, and that I have played cards for money in Nevada where it is perfectly legal, the major issue of this campaign. I explained the facts fully, including my personal finances and my campaign expenditures in detail on television on October 13, 1968. On October 16, in the second debate between my opponent and me, the first 20 minutes of questioning by representatives of three separate news media was devoted to this subject, and I answered every question that was asked. A story published in the Seattle *Post-Intelligencer* on October 24, 1968, disclosed that statements given by the Credit Manager of the Nevada hotel to *Times* reporters by Telephone had not been accurate or correct, and were given at a time when he was under the influence of drugs and medication. The investigation made by the *Post-Intelligencer* reporter was made by direct personal interviews in Nevada, as contrasted with the investigation made by the Seattle *Times* which was done largely by telephone.

A recent statewide poll conducted on October 22, 1968, indicates that the disclosure of my gambling activities, although perfectly legal, has caused some damage to my campaign for Governor. My opponent, Governor Evans, has not gained any votes because of this. The poll discloses, however, that voters previously committed to me have now become undecided. I am pleased and gratified that this matter has not yet caused any significant number of voters in this state to prefer my opponent, who has played a key role in this matter, but I am concerned that the question has caused doubts in some voters. I am convinced that this was precisely the aim of those person[s] who decided to make public the information concerning my card playing. I am further convinced that this information would never have been used in this campaign had it not been for my determination to investigate and pursue the allegations of corruption and payoffs in King County. To support this conclusion, it is important to look at the sources of the card playing information. There are three probable sources:

(1) the Governor's campaign staff and brain trust;

(2) the Nevada Hotel; and

(3) the bank which handled the checks involved. Not [sic], let's look at each one separately:

(1) *The Governor's campaign staff and brain trust.* As early as 1966, I was told by numerous people that the Republican State Chairman, C. Montgomery Johnson, told them that he had a document in his possession which was a "check" signed by me in five figures, payable to a Nevada hotel. Some of them stated that Mr. Johnson had exhibited the document to them. This document, of course, was the $10,000 line of credit, dated December 4, 1965, which was ultimately published in the Seattle *Times* on October 10, 1968. Mr. C. Montgomery Johnson, as Republican State Chairman, is extremely close to Governor Evans, and works closely with the Governor in his gubernatorial campaign, and on all political matters. In fact, the public opinion polls run by Central Surveys of Iowa, relied on by Governor Evans in his campaign for reelection, are purchased and paid for, not by the Evans campaign, but by the Republican

State Committee under the direction of C. Montgomery Johnson.

(2) On Sunday evening, September 29, 1968, a meeting of the Governor's Brain Trust was held in Seattle, Washington. I do not know the names of all persons present at that meeting, but I do know that James Dolliver, the Governor's Administrative Assistant, and C. Montgomery Johnson, the Republican State Chairman, were present. Mr. Johnson discussed the $10,000 check (line of credit document) at that meeting and it was determined then to turn the document over to a newspaper, which would follow up on the story and make it an issue in the political campaign. It is my understanding that the decision to do this was not an [sic] unanimous one, but that it carried by a majority vote. I am convinced that the Governor knew of this meeting, of its recommendation, and concurred in it. If he did not know of this meeting, and if he did not concur in its recommendation, clearly he has not been responsible for his own campaign. A man who is not responsible for his own campaign cannot be responsible for the government of this state.

On the very next day, September 30, 1968, the Director of General Administration, Mr. William Schneider, a cabinet officer of the Governor, came over to state archives and made a copy of my expense account voucher for December, 1965, covering the period when I had been in Nevada.

I am informed that the Governor's brain trust and campaign staff thereafter offered the story to three newspapers in Western Washington. These newspapers concluded that they were not interested. I hope that their conclusion was based on the belief that this material was totally irrelevant to the political campaign. The material was then offered to the Seattle *Times* which took the material and agreed to run the story.

On October 4, 1968, Mr. William Schneider returned to archives, made copies of additional documents. These copies were turned over to the *Times*. Nothing was done, however, by the *Times* until the morning of October 8,

1968. *Remember* that on October 7, I had indicated my intention to continue with the investigation of King County corruption, and made clear my willingness to cooperate with the King County Superior Court Judges in anticipation that a Grand Jury would be called.

(3) Now the question arises: "How did Mr. C. Montgomery Johnson and members of the Governor's brain trust obtain the line of credit document, and how did they or the Seattle *Times* obtain the additional information, some of it accurate, some of it inaccurate, which has recently been published?" There can only be two sources: (1) the banks involved; or (2) the Nevada Hotel. In either case, there is grave reason to be concerned. I hope we have not come to the day where banks in the State of Washington are willing to turn over records of personal accounts and personal transactions of one of their depositors for others to persue [sic]. I sincerely hope that is not the case—not for my own sake, but for the sake of everybody in our State who has a bank account.

The other source is even more disturbing. Credit managers of hotels in Nevada ordinarily do not turn over their records to political party chairmen or to metropolitan newspapers. It is a known fact that many prominent, well-known businessmen, elected officials, and men and women of substance in this country play cards on lines of credit for large amounts of money in Nevada. A reputable and respected hotel would simply not risk losing the confidence of its guests without a very good reason. Frankly, I do not know what that reason is, but I am very concerned.

(4) Why would the Seattle *Times* accept this material and believe it relevant, when three other newspapers (which have no particular connection or loyalty to me) turned it down, and why would they wait until October 8, *after I had made my report to the judges* to take action? We cannot know the answer for sure, but we do know the following:

The Seattle *Times* has historically and consistently been a major supporter of the King County Prosecutor. To my knowledge, it has never printed a word of criticism or any unfavorable comment on a man who has been in office for over 20 years. When the disclosures of Mr. Carroll's association with an official of Far West Novelty Company were made on August 21, 1968, the *Times* promptly and predictably came to his defense. If it obtained any explanation from him, it did not make that explanation public.

I have concluded that but for this investigation, the Seattle *Times* would not have attempted to make so much of my card playing. As recently as October 25, 1968, Mr. Ross Cunningham of the Seattle *Times* stated that he would vote for Governor Evans, but he added some very favorable comments about my conduct of the office of Attorney General, and some of my proposals in my campaign for Governor.

Why, then, would the Governor and his brain trust, the Seattle *Times*, the banks involved, and the Nevada Hotel, take this highly unusual action to defeat me?

1. In respect to Governor Evans, I think the answer is simple. He wants very much to remain Governor for another 4 years. A number of his close advisors are determined to do anything to see that he remains Governor, and they were the ones to whom he listened in deciding to take this course.

It is a much publicized fact that Governor Evans and Prosecutor Carroll were from different factions of the Republican Party, and that they have been feuding politically since 1966. That fact makes it all the more curious that Governor Evans came so quickly to the defense of Prosecutor Carroll when I began investigating the situation, and that he appears to have put no pressure on the Prosecutor to make a public statement.

2. In respect to Prosecutor Carroll, I think his actions over the past 3 months have made it clear that he wishes to remain Prosecutor and that he does not want my investigation to continue. Despite the Governor's statement in August, that he expected and wanted the Prosecutor to answer the questions and to hold a news conference, more than two months have passed without one word of explanation from Prosecu-

tor Carroll. Clearly, he does not want his role in the King County tolerance policy subjected to the investigation which will be completed if I am elected Governor.

3. The Seattle *Times'* defense of the King County Prosecutor is well known. The *Times* in an editorial recently urged, by name, everyone but the Prosecutor "to put an end to the tolerance policy of gambling in King County." It carefully avoided mentioning that in Spokane and Pierce Counties, it is the Prosecutor and no one else who has acted to end similar tolerance policies.

4. In respect to the other two participants—the banks and the Nevada Hotel—I do not know the reason for their interest or involvement, but the very fact that they have been involved should be cause for serious concern.

I think the timing, the participants, and the manner in which the information was disclosed make it clear that turning my card playing in Nevada into a campaign issue was prompted by one thing and one thing only—our investigation of corruption and payoffs in King County.

The vital question now before the public is: "What will happen to the investigation if I am elected, and what will happen to it if I am defeated by these tactics?"

If I am elected Governor, the investigation I have begun will continue. I will direct the new Attorney General, whoever he is, to continue the investigation, and I will use all the powers of the office of the Governor to insure that the investigation continues and is brought to a successful conclusion. It will be a thorough, painstaking and professional job. It will lay the basis for a Grand Jury which can return meaningful indictments if the evidence justifies such indictments, or if it does not it will clear the air. I expect this investigation to be as successful as the investigations I conducted in 1959 of official corruption in Snohomish County, and the investigative work I did prior to the conviction of the former King County Assessor in 1966.

If I am not elected, there are two possibilities.

The first possibility is that the investigation will be stopped when my term as Attorney General expires in January. I, of course, intend to continue the investigation as long as I hold public office, but as I have said, an investigation of this nature cannot be completed by January. Regrettably, I conclude that this is the most likely result.

No other public official on the city, county or state level has shown any willingness to exert the leadership necessary to see the investigation through. I see no candidate who, if elected, will carry through without strong support from the Governor's office. The incumbent Governor simply does not support this investigation.

There is another possibility, namely the calling of a Grand Jury by the King County Superior Court Judges. Without an independent prosecutor I believe this course would be futile. The public would have no confidence in an investigation in which those who are questioned investigate themselves. Under existing state law, there is grave doubt as to whether the judges could appoint a special prosecutor without the consent of the Prosecuting Attorney; however, if this hurdle is surmounted, the special prosecutor would need a staff of skilled investigators. I estimate that to retain a special prosecutor and an adequate staff of investigators would require the county commissioners to appropriate approximately $200,000. One thing is crystal clear. All national experts agree with my belief that a serious problem exists and that it must be cleaned up now.

Mr. Milton Rector, Director of the National Council on Crime and Delinquency, was in Seattle on September 24, 1968. At that time he stated flatly that a "tolerance policy" toward gambling means the payoff of public officials. He stated further: "If you know of any betting operation that's been around for more than a month, then you know the law enforcement officers know about it." Rector continued: "If the operation has been around for three months, then you can be assured of payoffs in the courthouse or the city hall." Referring to the tolerance policy, Rector said: "It's an open invitation for the syndicates to move in."

Mr. Ralph Salerno, a nationally known expert in the field of organized crime, retained by me to advise our investigative staff, put it even more directly. Noting that Seattle was ripe for organized crime now that it is big league in Sports, business, and population, Salerno said: "If the Seattle King County situation is not cleaned up right now by the Attorney General's investigation, it will be twenty years before anyone will be willing to tackle it again."

The question is what will happen now? I have attempted to set out the facts fully and objectively in this "white paper." I invite all persons mentioned here to do the same. The final decision is in the people's hands.

APPENDIX G

The Investigative Task Force Report of the
Seattle Police Department, September 14, 1970

*A probe into the illegal payoff
system and actions of bribery
within the Seattle Police Department*

September 14, 1970

The Honorable Wes Uhlman
Mayor
City of Seattle

Dear Mayor Uhlman:

This is a report of the Investigative Task Force which was
established to investigate charges of illegal payoffs and bribery in
the Seattle Police Department. The report is directed, and in a
sense is limited both in scope and in time, toward resolving those
specific allegations. The information accumulated by the Investigative Task Force indicated that payoffs and the acceptance of
bribes and gratuities among certain members of the Seattle Police
Department was a practice that had existed for many years.

The primary objective of the Task Force was to identify and
eliminate from the Seattle Police Department those officers that
were instrumental in maintaining and controlling the payoff sys-

237

tem in the department. The Task Force feels that it has been successful in this endeavor. Criminal charges have been filed against several of the officers involved.

It was necessary to purge those men who had violated the law and brought discredit to the department. The many honest and dedicated members of the Seattle Police Department must feel secure in the knowledge that they truly deserve the trust and confidence of the community, and that they in good faith can move forward in developing a fine and progressive police organization.

Sincerely

Signed

Edward M. Toothman
Acting Chief of Police

THE INVESTIGATIVE TASK FORCE REPORT
OF THE
SEATTLE POLICE DEPARTMENT

Systems of illegal payoffs and bribery in various forms have existed in the Seattle Police Department for many years. The purpose of this report is to relate briefly the scope of the payoffs, and to outline how the payoff system worked. With these objectives in mind, this report will also relate the events that prompted the creation of the Investigative Task Force, and the results of the investigation of the payoff system as it existed in more recent years. The investigation revealed that only a comparatively small number of police officers were engaged in the illegal payoff system at any given time. The great majority of the members of the department, past and present, were and are honest, performing their duties as they properly should. It is also noted that many of the participants in the payoff system as it existed until 1968, have left the employment of the Seattle Police Department, either because of normal attrition or as a result of this investigation.

The facts disclosed by the Task Force investigation show that the success of the payoff system hinged upon the implementation of the so-called tolerance policy established by the City Council.

While the Washington State Constitution prohibits gambling, the City of Seattle enacted provisions providing for the licensing of cardrooms. The Public Cardroom Ordinance, which was enacted in 1954 and rescinded in 1969, provided only for the licensing of cardrooms. The ordinance in no way implied that gambling was to be permitted or tolerated. The term "tolerance policy" was presumably created to identify a position adopted by the Council as to the leniency in requiring adherence to the State gambling law. Nothing in writing exists stating the policy. Through the years that the cardroom ordinance was in force, the policy of the City Council as to the leniency of enforcing gambling fluctuated with the times and personalities of those in office.

The cardroom ordinance sections themselves are innocuous as they ostensibly permit persons to play cards only, however, the ordinance opened the door for the setting up of facilities and equipment, i.e.—cardroom and card tables which were utilized for gambling purposes. All that remained was to establish a clientele. From this point it was relatively easy for cardroom operators to develop gambling operations. In order to implement a payoff system to permit gambling, it required only collusion between the cardroom operators and the police. It is from this basis that grafting, with all of the accompanying evils, prospered in the City of Seattle.

The payoff system that has been identified operated

primarily within the Patrol Division and the Vice Squad of the Police Department. Payoff activity within the Patrol Division was confined generally to two geographic areas of the city, i.e.—the lower downtown business district, and portions of the east central district. Gamblers and tavern operators, some of whom catered to homosexual clientele, were the primary participants in this payoff system to the police. Thus, for a price, gamblers and selected tavern owners could operate illegally without fear of police harassment or arrest.

The Vice Squad exerted control over gambling such as licensed cardrooms, stag activities and the private and often covert gambling games that moved about certain sections of the city. The Vice Squad set the ground rules and established the price for the illegal operation, and collected the payoffs usually on a monthly basis. As a rule it was the responsibility of one designated vice officer to make all the contacts with the people making payoffs. A portion of the money collected from the gamblers was divided among those vice officers involved in the payoff system. The remainder of the money was passed upward to selected command personnel. The number of people involved in the Vice Squad operation was few, so each individual share was considerable. In this manner the Vice Squad extracted protection payments from downtown cardrooms engaging in illegal gambling activities under the tolerance policy, and from a number of prominent gamblers most of whom were located in the downtown area.

The structure of the payoff system within the Patrol Division was similar to that of the Vice Squad but involved more people. For the most part, the uniformed officers who participated were assigned to work on a foot patrol beat in the 1st Avenue, Pike Street, and Chinatown areas, or were assigned to a patrol car in a selected patrol district located in the east central area of the city. An officer so assigned collected money from the taverns and clubs, and the gamblers located in his respective district. The patrolman kept a share of his collection, often dividing his take with his partner, and passed on the other half to his sergeant. The sergeant extracted his share and passed the balance to a superior officer. In many instances, the Patrol Division as well as Vice officers collected from the same establishments, each for the particular favor or service that they could offer the operator or gambler.

Testimony in the perjury trial of Assistant Chief M. E. Cook revealed that some officers realized as much as $600.00 per month, and that a Captain received as much as $700.00 to $900.00 per month. It was estimated that during one period of time, the Vice Squad was collecting about $6,000.00 monthly.

Officers were generally recruited into the system by older officers, after they had been carefully screened to determine their reliability and willingness to participate in the payoff system. The criteria for admittance was a display of tolerance and approval toward other officers' transgressions and a propensity for engaging in similar conduct. The best assignment for any beat officer participating in this illegal activity was the downtown business district. This was traditionally the most lucrative spot in the Patrol Division.

Although gambling was a major source of grafting by the police, a substantial amount of money was received by the police from the operators of taverns and other public establishments that catered to homosexuals. The technique used by the police was to harass the homosexual establishment to the point where the clientele ceased to patronize it. The operator then paid the police officers to remain away from the establishment in order to continue his business. The amount of the bribe would vary with the ability of the operator to pay.

In 1967, a tavern operator complained to the FBI, to the press and to the Chief of Police. As a result of his complaint, a Seattle newspaper published an expose of the payoff system which ultimately resulted in an inquiry by a blue ribbon committee appointed by the Mayor.

The blue ribbon committee made a number of recommendations to the Mayor and to the Chief of Police which were intended to correct some of the police practices which had come to their attention. One of their recommendations was that the International Association of Chiefs of Police (IACP) conduct a survey of the Seattle Police Department. The IACP conducted a six-months survey and issued a report that was critical of some of the administrative practices in the department. In December 1968, the Police Department was reorganized based on recommendations made by the IACP. Internal strife which occurred shortly thereafter forced the retirement of Chief F. C. Ramon in October 1969.

Major Frank Moore was appointed Interim Chief and served until the end of June 1970, pending the selection of a permanent Chief of Police. During this period of time, a Federal Grand Jury was called which resulted in the indictment of Assistant Chief M. E. Cook for perjury. Cook was accused of lying about his knowledge of the payoff system in the department, and was consequently charged and convicted of perjury.

Some of the witnesses at Cook's perjury trial testified that they had direct knowledge of a payoff system that had existed for over 30 years. It was indicated that the system apparently stopped in late 1968 after the departmental reorganization that had been recommended by the IACP.

During the trial, accusations were made involving personnel in the Police Department. Mayor Uhlman removed Frank Moore as Acting Chief and appointed Chief Charles Gain of Oakland, California to serve as Interim Chief pending the selection of a permanent chief. Chief Gain served from June 24, 1970 to August 8, 1970.

Interim Chief Charles Gain appointed a special Task Force on July 15, 1970 to investigate the alleged payoffs in the Seattle Police Department. Named as Commander of this Investigative Task Force was E. M. Toothman, retired Chief of Police of the Oakland Police Department. Chief

Toothman selected eight supervisory officers and two secretaries of the Seattle Police Department to assist in the investigation.

Chief Gain returned to his post in Oakland on August 8, 1970, and Toothman took his place as Acting Chief of the Seattle Police Department. Lawrence Waldt, Chief of the Hayward, California Police Department, was chosen to become the new Commander of the Investigative Task Force.

The Investigation

To date the Task Force has been in operation for eight weeks. At the outset, it was necessary to establish certain procedures in order to provide the necessary records and information. All information collected was reduced to writing which included transcriptions of tape recordings. To date 205 subjects have been interviewed by members of the Task Force. Persons interviewed consisted of active and retired police officers, and other individuals that could provide information pertaining to the investigation.

It was the intention of the Chief of Police to utilize the polygraph in conjunction with interviews of those persons who were under investigation. Two outside polygraph experts were employed to meet this need. To implement the planned series of polygraph tests, Chief of Police Charles Gain issued a General Order which stated that all officers, when requested, would submit to a polygraph test or face possible dismissal.

In response to this General Order, on July 28, 1970, the Seattle Police Officers Guild secured a temporary restraining order in Superior Court enjoining the Chief of Police from administering involuntary polygraph tests. This restraining order stated in part:

> . . . . . . the plaintiffs . . . . . . moves the Court for an order restraining the defendant, City of Seattle, its Chief of

Police, Charles Gain, from requiring the plaintiffs or any members of the Seattle Police Department to unwillingly submit to a polygraph test, or to answer questions to which the officer may properly invoke the protection of the Fifth Amendment to the United States Constitution, at the peril of facing dismissal or other penalty for failure to submit to said tests or answer said questions . . . . . .

The invoking of the restraining order imposed a serious roadblock to establishing the truth and hindered the efforts of the Investigative Task Force. It is interesting to note that under RCW 49.44.120 of the State of Washington, police officers are not exempt from being subjected to polygraph examination. The Corporation Counsel of the City of Seattle is appealing this restraining order.

The question is asked, "How extensive was the involvement in terms of numbers of officers?" It has been stated earlier that only a few districts were involved. At a given period, there were about 35 to 40 men working in these districts. Of that number, all were not involved. There is only speculation as to how many were. Of those who worked in the department during the last ten years, the Task Force identified about 70 to 80 as having been involved in payoffs. The majority of those persons had left the Police Department prior to the beginning of the investigation. As a result of the investigation, fourteen officers have either "vested" (left the department before having reached normal retirement age), retired, or were fired. Six officers have been charged criminally.

In developing the criminal cases, the only available evidence was the direct testimony of witnesses. There was no physical evidence. There was collusion between the operators from whom money was being extorted by the police in order that they could violate the law. As a consequence,

few operators were willing to talk. One of the greatest ob-
stacles to the successful investigation of these offenses was
the lapse of time. The grafting action ceased in 1968, more
than two years ago. No vestige of it remains. A number of
the operators are now out of business or have left the area.
Several have died. So in terms of time and the related
circumstances, it was difficult to gain information about
the activities of the payoff system.

Immediately prior to and during the course of the investigation, fourteen members of the department saw fit to
sever their service with the department. Those members
were:

Assistant Chief M. E. Cook	Retired
Assistant Chief George Fuller	Vested
Major Henry Schultheis	Retired
Major David Jessup	Vested
Captain Ralph Zottman	Retired
Lieutenant David Devine	Vested
Lieutenant Jay Brozovich	Retired
Lieutenant Milton Price	Vested
Sergeant David Buher	Vested
Sergeant Leo Ormsby	Retired
Sergeant Gerald Barmann	Vested
Detective Roy Hull	Vested
Police Officer Wesley Youngquist	Vested
Police Officer James Hinterberger	Disability (In Process)

The Task Force presented to the King County Prosecutor's Office evidence of bribery involving former members
and active members of the Seattle Police Department and
Washington State Liquor Control Board Retail Inspectors.
Information was presented in writing which, in some instances, included tape recorded statements made by wit-

nesses, victims and suspects. The following cases were presented to the Prosecutor's Office for review:

Detective Roy Hull	Seattle Police Department
Lieutenant David Devine	''
Officer Robert Gordon	''
Officer Wesley Youngquist	''
Sergeant Gerald Barmann	''
Lieutenant Jay Brozovich	''
Sergeant Donald R. Kuehl	''
Officer Harvey H. Noot	''
Sergeant Leo F. Ormsby	''
Officer Jack E. Rinker	''
Captain Ralph Zottman	''
Inspector Malcolm Nelson	Washington State Liquor Control Board
Inspector John C. Wilson	''

In several of the cases submitted, the evidence proved to be insufficient to justify the filing of criminal charges. With reference to these cases, it was also felt that the information was too inconclusive at this time to justify department disciplinary action. The investigation is still continuing and as further information is developed, appropriate action will be taken.

Of the cases submitted, the following criminal filings have been made to date:

Detective Roy Hull	Bribery
Lieutenant David Devine	Bribery
Officer Wesley Youngquist	Grafting
Sergeant Gerald Barmann	Grafting
Lieutenant Jay Brozovich	Grafting
Captain Ralph Zottman	Grafting

The attorneys who represented Lieutenant Brozovich, Police Officer Youngquist, Sergeant Barmann and Captain Zottman met with representatives of the Prosecutor's Office and agreed to waive the Statute of Limitations and plead their clients guilty to Grafting.

Grand Jury

At this time most of the investigative work that the police can accomplish has now been completed by the Task Force. Any additional investigation can be done by the Internal Investigations Division of the Police Department.

During earlier periods of this Task Force investigation, there were those who publicly expressed a desire to have the County Grand Jury immediately called to look into the police payoff scandal. It was suggested that the Grand Jury be delayed until the completion of the Task Force investigation. If the Grand Jury is now to be called on the matter, the information developed by the Task Force will be of value and should expedite the hearing.

Evaluation

With the removal from the department of those officers known to have been involved, and the filing of criminal charges against several, the department through its own efforts has purged itself of most of the guilty officers. There are, of course, some officers who have not been exposed, so they will probably go unpunished, except by the knowledge of their guilt. Darkness, however, does not protect a man from his own conscience.

Because a police officer takes an oath to perform his duty

and serve his community, the degree of his responsibility is greater than that which might be expected from the average citizen. Thus, the penalty for his failure is usually more severe. It must be remembered, however, that there were many persons other than police officers that were involved in the payoff system.

There were first, the Chiefs of Police who during their respective tenures failed to exercise adequate controls to prevent the criminal activities of the officers. Secondly, there were the gamblers and homosexuals who paid off to the police to protect their own interests. Under the law, they are as guilty as the officers. (They were not charged because it was necessary to use them as witnesses.) Thirdly, the Mayors and Councilmen in the past who conceived and perpetuated what was known as the "tolerance policy" carry a major part of the responsibility for the shaping of conditions that spawned crime and corruption in the Seattle Police Department.

Laws and policies, rules and regulations, as such, cannot guarantee an honest police department. Only the knowledge, integrity and continuing vigilance of the Chief, requiring the highest order of accountability from each member of the department can assure that the police department remains free of graft and corruption. The community is entitled to assurance as to this matter.

In the past there has existed internal laxity of police control and the accompanying color of political infringement and intrigue both in and out of the police department. For this reason it is recommended that there be a periodic review of the department by an impartial professional police investigative body until there has been demonstrated a sincere intent to maintain a graft free police department and government. In this way, those who would violate the public trust could be identified and appropriate action taken.

APPENDIX H

IN THE SUPERIOR COURT OF THE STATE OF WASHINGTON FOR KING COUNTY

STATE OF WASHINGTON,

        Plaintiff,

vs

CHARLES M. CARROLL, CHARLES O. CARROLL,   NO.
RAYMOND L. CARROLL, CHARLES R. CONNERY,
M. E. COOK, W. W. COOK, ROBERT D. COVACH,
ALBERT KRETCHMAR, LYLE J. LA POINTE,
ROBERT D. McNEILLY, WILLIAM F. MOORE,
JACK D. PORTER, FRANK C. RAMON,   INDICTMENT
HENRY SCHULTHEIS, LEE W. SCOTT,
RONALD A. SMITH, H. R. SWINDLER,
CHARLES K. WAITT and WILLIAM J. WALSH,

        Defendants.

The defendants named above are accused by the Grand Jury of the County of King, State of Washington, by this indictment, of the crime of conspiracy against governmental entities, committed as follows:

They, the said CHARLES M. CARROLL, CHARLES O. CARROLL, RAYMOND L. CARROLL, CHARLES R. CONNERY, M. E. COOK, W. W. COOK, ROBERT D. COVACH, ALBERT KRETCHMAR, LYLE J. LA POINTE, ROBERT D. McNEILLY, WILLIAM F. MOORE, JACK D. PORTER, FRANK C. RAMON, HENRY SCHULTHEIS, LEE W. SCOTT, RONALD A. SMITH, H. R. SWINDLER, CHARLES K. WAITT and WILLIAM J. WALSH, in the County of King, State of Washington, during the period of time intervening between approximately the 1st day of January, 1950, the exact date being to the Grand Jury unknown, and continuously thereafter until the date of this indictment, while being public officers

Indictment   1.

CHRISTOPHER T. BAYLEY
Prosecuting Attorney
W554 King County Courthouse
Seattle, Washington 98104
344-2550

and thereafter, did unlawfully, willfully, feloniously and knowingly, conspire, combine, confederate, and agree together and with diverse other persons, including but not limited to other public officials and persons engaged in gambling and other illegal activities, who are unindicted herein, and whose names are to the Grand Jury in some cases known and in other cases unknown, to commit offenses against the State of Washington and to defraud the State of Washington, the City of Seattle and the County of King, that is, to promote, engage in,carry on, assist, aid, encourage, allow, facilitate, and conceal (1) the bribery of public officers; (2) the asking and receiving of bribes; (3) the conducting of gambling and lotteries, including but not limited to the operation of coin-operated gambling devices, bingo, and cardrooms; (4) violations of the liquor law of the State of Washington; (5) extortion and blackmail; (6) prostitution; (7) the asking and receiving of compensation upon an understanding that violations of the laws of the State of Washington would be concealed; and (8) other schemes whereby the members of the conspiracy sought to enrich themselves by unlawful means, all as prohibited by the laws of the State of Washington; CONTRARY TO RCW 9.22.040 AND AGAINST THE PEACE AND DIGNITY OF THE STATE OF WASHINGTON.

MANNER AND MEANS

The conspiracy was carried out in the following manner and by the following means:

I

That gambling, coin-operated gambling devices, lotteries, prostitution, bribery, extortion, blackmail, violations of the liquor laws, and other illegal activities, which, although prohibited by the laws of the State of Washington,were tolerated, permitted and protected by certain elected and

Indictment   2.

appointed officials of the City of Seattle and the County of King, officials whose duty it was to enforce the law.

II

That proceeds from the illegal activities which were allowed under this tolerance policy were shared with certain elected and appointed officials of the City of Seattle and County of King who allowed these illegal activities to operate.

III

That public officials shared in these proceeds by means of a payoff system which operated both by payments from the operators of these illegal activities or their agents to high level officials, sometimes in the form of covert campaign contributions, and by an organized system of payoffs through the structure of the law enforcement agencies of the City of Seattle and the County of King.

IV

That as such payments were made both to high level officials and to certain individuals through the ranks of the law enforcement agencies of the City of Seattle and County of King, actions were taken by these persons which tended to insure the preservation and protection of the policy of tolerating the operation of gambling and other illegal activities and to insure the continuation of the sharing through the payoff system of the proceeds from these illegal activities with certain elected and appointed officials of the City of Seattle and County of King.

V

That these actions included non-enforcement of certain criminal statutes involving, among other things, gambling, lotteries, prostitution, bribery, extortion, blackmail and liquor laws; decisions as to how and whether to prosecute

Indictment   3.

certain violations of the law; the recruitment and promotion of
personnel in certain key positions; the designing, promoting, and
enforcement of City and County ordinances which licensed and
regulated illegal activities; the formulation, interpretation
and administration of policies and procedures governing the
issuance of licenses to and the regulation of illegal activities;
the exercise of political influence through the solicitation of
and offering and giving of financial support to certain candidates
for public office.

VI

That payments to high level officials of the City of
Seattle and County of King, sometimes in the form of covert
campaign contributions, were made or arranged for at meetings
attended by certain members of the conspiracy who were high
level officials or who were gambling operators or their agents.

VII

That the foundation of the payoff system within the
Seattle Police Department was payments by operators of various
establishments to individual members of the Seattle Police
Department such as beat patrolmen, vice detectives and prowler
car officers to guarantee immunity from enforcement and harassment.
The amounts paid by individual operators varied from $10 to
$1,000 per month, depending on the operator's ability to pay
and the nature of his business.

VIII

That the officers who collected this money would keep
a portion for themselves, generally one-third to one-half of
the amounts collected, and pass the remainder up through the
chain of command, with each person in the chain of command in
turn keeping a portion and passing a portion. Individual

Indictment   4.

members of the Seattle Police Department received as much as
$1,000 per month as their personal share. In addition, certain
other officers would receive money in return for their silence
and acquiescense.

IX

That members of the conspiracy whose duty it was to
enforce the law had knowledge, direct and indirect, of violations
of certain criminal statutes, involving among other things,
gambling, lotteries, prostitution, bribery, extortion, blackmail
and liquor law violations, and took no action or took action
which was influenced, directly or indirectly, by their membership
in and their profit from the conspiracy.

X

That for the purpose of the continuation of the tolerance
policy and the concealment of the payoff system, members of the
conspiracy were maintained in key positions in the law enforcement
and regulatory agencies in the City of Seattle and County of
King and when a member of the conspiracy was transferred,
retired or died, he was replaced with another member of the
conspiracy. This replacement took place both within and between
the various law enforcement and regulatory agencies of the
City of Seattle and County of King.

XI

That members of the conspiracy designed, promoted, supported
and enforced City and County ordinances which licensed and
regulated cardrooms, coin-operated gambling devices and other
coin-operated machines.

XII

That members of the conspiracy formulated, interpreted and
administered policies governing the issuance of licenses for
and the regulation of the activities described in Paragraph XI

Indictment   5.

CHRISTOPHER T. BAYLEY
Prosecuting Attorney
W554 King County Courthouse
Seattle, Washington 98104
344-2550

so as to guarantee the establishment and perpetuation of a monopoly of coin-operated gambling devices and mechanical amusement devices by other members of the conspiracy and to insure continuing payment to members of the conspiracy who were public officials.

XIII

That members of the conspiracy gave financial contributions to candidates for the positions of Mayor and members of the City Council of the City of Seattle, and Prosecuting Attorney and Sheriff of the County of King, who would support the policy of tolerating the operation of gambling and other illegal activities.

OVERT ACTS

That in order to effect the objects of said conspiracy, the following acts were committed:

I

During the period of time intervening between January 1, 1956 and January 1, 1967, unindicted co-conspirator EDGAR TRUE CORNING received regular monthly shares of payoff monies from his subordinates and shared a portion of the same with his superiors.

II

During the period of time intervening between January 1, 1956 and December 31, 1963, the defendant WILLIAM J. WALSH received money from unindicted co-conspirator EDGAR TRUE CORNING.

III

During the period of time intervening between January 1, 1959 and December 31, 1967, the defendant RONALD A. SMITH gave money to his superior officers in the Seattle Police Department.

Indictment   6.

CHRISTOPHER T. BAYLEY
Prosecuting Attorney
W554 King County Courthouse
Seattle, Washington 98104
344-2550

IV

During the period of time intervening between January 1, 1960 and December 31, 1968, the defendant LYLE J. LA POINTE received money from unindicted co-conspirator STANLEY N. STEVENSON.

V

During the period of time intervening between January 1, 1960 and November 15, 1968, the defendant HENRY SCHULTHEIS received money from unindicted co-conspirator LLOYD ZEEK.

VI

During the time intervening between January 1, 1960 and June 7, 1967, the defendant HENRY SCHULTHEIS received money from unindicted co-conspirator WILBUR FARMER.

VII

During the period of time intervening between January 1, 1962 and December 31, 1967, the defendant CHARLES M. CARROLL acted as Chairman of the License Committee of the Seattle City Council.

VIII

During the period of time intervening between May 1, 1962 and September 1, 1968, the defendant H. R. SWINDLER gave money to his superior officers in the Seattle Police Department.

IX

During the period of time intervening between January 1, 1963 and December 31, 1968, the defendant ALBERT KRETCHMAR gave money to Seattle Police Department Officer DAVID W. JESSUP.

X

During the period of time intervening between January 1, 1963 and December 31, 1968, the defendant M. E. COOK gave money to Seattle Police Department Officer DAVID W. JESSUP.

Indictment   7.

CHRISTOPHER T. BAYLEY
Prosecuting Attorney
W554 King County Courthouse
Seattle, Washington 98104
344-2550

XI

During the period of time intervening between January 1, 1963 and December 31, 1968, the defendant M. E. COOK gave money to unindicted co-conspirator JAMES V. FINERAN.

XII

During the time intervening between February 1, 1963 and August 31, 1963, the defendant CHARLES R. CONNERY gave money to his superior officers in the Seattle Police Department.

XIII

During the period of time intervening between August 1, 1963 and February 28, 1964, the defendant ROBERT D. COVACH met with deceased co-conspirator BEN CICHY.

XIV

During the period of time intervening between August 1, 1963 and September 30, 1963, the defendant CHARLES O. CARROLL, JACK D. PORTER and FRANK C. RAMON met with deceased co-conspirator BEN CICHY.

XV

That at the meeting described in the preceding paragraph deceased co-conspirator BEN CICHY gave defendant JACK D. PORTER approximately $2,000.

XVI

During the period of time intervening between December 1, 1963 and November 30, 1968, the defendant RAYMOND L. CARROLL gave money to his superior officers in the Seattle Police Department.

XVII

During the period of time intervening between February 1, 1964 and March 31, 1964, the defendant M. E. COOK met with defendant CHARLES O. CARROLL and J. D. BRAMAN.

Indictment   8.

CHRISTOPHER T. BAYLEY
Prosecuting Attorney
W554 King County Courthouse
Seattle, Washington 98104
344-2550

XVIII

During the time intervening between February 1, 1964 and March 31, 1964, at the meeting described in the preceding paragraph, defendant M.E. COOK gave J.D. BRAMAN one thousand dollars.

XIX

During the period of time intervening between February 1, 1964 and March 31, 1964, defendant CHARLES O. CARROLL met with J.D. BRAMAN and then arranged for J.D. BRAMAN, in the company of defendant CHARLES O. CARROLL'S assistant, MARVIN STENHOLM, to visit and receive sums of money from unindicted co-conspirators BEN CICHY, ROBERT MURRAY, CALVIN DECKER and A.F. SANTOS.

XX

During the period of time intervening between November 1, 1964 and January 1, 1967, the defendant WILLIAM J. WALSH received a sum of money from the unexpended campaign funds of the defendant JACK D. PORTER'S campaign for office of Sheriff of King County.

XXI

During the period of time intervening between September 1, 1964 and December 1, 1967, the defendant ROBERT D. McNEILLY gave money to his superior officers in the Seattle Police Department.

XXII

During the period of time intervening between January 1, 1965 and December 31, 1969, defendant FRANK C. RAMON received liquor from unindicted co-conspirator DAVID W. BUHER.

XXIII

During the period of time intervening between January 1, 1965 and January 1, 1969, unindicted co-conspirators and Seattle Police Department Officers JOHN W. CARLSON and

Indictment   9.   CHRISTOPHER T. BAYLEY

Prosecuting Attorney
W554 King County Courthouse
Seattle, Washington 98104
344-2550

RONALD C. McNAUGHT received money from persons conducting gambling who are unindicted co-conspirators and whose names are to the Grand Jury in some cases known and other cases unknown.

XXIV

That on or about February 16, 1966, the defendant JACK D. PORTER received one thousand dollars from unindicted co-conspirator CHARLES DANIEL BERGER.

XXV

On or about January 1, 1967, the defendant CHARLES K. WAITT became the Director of Licenses for King County.

XXVI

During the period of time intervening between January 1, 1967 and November 30, 1967, deceased co-conspirator BEN CICHY gave the defendant CHARLES M. CARROLL approximately two thousand dollars.

XXVII

During the period of time intervening between January 1, 1967 and December 31, 1967, the defendants WILLIAM F. MOORE, W. W. COOK and H. R. SWINDLER met.

XXVIII

During the period of time intervening between January 1, 1967 and July 31, 1969, the defendant WILLIAM F. MOORE met with Seattle Police Officer DAVID W. JESSUP.

XXIX

In March, April or May of 1967, the defendants M. E. COOK, LYLE J. LA POINTE and HENRY SCHULTHEIS met at the home of defendant HENRY SCHULTHEIS.

XXX

At the meeting described in the immediately preceding paragraph, the persons named therein agreed to each contribute $100 per month from their respective shares of the payoff monies to a pool of money to be thereafter delivered by defendant LEE W. SCOTT, then a King County Deputy Sheriff, to defendant

CHRISTOPHER T. BAYLEY
Prosecuting Attorney
W554 King County Courthouse
Seattle, Washington 98104
344 2550

Indictment   10.

and then Chief of Police FRANK C. RAMON.

XXXI

During the period of time intervening between June 1, 1967 and June 1, 1969, the defendant ROBERT D. McNEILLY instructed unindicted co-conspirator JAMES HINTERBERGER to take money from persons arrested for public intoxication.

XXXII

During the period of time intervening between June 1, 1967 and June 1, 1969, the defendant ROBERT D. McNEILLY received money from unindicted co-conspirator JAMES HINTERBERGER.

XXXIII

During the period of time intervening between December 1, 1967 and August 31, 1968, the defendant W. W. COOK gave money to his superior officers in the Seattle Police Department.

XXXIV

During the period of time intervening between January 1, 1968 and August 31, 1968, defendant CHARLES O. CARROLL met with deceased co-conspirator BEN CICHY.

XXXV

On or about the 22nd day of August, 1968, the defendant WILLIAM F. MOORE met with Seattle Police Officer GARY BERMAN.

XXXVI

During the period of time intervening between August 1, 1968 and December 31, 1968, unindicted co-conspirator DAVID W. BUHER gave to GEORGE W. FULLER a list of those who paid the vice squad of the Seattle Police Department.

XXXVII

On or about the 31st day of December, 1968, the defendant H. R. SWINDLER became head of the Internal Investigations Division of the Seattle Police Department.

Indictment   11.

CHRISTOPHER T. BAYLEY
Prosecuting Attorney
W554 King County Courthouse
Seattle, Washington 98104
344-2550

XXXVIII

During the time intervening between January 1, 1966 and
November 31, 1966, the defendant CHARLES O. CARROLL received
$500 from unindicted co-conspirator CHARLES DANIEL BERGER.

XXXIX

On or about the 1st day of November, 1969, the defendant
WILLIAM F. MOORE became acting Chief of Police of the Seattle
Police Department.

XL

During the time intervening between August 15, 1970 and
August 27, 1970, the defendant CHARLES O. CARROLL met with
unindicted co-conspirator GERALD BARMANN.

XLI

During the period of time intervening between August 27,
1970 and November 25, 1970, the defendant CHARLES O. CARROLL
telephoned United States Attorney STAN PITKIN and requested that
the United States of America grant immunity from prosecution to
unindicted co-conspirator JASPER BROZOVICH.

XLII

On or about the 2nd day of October, 1970, the defendant
CHARLES O. CARROLL authorized a letter purporting to grant
immunity from state prosecution to JASPER BROZOVICH for any
actions taken by him while a public officer.

XLIII

During the period of time intervening between June 1,
1971 and July 20, 1971, the defendants H.R. SWINDLER and WILLIAM
F. MOORE met with unindicted co-conspirator SIDNEY STEVENSON.

XLIV

During the year 1967, defendant CHARLES M. CARROLL
appropriated to his personal use the sum of $2,400 which he had

Indictment   12.

CHRISTOPHER T. BAYLEY
Prosecuting Attorney
W554 King County Courthouse
Seattle, Washington 98104
344-2550

received as campaign contributions.

CONTRARY TO RCW 9.22.040 AND AGAINST THE PEACE AND DIGNITY
OF THE STATE OF WASHINGTON.

A TRUE BILL

DATED: JULY _____, 1971

FOREMAN OF THE KING COUNTY GRAND
JURY

PRESENTED BY:

CHRISTOPHER T. BAYLEY
Prosecuting Attorney

RICHARD G. McBROOM, JR.
Chief Special Deputy Prosecuting
Attorney

Indictment   13.

UNITED STATES DISTRICT COURT
WESTERN DISTRICT OF WASHINGTON
NORTHERN DIVISION

UNITED STATES OF AMERICA,)
)
           Plaintiff)
)
    v.   )
)
FRANK COLACURCIO, CHARLES)
DANIEL BERGER AND HARRY)
HOFFMAN)
)
        Defendants)
_____)

NO. 51898

INDICTMENT

    The Grand Jury charges:

COUNT I

    That from on or about June 1, 1965, the exact
date being to the Grand Jury unknown, and continuously
thereafter, until September 24, 1969, the defendants, Frank
Colacurcio, Charles Daniel Berger and Harry Hoffman, all
of whom are hereinafter called the defendants, did, within
the Northern Division of the Western District of Washington,
and within the jurisdiction of this Court and elsewhere,
knowingly, willfully, unlawfully and feloniously conspire,
combine, confederate, and agree together with each other to
commit offenses against the United States, more particularly
to violate Title 18 U.S.C., Section 1952, by using facilities
in interstate commerce, to wit: truck facilities between
Englewood, Colorado and Seattle, Washington and telephone
facilities between Englewood, Colorado and Seattle, Washington, as well as the use of the mail between Seattle, Washington and Englewood, Colorado, with the intent to promote,

manage, carry on and facilitate the promotion, management
and carrying on of business enterprises involving gambling
offenses, that is to say, operating bingo games in violation
of the revised Code of Washington, Sections 9.47.010,
9.47.030 and 9.59.010 and thereafter perform acts to promote,
manage, carry on and facilitate the aforesaid unlawful
activity, all in violation of Title 18, U.S.C., Section 1952.

The Grand Jury further charges that the said unlawful
combination, conspiracy, confederation and agreement was to
be accomplished by the means and in the manner following:

1. That the defendant, Charles Daniel Berger, would
operate gambling enterprises involving bingo in violation
of the laws of the State of Washington on behalf of the
defendants.

2. That the defendant Charles Daniel Berger would
deliver to the defendant Frank Colacurcio, on or about
the last day of each month, the sum of $1,000 in cash for
each location in the city of Seattle where he was conducting
gambling enterprises involving bingo, to wit: the Alfa
Club, 1504-1/2 First Avenue, the Lifeline, 1431 First Avenue
and the DAV, 7104 Greenwood, N., and the defendant Frank
Colacurcio and others, whose names are to the Grand Jury
unknown, would guarantee that the Seattle Police Department
would maintain a tolerance policy and would not enforce the
gambling and lottery laws of the State of Washington with
regard to said gambling enterprises involving bingo.

3. That the defendants and co-conspirators would,
using facilities in interstate commerce, to wit: truck

transportation facilities and telephone communication
facilities between the states of Washington and Colorado,
cause the transportation in interstate commerce of the
equipment necessary to promote, establish and carry on

business enterprises involving gambling as heretofore
described.

OVERT ACTS

That in order to effect the objects of said conspiracy, the following acts were committed:

1. That on or about July 28, 1965, a Washington
corporation entitled Senior Citizens of Washington Club
of Seattle was incorporated by defendant Harry Hoffman
and others to promote, manage, establish and carry on a
gambling enterprise in violation of the laws of the State
of Washington.

2. That on or about July 28, 1965, the defendant
Harry Hoffman became a director of the Senior Citizens of
Washington Club of Seattle, a Washington corporation.

3. That on or about September 24, 1965, the
defendant Harry Hoffman and others caused the name of the
Senior Citizens of Washington Club of Seattle to be changed
to the Alfa Club, Inc., a Washington corporation.

4. That on or about the last day of each month
between June 1965 and September 1969 at various locations
within the city of Seattle, including Ciro's Restaurant,
109 Pine Street and the Firelite Room of the Moore Hotel,
2nd and Virginia Streets, cash payments were made to the
defendant Frank Colacurcio in person by the defendant
Charles Daniel Berger or by persons acting on his behalf.

5. That on or about June 28, 1965, the defendant
Charles Daniel Berger did, using a facility in interstate
commerce, to wit, a telephone, order from Bingo King

Company of Englewood, Colorado, 1500 shuttertype bingo
cards imprinted with the inscription "SENIOR CITIZENS,
1504-1/2 First Avenue, Seattle, Washington", ten cartons
of paper throwaway bingo sheets containing 10,500 sheets

per carton, 38 tables and 144 chairs together with other goods usable in a gambling enterprise involving bingo.

6. That on or about June 28, 1965, the Bingo King Company of Englewood, Colorado, did forward from Englewood, Colorado, to 1504-1/2 First Avenue, Seattle, Washington the equipment described in overt act No. 5.

7. That on or about February 13, 1969, Bingo King Company of Englewood, Colorado did forward from Englewood, Colorado, to Seattle, Washington, 20 cartons of paper throwaway bingo sheets containing 10,500 sheets per carton and 12 cartons of double admission tickets.

8. That on or about February 13, 1969, prior to the shipment of the equipment referred to in the previous overt act, defendant Charles Daniel Berger, or persons acting under his control and direction whose identity is at the present time to the Grand Jury unknown, did, using a facility in interstate commerce, to wit: a telephone, request that Bingo King Company of Englewood, Colorado ship said equipment in interstate commerce from Englewood, Colorado, to Seattle, Washington.

9. That on or about March 4, 1969, Bingo King Company of Englewood, Colorado, did forward from Englewood, Colorado, to Seattle, Washington, 20 cartons of paper throwaway bingo sheets containing 10,500 sheets per carton.

All in violation of Title 18, U.S.C., Section 371 and 18 U.S.C., Section 2.

[Counts II-V not included here.]

STAN PITKIN
United States Attorney

STUART F. PIERSON
Assistant U. S. Attorney

1012 U. S. Courthouse
Seattle, Washington 98104

(206) 442-4735

Presented to the Court by the foreman of the Grand Jury in open Court,
in the presence of the Grand Jury and
FILED in the U. S. DISTRICT COURT
at Seattle, Washington.

April 27 19 71

CHARLES J. SCHAAF, Clerk

By _____ Deputy

UNITED STATES DISTRICT COURT
WESTERN DISTRICT OF WASHINGTON
AT SEATTLE

UNITED STATES OF AMERICA,

        Plaintiff,

    v.

RICHARD J. POWERS and
JAMES A. ALFIERI,

        Defendants.

NO. 52231

INDICTMENT

The Grand Jury charges:

COUNT I

That from on or about October 1, 1970, the exact date
being to the Grand Jury unknown, and continuously thereafter,
until April 29, 1971, the defendants, RICHARD J. POWERS and
JAMES A. ALFIERI, did, within the Western District of Washington, and within the jurisdiction of this Court and elsewhere, knowingly, willfully, unlawfully and feloniously conspire, combine, confederate, and agree together with each
other to commit offenses against the United States, to wit:
to corruptly endeavor to influence, intimidate, and impede a
witness in the United States District Court for the Western
District of Washington in the discharge of her duty in the
pending cases of United States v. McCullough, No. 52120, and
United States v. Colacurcio , No. 51898; all in violation of
18 U.S.C. § 1503.

The Grand Jury further charges that the said unlawful
combination, conspiracy, confederation and agreement was to

be accomplished by the means and in the manner following:

1. The defendants RICHARD J. POWERS and JAMES A. ALFIERI would endeavor to induce Mrs. Betty Lou Luke, a witness in the aforesaid cases of United States v. McCullough and United States v. Colacurcio, to receive a payment in lawful United States currency in order to facilitate the evasion by the same Mrs. Betty Lou Luke of service of subpoenas of the United States District Court for the Western District of Washington commanding her presence at the times and places of trial of the aforesaid cases of United States v. McCullough and United States v. Colacurcio.

2. The defendants RICHARD J. POWERS and JAMES A. ALFIERI would endeavor to induce the same Mrs. Betty Lou Luke to join them in efforts to conceal actions taken in furtherance of their unlawful combination, conspiracy, confederation and agreement.

OVERT ACTS

That in order to effect the objects of said conspiracy, the following acts were committed:

1. On or about November 18, 1970, defendant RICHARD J. POWERS endeavored to induce the same Mrs. Betty Lou Luke to come to the law offices of defendants RICHARD J. POWERS and JAMES A. ALFIERI on the following day, November 19, 1970.

2. On or about November 19, 1970, defendants RICHARD J. POWERS and JAMES A. ALFIERI described a plan to the same Mrs. Betty Lou Luke in the following manner: In order to facilitate her evasion of the service of subpoenas commanding her presence as a witness for the United States at the trials of the aforesaid cases of United States v. McCullough and United States v. Colacurcio, the same Mrs. Betty Lou Luke would receive ten thousand dollars ($10,000.00) and defendant

JAMES A. ALFIERI would receive two thousand, five hundred dollars ($2,500.00).

3. On or about November 20, 1970, defendant JAMES A. ALFIERI endeavored to guide the same Mrs. Betty Lou Luke to the Firelite Restaurant and Lounge, Second and Virginia Avenue, Seattle, Washington for the purpose of meeting Frank Colacurcio and for the purpose of obtaining twelve thousand, five hundred dollars ($12,500.00); and, upon return to the law offices of RICHARD J. POWERS and JAMES A. ALFIERI, defendant JAMES A. ALFIERI endeavored to induce the same Mrs. Betty Lou Luke to leave Seattle, Washington in order to conceal the aforesaid unlawful combination, conspiracy, confederation and agreement.

4. On or about December 8, 1970, as indicated in part by a tape recording taken pursuant to order of the United States District Court for the Western District of Washington at Seattle, defendant RICHARD J. POWERS met with the same Mrs. Betty Lou Luke in his law office and there endeavored to induce her to evade service of subpoenas, not then served, commanding her presence as a witness for the United States at the trial of the aforesaid case of United States v. Colacurcio, suggesting then that she might later receive monetary payment in an undetermined amount in exchange for such evasion, and that such evasion would protect her from the realization of threats against her life and the lives of her children, which threats she had received during the months of October and November, 1970.

·5. On or about February 19, 1971, defendant RICHARD J. POWERS met with the same Betty Lou Luke in his law office and there advised her of the continuing plan for her to evade service of subpoenas, not then served, commanding her presence as a witness for the United States at the trial of the aforesaid case of United States v. Colacurcio.

6. On or about March 12, 1971, as indicated in part by a tape recording taken pursuant to order of the United States District Court for the Western District of Washington at Seattle, defendant RICHARD J. POWERS met with the same Mrs. Betty Lou Luke in his law office and there endeavored to induce her to evade service of subpoenas, not then served, commanding her presence as a witness for the United States at the trial of the aforesaid cases of United States v. McCullough, which had been reset for trial on March 22, 1971, and United States v. Colacurcio.

7. On or about March 12, 1971, as indicated in part by a tape recording taken pursuant to order of the United States District Court for the Western District of Washington at Seattle, defendant JAMES A. ALFIERI met with the same Mrs. Betty Lou Luke in his law office and there described to her a method for concealment of actions taken on November 20, 1971, in furtherance of the aforesaid unlawful combination, conspiracy, confederation and agreement.

All in violation of 18 U.S.C. §§ 2 and 371.

[Counts II-V not included here.]